D0992096

Macaulay and the Whig Tradition

Macaulay and the Whig Tradition

Joseph Hamburger

The University of Chicago Press
Chicago and London

JOSEPH HAMBURGER is Professor of Political Science
at Yale University.

The University of Chicago Press, Chicago 60637
The University of Chicago Press, Ltd., London

© 1976 by The University of Chicago
All rights reserved. Published 1976
Printed in the United States of America
80 79 78 77 76   87654321

Library of Congress Cataloging in Publication Data
Hamburger, Joseph, 1922–
    Macaulay and the Whig Tradition.
    1. Macaulay, Thomas Babington Macaulay, Baron,
1800–1859.   2. Great Britain—Politics and
government—19th century.   I. Title.
DA3.M3H27   941.081'092'4 [B]   75-27892
ISBN 0-226-31472-3

IN FOND MEMORY OF MY FATHER

Contents

There has been so much written about Macaulay, including recent publications of considerable value, that yet another book can be justified only if it does not repeat what has become the familiar, almost the standard, interpretation of Macaulay as politician and historian.

I believe that Macaulay has been regularly misunderstood as a consequence of an established tradition of interpretation in which he is labeled Whig or liberal Whig. Related to this, he also is portrayed as a spokesman for the middle class, as a believer in progress, civil liberty, toleration, science, and laissez-faire; and his characteristic attitudes are said to have been complacent, arrogant, insensitive, optimistic, and materialistic. This image of Macaulay took shape in his own time and was firmly established by late Victorian writers such as Matthew Arnold, Leslie Stephen, and John Morley. Since then, most critics have accepted and expanded this image, until by now there is a conventional interpretation, even a stereotypical view, that is difficult to overcome.

It is my purpose in this book to call this established interpretation into question, particularly that part of it that uses the labels Whig and liberal Whig in a way that gives no recognition to the trimming component in his thinking. To some, it is true, Whiggism and trimming are the same thing; but not in the conventional interpretations of Macaulay in which the trimming theme has been largely ignored. Reliance on the Whig label has concealed the fact that Macaulay thought of himself as a trimmer and that the idea of trimming entered into much of what he did and wrote. Thus, use of the Whig label has caused neglect of Macaulay's intentions and the main theme in his writings. To merely say that he was a Whig or a liberal Whig (or that he believed in laissez-faire, progress, and toleration) is to say what was partly or sometimes true; but it does not get at what was distinctively true of him, and therefore, although plausible, these conventional labels and attributions also seriously distort the truth.

I will argue that from an early period, while he was still at Cambridge, Macaulay held the position of the classical trimmer, whose highest priority was not the achievement of progress but the reduction of the great danger of civil war that arose from extremist politics, and for whom reform was only a means to the more important goal of achieving balance and stability. I will try to show that this is the main and distinguishing theme in his writing and in his politics, and that he developed this point of view before he became a Whig, and that the Whigs were attractive to him because that party appeared to provide the most likely means of injecting trimming policies into the deliberations of politicians. Of course trimming was intermixed with Whiggism—a development to which Macaulay contributed in a significant way; but in my view Macaulay's Whiggism was derived from his trimming, and his trimming could have, and occasionally did, lead to antiliberal and anti-Whig views. Furthermore, I believe it can be shown that the trimming theme provides an underlying structure and coherence, even if not perfect unity, to what he did as both essayist and historian, as man of letters and as politician.

I will present a fundamentally different interpretation of Macaulay's politics from that of Macaulay's most recent biographer. In view of this difference, it is perhaps unnecessary to do more than mention that my book was completed before I had an opportunity to read that biography, which did not affect my interpretation in any way. On the contrary, in response to that book I have made a small number of changes, mainly in the notes, in order to give sharper definition to the differences in interpretation. In addition, I have recently made changes and additions called for by the discovery of new evidence, notably Macaulay's unfinished "History of France, from the Restoration of the Bourbons to the Accession of Louis Philippe" and the ample diaries of the seventh earl of Carlisle, which provide much more evidence about Macaulay's opinions than Trevelyan used in his biography.

There are so many ways in which one might write about Macaulay that perhaps it would be as well to say what this book does not deal with. It draws, where appropriate, on his important writings on India and codification, as well as on his poetry, but these subjects are treated as subsidiary. Nor is this an intellectual biography with a chronological format, emphasizing all the experiences and influences that shaped its subject.

In using Macaulay's historical writing as evidence of his political outlook I have made no attempt to assess the accuracy of his historical judgments or to evaluate his work as if he had been a professional historian. The professionals have heavily criticized him. They have found him wrong in certain matters of fact, and they have not accepted some of his judgments. Certainly the questions he thought most important are no longer fashionable among academic historians. And he has been charged with political prejudice—with writing history from an exclusively Whig point of view. Of course, Macaulay was not a professional historian (which does not excuse his errors of fact). He wrote in a different genre: recognizing that examples from the past would affect future developments, especially in a country where the force of tradition was so great, Macaulay set out to shape historical memories in order to influence the way politics would be conducted. But even if we were to accept the more extreme criticisms that charge Macaulay with being obsolete in his approach, wrong in his facts, and prejudiced in his judgment, his historical writings yet remain an excellent source of evidence for his understanding of politics. The way he interpreted the past, even when incorrect, is no less important and revealing a part of his outlook than it would be if he saw the past in a way that is agreeable to contemporary historians.

I am especially pleased to express my appreciation for my son Philip's help in finding Macaulay's unfinished "History of France." By asking probing questions, by searching wills at Somerset House, and by prodding me to follow up improbable but conceivably fruitful clues after I had all but given up the search, he was instrumental in locating the document. He displayed imagination and an eagerness to solve problems, qualities he shares with his sister and brother. Observing such things adds to the gratification of parenthood.

Grants and fellowships from the American Council of Learned Studies, the Earhart Foundation, and the Guggenheim Foundation have made it possible to pursue the research and writing of this book. I am glad to have this opportunity to publicly express my considerable gratitude to them.

I have greatly enjoyed and also appreciated the benefits of conversation about Macaulay with John Clive, Don Kagan, Jane Millgate, Tom Pinney, and Dr. Robert Robson. I am grateful to Mr. Alistair Elliot, Professor Harvey Mansfield, and Professor Thomas Pinney for having answered inquiries, and to Mr. Trevor Kaye for his kind help at Trinity College Library. John Clive kindly allowed me to use his microfilm copies of Macaulay papers at the Huntington Library. The late A. N. L. Munby kindly allowed me to examine his Macaulay collection. Mr. and Mrs. Houghton were generous, as always, with the resources of the Wellesley Index and their own researches. And Dr. Robert Robson, by generously allowing me to use his typescripts of Macaulay's Journals, greatly reduced the difficulty I had in reading Macaulay's handwriting.

Many persons and institutions have kindly allowed me to publish extracts of manuscripts in their possession, and I would like to record my gratitude to them: Mr. George Howard (the Diaries of the 7th earl of Carlisle at Castle Howard, Yorkshire); Longman Group Ltd. (Macaulay's unfinished "History of France, from the Restoration of the Bourbons to the Accession of Louis Philippe"); the Master and Fellows of Trinity College, Cambridge (Macaulay Papers, Macaulay's Journals, Whewell Papers, Munby collection); The National Trust for Places of Historic Interest or Natural Beauty (Macaulay's annotations in books at Wallington); The Huntington Library, San Marino, California (Selina Macaulay's Journal, Zachary Macaulay Papers); University College London Library (Brougham Papers); University of London Library (Booth Papers); British Library Board (Holland, Mackintosh, and Napier papers); The Trustees of the National Library of Scotland (Macaulay letters); Pierpont Morgan Library, New York (Macaulay letters); John Rylands Library, Manchester (Macaulay letters); Bibliothèque Publique et Universitaire, Geneva (James Mill letters), and Josiah Wedgwood and Sons

Limited (an A. V. Dicey letter). Quotations from Crown copyright records in the Public Record Office appear by permission of the Controller of Her Majesty's Stationery Office, London.

The epigraphs are taken from Acton's "Inaugural Lecture on the Study of History (1895)," in *Lectures on Modern History,* edited by John N. Figgis and R. V. Laurence (London, 1918), page 28; and a letter to F. Moore Bayley, 23 December 1901, in Randolph S. Churchill, *Life of Winston S. Churchill,* volume 2, *Young Statesman, 1901-1914* (Boston: Houghton Mifflin, 1967), page 31.

J. H.

Whatever a man's notions of these later
centuries are, such, in the main, the man
himself will be. Under the name of History,
they cover the articles of his philosophic,
his religious, and his political creed.

LORD ACTON

... we wretched, unorganized middle-thinkers ...

WINSTON S. CHURCHILL

A great deal is learned about a political outlook by knowing whether it hopefully cultivates aspirations for high achievements or more modestly aims to avoid disaster—whether it is animated by optimism and vision or by foreboding and nightmares. In Macaulay's case it was a matter of nightmare. Despite his reputation for optimism, there was about his thinking an atmosphere of gloom. Not that society was without its achievements and good prospects. But all this was vulnerable, for political skill and good sense might not be sufficient, and passion and shortsightedness could well prevail.

When Macaulay looked beneath the surface to discern the forces that shaped events, he saw two classes in postures of mutual antipathy; these classes existed in all societies, though the issues that divided and the purposes that motivated the contestants naturally varied. In the seventeenth century the conflict was between religiously inspired political dissenters and the Stuarts; in his own day, between the Radicals and the largely aristocratic ruling class. In all societies there would be established classes and those discontented with them. They threatened each other, but above all they undermined the social order. The discontented were, or could become, rebellious: they threatened anarchy. But even more serious, in Macaulay's view, was the unyielding response of the established, privileged classes, who typically sought to suppress rebelliousness without relieving understandable grievances. Because this class instinctively wished to suppress and even persecute, it threatened tyranny. It was not a matter of choosing between them, anarchy from one, tyranny from the other, for the success of either could be only temporary. The predominance of either would always provoke a strong and effective reaction by the other, and, once this happened, a third alternative was not likely to be available; for it was the diminution of the center that made possible the prominence and the success of the extremes.

This understanding of the political situation was made plausible by developments during the early part of the century. Born in 1800, Macaulay during the period of his youth and early manhood witnessed the growth of Radicalism and the Tory response to it. He had observed the variety of ways in which the discontents of the working people were expressed during the years of depression following Waterloo. There was a great increase of the Radical press and petitioning to Parliament on behalf of Radical causes. There were outbreaks of machine-breaking and the attack on the prince regent in 1817; and the plot to assassinate the cabinet in 1820 appears to have impressed Macaulay sufficiently that he recalled it in his fifties, when he was writing his *History*.[1] While he was a student at Cambridge, there was the Peterloo Massacre; this was the occasion of a dispute with his father, who, because the son felt indignant, feared that he might have become a democrat. He also witnessed a good many riots. He was present at Hunt's tumultuous procession in London in September 1819; he observed town-gown rioting at Cambridge after the queen's trial in 1820; and he was an active supporter of a candidate at Leicester in 1826, where there was rioting that gave Macaulay an opportunity to rescue a woman who was being roughly handled by a mob.[2] Macaulay was an observer of more than surface disturbances; he also was aware of the inclination to Radicalism among the middle classes, and he noted the rise of a Radical intelligentsia that could mobilize middle-class discontents against the government.

A strong and angry Radical movement was only part of the problem. The established order, with the Tory government as its spokesman, responded to the Radicals with vigor and sometimes ferocity. Press prosecutions increased with the number and circulation of Radical newspapers. Habeas corpus was briefly suspended in 1817, and the infamous Six Acts were on the statute books for six months in 1819. State trials in which Brandreth, Watson, and Thistlewood were condemned to death displayed the spirit in which Eldon, Sidmouth, and Ellenborough defended the constitution.

With the Tory government drawn up in battle array against a fragmented but ubiquitous Radical movement, it is not surprising that destructive conflict appeared to be the distinguishing characteristic of the age. This impression gained force from the weakness of moderate voices. Eldonine Toryism seemed to predominate over moderation among the Tories; and the Whigs, long out of office, were weak and dispirited. Macaulay's view that the fundamental antagonism was between unyielding Toryism and the Radicals was shared by some of the leading intellectual figures of the period, who saw the antagonism between Whig and Tory as a trivial factional quarrel within the aristocracy, while believing that the real conflict was between the aristocracy and "the people," represented by the Tories and the Radicals. In this climate of opinion Macaulay formed his early judgments about politics and developed his concern about the gravitation of opinion to extremes and the diminution of the center.

Conflict between a defensive and fearful governing class and an aggrieved, angry Radical movement appeared to be intensified by the antagonists' expectation of unreasonableness and hostility from each other. The government, in face of increasing symptoms of discontent, became more fearful and coercive. Armed with legislation and determined to seek opportunities to prosecute editors, printers, and even vendors of the proliferating Radical press, the government elicited renewed hostility from the Radical intelligentsia, perhaps even stimulating the growth of Radicalism. The same suppressive policy was directed against attempts to demonstrate Radical sentiments in public meetings and by processions. The government attempted to enforce compliance with uncongenial laws, but this only aggravated disaffection. The result was increased prominence and support for a Radical movement that gave expression to the grievances and hostilities of the disaffected — whether the impoverished, the displaced, or the unenfranchised. The government and its supporters, feeling threatened yet unwilling to make concessions, cried anarchy. On the other side, the disaffected, faced with attempts at strict enforcement of severe laws, cried out at oppression.

With the benefit of hindsight that looks back on the nineteenth century as one of comparative stability, Macaulay's concern may appear to have been somewhat fanciful. In retrospect, the governing class was, on the whole, conciliatory; even the Tories soon demonstrated a willingness to yield to popular pressure and genuine grievance, as the events of 1829 and 1846 indicate. And most of the discontented were relieved before they became totally disaffected; over the decades most potentially rebellious groups were given a sense of attachment to society. Yet in Macaulay's time a rational and sophisticated person need not have expected this outcome. Symptoms of disaffection were to be found in various places: agricultural workers burned hayricks and broke threshing machines; the beginnings of trade-union organization led to strikes, some of them violent; there had been cases of machine-breaking in factories; and even some of the middle classes, many of them not enfranchised, were organizing extraparliamentary opposition to established institutions. Furthermore, as mentioned, during Macaulay's youth, and until he was almost thirty, the government's response to these discontents was determined by the ultra-Tories: it was uncompromising and unyielding, anxious to extend and strictly enforce the law.

Macaulay interpreted contemporary developments in the light of his understanding of historical change, particularly the change that occurred during the seventeenth century. He put forth what can be called a theory of history as early as 1822 in his remarkable "Essay on the Life and Character of King William III," which was awarded the Greaves Prize at Trinity College. In it he described society as simultaneously threatened by resistance bordering on rebellion and by coercion leaning to despotism. British government and society "were in a state not of amalgamation, but of conflict, — not of equilibrium but of alternate elevation and depression."[3] As a consequence there were alternating conditions of anarchy and despotism. This situation had prevailed throughout history, and the pattern of alternating regimes during the seventeenth century was to be understood in these terms. Thus the pendulum had swung between the early Stuarts and the Puritans and parliamentary forces; then back to Charles II, who was threatened by Whig rebellion during the early 1680s; and then, with James II, back once more in the direction of despotism, which produced renewed resistance.

The nation might not reach the extreme of anarchy or despotism, but movement in the direction of either created a fear that it would continue, and it was this fear that brought about the reverse movement. Thus, in the 1680s, "civil war, anarchy, regicide were apprehended from the violence of the [Whig] opposition." Consequently "the people rallied round the throne, and seemed eager to expiate turbulence by servility." Generalizing, Macaulay noted that the friends of liberty tended to outrage moral feelings and offend worldly interests by seeking excessive vengeance for past abuses and urging too great change; the result was to "alarm the timid, disgust the good, and drive a nation to seek in slavery a refuge from commotion."

Each extreme provoked its opposite. "Anarchy in turn generated tyranny. Tyranny had now again produced resistance and revolution." In an unfortunate society there was an alternation from one condition to the other:

> Each is the cause and the effect of its antagonist. Since the first recorded origin of government they have followed each other in perpetual succession, reciprocally producing and produced. Society, when once drawn out of that happy central point in which alone it can repose, continues to oscillate between these extremes, instead of resting again in the medium.

The remedy for this condition was to establish that "central point" that provided for order without despotism and liberty without anarchy. This would be achieved by bringing the two antagonistic forces into a state of amalgamation and harmony. Those who feared despotism would have to recognize the value of order, and those who feared anarchy would have to recognize the value of liberty. William III was significant because he interrupted the cycle and took a major step toward achieving harmony.[4]

Macaulay applied this type of analysis in his historical writing, not only about England but about France as well, and also in his diagnosis of contemporary politics.[5] In the prize essay of 1822 it was stated as a matter of generalization that still had relevance to politics. It is not surprising, then, that Macaulay's first sustained analyses of the contemporary political situation, published in the later 1820s, were couched in the same terms.

In these later essays he again saw the most important political struggle as taking place between the government—and particularly the Tory party, representing the privileged, landed class—and what he called the lower orders, for whom the Radical politicians were the spokesmen. Ignoring the conventional contests between Government and Opposition, Tories and Whigs, Macaulay thought that "the history of our country, since the peace of 1815, is almost entirely made up of the struggles of the lower orders against the government, and of the efforts of the government to keep them down." Both were extreme parties. Those among the lower orders "who have any opinions at all are democrats already," i.e., Radicals. In addition, there was a "Republican sect"—what might be called a Radical intelligentsia—that was antitraditional, zealous, and arrogant. Analogous to the Puritans and Jacobins, these men, who were educated and from the middle class, could provide the leadership to a growing Radical Movement.[6] On the other side, the government also adopted an extreme position, as the suspension of habeas corpus and the antisedition laws made clear. From the one side there was suppression; from the other, hostility and the threat of rebellion.

If a conflict between these extreme parties occurred, it would be the consequence of unyielding Tory policy provoking those with grievances into a revolutionary posture. The working classes normally lived at a marginal level of existence; thus the vast body of laborers and artisans usually had legitimate grievances arising out of distress and privation. They were also prone to be radical because "it is on persons in this station that the abuses of our system press most heavily; while its advantages, on the other hand, are comparatively little felt by them." Already inclined to radicalism, in this situation they could easily become openly hostile. A Tory government could not exist for one year "without incensing the lower classes of the English to frenzy, by giving them up to the selfish tyranny of its aristocratical supporters." It would not be too much to say of the working classes "that in a season of distress, they are ripe for any revolution."[7]

The revolutionary opposition to the Tory government would include the middle class as well, for it too would be provoked into a revolutionary posture. Normally the middle class had an interest in moderation and an inclination to it as well. Without endorsing Radicalism, it looked for improvements; and without being blindly loyal, it had a stake in the prevailing institutions. But its moderation could not be counted on. If its growing desire to see the removal of faults in the system were disappointed, the middle class would be made more radical. They would enter into an alliance with the working classes, placing "at the head of the multitude persons possessing all the education, all the judgement, and all the

habits of co-operation, in which the multitude itself is deficient."
Then the Radical intelligentsia would take on greater importance,
and a potentially large and numerous revolutionary party would
appear. Something like this had begun to emerge at the time of the
queen's trial in 1820, and it would take place again if the Tories
(that is, the non-Canningite Tories) returned to office. Committed,
as Macaulay saw them, to a policy of suppression and opposed to
change, they "would goad every Reformer in the country into a
Revolutionist" and make an alliance between middling and lower
orders inevitable.[8]

Macaulay's fear was not the conventional fear of a revolution in
which the masses overwhelm the governing and propertied classes.
Of course he had the conventional picture of radicalism as a kind of
anarchy, and he feared its spread among the angry working classes.
But he had an equally frightening view of the extreme opposition to
it as a kind of despotism, and he saw evidence of this in the
willingness of the government to suppress radicalism. One side was
angry; the other was afraid and had great strength. What
Macaulay feared was that antagonism between two powerful and
determined groups — a powerful extraparliamentary opposition,
dominated by doctrinaire Radicals, and the government, dominated by the ultra-Tories — would cause the political process to be
monopolized by impassioned spokesmen for extreme views; there
would be "an insolent oligarchy on the one side and infuriated
people on the other." At the end of this road there was the
nightmare of civil war.[9]

Macaulay's observation of political conflict in the post-Waterloo period led him to believe that the situation threatened to take
on some of the characteristics that prevailed in the seventeenth
century, and this perception was reinforced by his belief that there
was a tendency in all societies to develop in this way. This is the
context of Macaulay's rationale for reform and for his defense of
the Canning coalition government in 1827. By putting the
ultra-Tories into opposition, the Canning coalition would prevent
the radicalization of middle-class reformers and the incensing of
the working classes, and it would keep at bay the threat of an
alliance between middle and working classes. It in fact caused a
split in the Tory party. Thus Canning's success would isolate both
extremes — Tories and Radicals — and prevent their growth. At the
same time, the coalition government was expected to take mea-

sured steps toward commercial reform and Catholic emancipation. This gave hope that the middle classes would remain moderate and that the center would be maintained.[10]

This hope was short-lived, since the Canningite government lasted for so brief a period. With the return of the ultra-Tories under Wellington, Macaulay again felt that the greatest problem was the push to the extremes. He feared a retreat from the center by those who admired either rebellion or oppression but nothing between. There were those who "cannot be a friend to liberty without calling for a community of goods, or a friend to order without taking under [their] protection the foulest excesses of tyranny." And again, "There are those who will be contented with nothing but demolition; and there are those who shrink from all repair. There are innovators who long for a President and a National Convention; and there are bigots." The alternative was to find a government that would reconcile antagonists and judiciously reform the system of representation. Such a policy, "by so widening the base of the government as to interest in its defence the whole of the middling class . . . [would] succeed in averting a struggle to which no rational friend of liberty or of law can look forward without great apprehensions."[11]

Meanwhile Macaulay felt apprehensive, for during the late 1820s, with the ultra-Tories dominant and the Whigs still in opposition (not having been in office for a generation, except for their meager participation in the short-lived Canningite governments), conflict between an insensitive and even oppressive government and a discontented and rebellious people appeared to be increasingly likely:

> Already we seem to ourselves to perceive the signs of unquiet times, the vague presentiment of something great and strange which pervades the community; the restless and turbid hopes of those who have every thing to gain, the dimly-hinted forebodings of those who have every thing to lose. Many indications might be mentioned, in themselves indeed as insignificant as straws; but even the direction of a straw, to borrow the illustration of Bacon, will show from what quarter the hurricane is setting in.[12]

This was the mood with which he faced the Reform Bill agitation, and it was the expectation of this kind of conflict that shaped his interpretation of the constitutional crisis of 1831-32.

In his nightmare of civil conflict Macaulay pictured the antagonists in the postures that characterized the religious conflicts of the seventeenth century. There would be two extreme antagonists—the visionaries and the defenders. On the one side were enthusiasm and zeal, which created in the discontented both unrealistic expectations and destructive wishes. On the other side, among the defenders of order, there were dogmatism and fear, which made them unwilling to allow changes. Religion provided the model of the sectarian zealot who manipulated mass passions, thereby giving reality to the threat of anarchy and revolution. And it also provided an example of the misguided, unyielding defender of order who persecutes and suppresses, thereby helping to undermine what he would defend.[13] Religion also provided the model for the way these two types of antagonists would engage each other. Doctrinaire, dogmatically assured, and hostile, they would be uncompromising in battle, bitter in defeat, and without mercy when victorious. These ingredients would create the pattern of historical change outlined in 1822.

When Macaulay encountered immoderate Radicalism, with its sweeping criticisms of established arrangements and its utopian standards of judgment, he understood it in the context of religious radicalism. The religious enthusiasts had bred political Radicalism; and he thought that the secular political Radicals of his own time called on passions that had a religious dimension. Both encouraged discontent, criticism, and, in the end, separatism and rebellion, and Macaulay used such terms as "zealot," "demagogue," "sectarian," and "enthusiast" interchangeably for both.

Because their religious outlook had political implications, the Puritans, especially during the reign of Charles I and the Civil War, typified the religionists on whom Macaulay based his image of all other radicals. The Independents, the root-and-branch men, were, "to use the kindred phrase of our own time, radicals."[14] Encouraging men to seek guidance directly from the deity, the Puritans undermined other institutions besides the church; they were opposed to established churches, but they tended to be antiauthoritarian in politics as well. Religious fanaticism became political and thereby threatened the established order. Solely concerned with their relation to the deity, the Puritans felt "contempt for terrestrial distinctions. The difference between the greatest and meanest of mankind seemed to vanish, when compared with the boundless interval which separated the whole race from him on whom their own eyes were constantly fixed." In the political realm, although the Puritan "prostrated himself in the dust before his Maker ... he set his foot on the neck of his king." The religious zeal of these fanatics was the source of their single-mindedness and immutable purpose in debate and in battle.[15]

Against this background, it is noteworthy that Macaulay thought of the disciples of Jeremy Bentham and James Mill—the so-called Philosophic Radicals—as playing a role comparable to the Puritans' in the mid-seventeenth century:

> Even now [1827], it is impossible to disguise, that there is arising in the bosom of [the middle class] a Republican sect, as audacious, as paradoxical, as little inclined to respect antiquity, as enthusiastically attached to its ends, as unscrupulous in the choice of its means, as the French Jacobins.... Metaphysical and political science engage their whole attention. Philosophical pride has done for them what spiritual pride did for the Puritans in a former age; it has generated in them an aversion for the fine arts, for elegant literature, and for the sentiments of chivalry. It has made them arrogant, intolerant, and impatient of all superiority. These qualities will, in spite of their real claims to respect, render them unpopular, as long as people are satisfied with their rulers. But under an ignorant and tyrannical ministry ... their principles would spread as rapidly as those of the Puritans formerly spread, in spite of their offensive peculiarities.[16]

Of course Macaulay was aware of the differences. But when he thought of the way in which the Radical intelligentsia of his day might lead the combined middle and working classes in revolution, he pictured its leaders as being like the Puritans.

Turning to the other side, he saw the defenders of the established order as tradition-bound and rigid, insisting on maintaining particular institutional forms instead of looking beyond the forms to the purposes that might be compatible with a variety of institutional arrangements. Uncompromising and determined to maintain society as it was, they were willing to persecute and suppress in order to stamp out any demand for change. In Macaulay's view, they were bound to be ineffective, for such methods provoked without eliminating demands; indeed, instead of eliminating the enemy, they strengthened him. The typical spokesman for this outlook was Laud, and he was assimilated, in Macaulay's mind, to the Tories. Like him, they wished to preserve and to do so by suppressing anyone who challenged existing arrangements; like him, they were dogmatic, intolerant, and unyielding. Macaulay saw the Tory prosecutions of the press and their restrictions on expression of grievances during the post-Waterloo years as comparable, at least in intention and rationale, to Laud's persecution of the Puritans. To Macaulay, Laud was the archetypical Tory, and contemporary Tories were modern-day Lauds.

With Laud and the Puritans as prototypes of Tories and Radicals, the earlier struggle became the model for Macaulay's nightmare of civil war in the nineteenth century. The parallel did not depend on the survival of intense religious feeling. Macaulay was aware of the progress of secularization and of course welcomed it. Yet he assumed that destructive conflict would continue to be a problem, for it arose from circumstances that were ubiquitous.[17] When institutions violated the prevailing sense of justice and ceased to satisfy needs, governing establishments would become the object of distrust and anger, and the established classes would become fearful and vindictive. This could take place in connection with issues of economic policy and party politics, just as it had in the seventeenth century, in connection with religious and constitutional questions. There would be zeal, distrust, and hostility over questions of economics and class, just as there had been over religion. There would be enthusiasm and exclusiveness; and there would be dogmatism and intolerance. There would be rejection of established institutions; and there would be rigid defenses of them. With both visionary critics and orthodox defenders of the social order in mind, Macaulay was sensitive to the way that class differences in his own time could develop into conflict similar to that of the seventeenth century. Thus his descriptions of Lord Eldon and Laud were interchangeable; and his image of the fanatic was the same, whether he had a militant Puritan or a Jacobin or certain contemporary Radicals in mind.

Macaulay's preoccupation with civil conflict, and his belief that it originated in the mutual hostility of fanatical spokesmen at the extremes, affected his attitude to religion. When combined with fear, anger, and discontents, religion encouraged men to be immoderate and pushed them to extremes. It then became, in Macaulay's eyes, fanaticism, indeed, a sort of madness. It was not Augustan tastes that led him to disapprove of religious enthusiasm; much more emphatically, it was his observation that intense religion caused men to conduct themselves in ways that were politically undesirable. He regarded those possessed by it as having a disease. If the disease became epidemic, it was awesome, for it had the strength to convulse nations, cause revolutions, and sustain fierce wars — including civil wars. On the other hand, if intense religiosity did not exist, there would be a better chance that fear and anger would be reduced and discontents relieved by adjustments made through the political process. Then the political realm would be uncontaminated by aspirations and enmities associated with religion, and politics could be practiced without the distorting effects of utopian desires for change and romantic dreams of restoration. Politicians could then debate, adjust, compromise. With religion kept moderate, conciliatory politics would become possible. But if it became extreme, religion was a source of conflict and an obstacle to conciliation.

It was not religion as such, but religious fervor that Macaulay opposed. Tepid, conventional religion was acceptable, for it was useful to society. It restrained appetites, consoled those in want and calamity, allowed one to go to the grave without despair, and was "the restraint of those who are placed above all earthly fears."[18] Thus he defended the Church of England for serving these purposes and for being a bulwark against fanaticism.[19] He was also critical of those who were immoderately antireligious in public. Voltaire's "hatred of Xtnty is positively a disease." He disapproved of the poet Thomas Campbell as "the only man whom I ever heard talk against Christianity boisterously and indecently in a large mixed company," adding, however, with evident gratification, that no one answered him.[20]

Observing a connection between religious extremism and civil conflict, Macaulay in his historical writings was severe on those who displayed intense religiosity. Bunyan and Fox and many others he described as being bizarre and sometimes dangerous. Contemporary manifestations of religiosity, whether appearing among the prominent or the obscure, he treated with disdain and ridicule. Although lacking the potential for great consequence

that he associated with religion in the seventeenth century, intense
religion in his own time seemed to remind him of past threats to
the political order. The examples are innumerable. There are
unsympathetic references to Joanna Southcote, Quakers, and
Muggletonians. His Journals record the visit of "a mad Sweden-
borgian" who pestered him with "his grievances and his revelations."
Even when he recalled the Evangelical preacher Buchanan, whom
he admired, he could not help mentioning that his many fine
qualities were combined "with a little or rather not a little
fanfaronade and humbug." The Methodists elicited the same
reaction. "The controversialists [among them] . . . are so absurd
and malignant that one is always against the last speaker."[21]
Although these judgments may have reflected Macaulay's personal religious outlook, they were also consistent with the political
criteria with which he evaluated religion. Thus, while religiosity
rarely failed to elicit his disdain, neither did it fail to excite his
sense of danger.

His depreciatory comments were especially directed at anything
Puritanical. He visualized a Puritan household at the time of the
Restoration as one in which there were "Geneva bands, heads of
lank hair, upturned eyes, nasal psalmody, and sermons three
hours long." Apart from being distasteful, such an austere
environment was self-defeating, because it might send forth one
who would become the greatest rake of his time, one whose
dissoluteness would make the most dissolute Cavalier stand aghast.
A favorite Macaulay bugbear was Exeter Hall, which was associated with enthusiastic religious movements. It was his reference to
the "bray" of Exeter Hall during the debate on the Maynooth
grant that caused outrage, especially among some of his Edinburgh
constituents.[22] He was equally affronted by assertive Catholicism.
He found the Puseyites annoying; Tract Ninety was "the quintes-
sence of Jesuitism." He confessed feeling "the same disgust at the
Anglo Catholic and Roman Catholic cants which people after the
Restoration felt for the Puritan cant"; and he wrote, "I hate
Puseyites and Puritans impartially."[23] Macaulay knew that the
power of religion was diminishing in the face of science and
reason, but religious extremists in his own time symbolized the
fanaticism that would always be a problem, and they reminded
him of the way that visionaries, by working on the discontented,
can bring nations nearer to civil war.

It was his refusal to participate in the strong sectarian feelings of his constituents that led to his only experience of electoral defeat. In 1845 he supported the Conservative proposal to make a modest government grant to Maynooth, a Catholic college in Ireland. A large body of his constituents turned against him. Feelings ran high, and at his election meetings in 1847 he was frequently interrupted with hisses and groans. He had served as Member for Edinburgh since 1839 and had been reelected twice, but now he was defeated, an experience that must have given personal meaning to his observation about Catholic emancipation: that "it proved far less easy to eradicate evil passions than to repeal evil laws."[24] Long after this defeat, during another encounter with militant Protestant feeling in Edinburgh, he commented on "the excessive malignity and unreasonableness of the voluntaries. I have no particular love for establishments and priests," he said, "but the rancour of these men disgusts me." In a different context, but probably with these events in mind, Macaulay wrote about "the bigotry of the schismatics who domineered in the north," and he criticized a seventeenth-century Scottish politician (Melville) for having shrunk "from uttering a word so hateful to the theological demagogues of his country as Toleration."[25]

These views about the political uses and the potentially dangerous consequences of religion are not inconsistent with what is known about Macaulay's personal religious beliefs. It is difficult to be certain about them, for he was reticent and guarded. When asked on the hustings, he professed belief in Christianity in tepid and conventional language.[26] He sometimes attended church, believing that one should pay a decent respect to forms. In the same spirit, and from prudence and in deference to his father as well, he restrained in public his powerful impulse to ridicule religiosity; but behind this conventional posture Macaulay's real views were almost certainly more skeptical and irreverent, although they must have varied over the years. One finds him engaged in a debunking skepticism and enjoying mildly blasphemous verse, which suggests that he shared the doubts of his "advanced" contemporaries.[27] One may even speculate that he had himself in mind when he noted that "in every age there are many concealed atheists who keep their opinions to themselves."[28] If he did, such moments must have been few; but there were many others when his observation about the typical Roman Catholic country gentleman of the seventeenth century was applicable to him: "he held his hereditary faith, as men generally hold a hereditary faith, sincerely, but with little enthusiasm." The frequency of such possibly autobiographically inspired observations suggests that Macaulay was without strong religious commitment.[29] Gladstone sensed this, for in commenting on Macaulay's religious views he concluded that "there are passages which suggest a doubt whether he had completely wrought the Christian dogma, with all its lessons and all its consolations, into the texture of his mind."[30] Living at a time when many educated contemporaries bravely faced challenges to their religious beliefs and suffered agonies of doubt, Macaulay does not appear to have shared such experiences. He recognized the reality of strong religious feeling in others, but he could not quite believe in its necessity. Applied to the context of his own time, his observation on Shakespeare's religious creed appears relevant. Shakespeare, Macaulay thought, "was probably rather floating between, as the mass of a nation will do during some great national change of faith."[31] Situated somewhere between conventional views and the agnosticism that was to become frequent later in the century—and perhaps nearer to the latter—Macaulay too seems to have faced change by "floating between."

His readiness to be irritated by religiosity may have been related to his exposure to it among his own family. His father, Zachary Macaulay, was an active and prominent member of the Evangelical group associated with Clapham, and his mother came from a Quaker family. The piety and intense religious commitment of the Clapham side seems to have predominated during Macaulay's youth. It was carried so far as to discourage the reading of novels, but this did not prevent Macaulay from becoming an avid reader of fiction, including what he admitted to be "trash." His father apparently had hoped that he would devote himself to the church and take orders.[32] As an adult he certainly recalled the words, the atmosphere, and the sayings of some of the prominent members of the group. The Clapham sect, as it came to be known, proselytized vigorously. It was responsible for such organizations as the Sunday School Society, the Religious Tract Society, the Church Missionary Society, and the British and Foreign Bible Society.[33] It also tried to spread the influence of Christian principles, both within the Anglican community and in the wider social realm as well. This was evident in the Society for the Reformation of Manners and in the influential Anti-Slavery Society. Macaulay's father, in addition to playing a leading role in the antislavery movement, was editor of the *Christian Observer*, an evangelical periodical heavily laden with theological discussion, sermons (many of them composed by Zachary), reviews of religious books, biographical sketches of religious figures, reports on organizations in which the Evangelicals were interested, and comments on manners and customs in the light of a religious understanding. The contents of the *Christian Observer* provide a clue to the spirit in which Macaulay's family life was conducted.[34]

Macaulay reacted against most of this. In addition, although less important, his mother's Quaker connection should be kept in mind, not only when one is considering his personal antipathy to the Quakers and his harsh historical judgments of them, but also as one tries to understand his reaction to religiosity. Given his mixed religious background, his observation on Sir William Temple appears to have autobiographical significance. Temple, he said, was one "who had been disgusted by the morose austerity of the Puritans, and who, surrounded from childhood by the hubbub of conflicting sects, might easily learn to feel an impartial contempt for them all."[35]

The Evangelical background, in addition to its religious emphasis, included a political theme that had great significance for Macaulay. Zachary and most of the other prominent Evangelicals were not orthodox Tories; yet, despite their renowned humanitarianism, they exemplified that part of Macaulay's image of the Tory as one who repressed and persecuted. In 1802 the Evangelicals founded the Society for the Suppression of Vice, and Zachary was "an active member," serving on its executive committee and soliciting funds for it. The Society was part of the reaction to the French Revolution. Noting "that a general disrespect prevails for authority," and holding that "without the security of laws, the corrupt propensities of man could not be restrained, nor moral order and human society exist," it defined its object as being "to assist the state in the preservation of moral and religious order." Among its methods was the initiation of prosecutions (which the law allowed, even though it was a private body), including prosecutions for blasphemous libel. Many Radical editors, publishers, and vendors faced this charge, though it was their politics, as well as their irreligion, that was often the target.[36] Although the Society thought of itself as avoiding the political realm and did not initiate prosecutions for sedition, its prosecutions for blasphemous libel had a political dimension, since those prosecuted — men like Carlile and Davidson — were Radicals and had political purposes in publishing the religious doctrines that made them vulnerable to prosecution. In 1819, for example, Richard Carlile faced a prosecution initiated by the Society; Carlile was guilty of the "foulest sedition, and the most horrible blasphemy," according to Zachary.[37]

Despite his genuine concern about economic distress, Zachary was nervous about the breakdown of social order, and he wanted the government to be even more vigorous in its prosecution policy. He thought the ignited state of Manchester was due largely to "the criminal supineness of the Government in not having more vigilantly laboured to repress the host of seditious writers, the *Black Dwarfs, Medusas, Deists, Observers* [all Radical journals], (not meaning, of course, one [*Christian*] *Observer*), which have been so industriously exciting the evils which now threaten to overwhelm the country." He wanted the government to do nothing less than to accomplish "the radical extirpation of these grand germinal movers of sedition and rebellion."[38] He defended the Peterloo magistrates and approved of the Six Acts. After the Peterloo trials, Zachary said, "We are congratulating ourselves on the conviction of Burdett and Hunt."[39] Young Macaulay, when he portrayed the imprudent Tory policy that could provoke revolution, had attitudes like these in mind.

Macaulay's rejection of Evangelicalism, far from being simply a matter of theological differences or personal uncongeniality, was directly connected with his evaluation of religion in political terms. He could see two politically relevant dangers in Evangelicalism. First, his fear that religion could too easily become enthusiastic and fanatical made him unsympathetic to any movement devoted to stimulating religiosity. Second, and much more important, Macaulay could not approve his father's eagerness to suppress political radicalism nor the Evangelicals' initiative in such matters. Indeed, in the light of Macaulay's understanding of the twin dangers to constitutional stability, Zachary and the

Evangelicals were particularly objectionable, for they seemed to combine a touch of both the fanatical enthusiasm of the Puritans and Laud's inclination to persecute.

Alert to the "religious" dimension of politics, and having adopted categories of analysis derived both from the history of religious and political conflict, particularly of the seventeenth century, and from the literature of antiquity, as evidenced in the prize essay of 1822, Macaulay began his political career (and his preparations for his career as a historian) with the assumption that the most important political task was to control the inevitable centrifugal tendencies that made destructive civil conflict a real possibility. Because his political orientation had these origins, his historical writings were intimately connected with his responses to contemporary politics. Indeed, when he first wrote (in 1822) about the problem of civil conflict in the seventeenth century, Macaulay observed that "at the present period [it] suggests reflections peculiarly solemn and important."[40]

Macaulay saw anarchy and tyranny—or, as they became in the nineteenth century, revolution and repression—as twin political dangers: the one would come from the success of Radicalism, the other from extreme Toryism. They would be alternating evils, and they would produce civil conflict, even civil war. To avoid them, it was necessary to have political institutions that flexibly protected the center. Indeed, this was the virtue of the constitution that emerged after 1688, and it was the deficiency of the French constitution. It was also necessary for politicians on all sides to be conciliatory—to avoid rigidity, utopianism, and vindictiveness. Flexibility and conciliation could not be guaranteed even with the constitution produced by the Revolution of 1688, yet their absence would create a threat to the constitution itself and to the social order.

The situations that called for these qualities were created by uncoordinated changes within society, which produced conflict and grievances. Macaulay feared the remedies favored by both the discontented and the complacent, of both Radicals and Tories. Each posed a threat to the constitutional order, which with its legacy of institutions provided wise men with an opportunity to resolve conflicts without either violence or suppression.

These dangerous situations were created by what Macaulay called "noiseless revolutions"—the slow, gradual, accumulating changes that rarely attracted the notice of those historians who confined their attention to decisive and dramatic events in the political or military arena. These noiseless changes were visible only to the observer who examined developments over a long period of time. They included changes in economic conditions from poverty to opulence and changes in morals and manners from ferocity to humanity. They also included changes in the useful and ornamental arts, the rise of religious sects, and changes in literary taste, dress, public amusements, domestic life, and conversation. These developments were noiseless revolutions because

> their progress is rarely indicated by what historians are pleased to call important events. They are not achieved by armies, or enacted by senates. They are sanctioned by no treaties, and recorded in no archives. They are carried on in every school, in every church, behind ten thousand counters, at ten thousand firesides. The upper current of society presents no certain criterion by which we can judge of the direction in which the under current flows.[1]

These changes need not lead to severe dislocations. There had been noiseless revolutions with welcome results; for example, there was the emergence of ministerial or cabinet government. Before 1693 the House of Commons was ungovernable, with offices divided between the two great parties and men in office caballing and haranguing one another, moving votes of censure, and attempting to impeach one another. All this had changed by 1696, by which time the principal servants of the crown were in the same party; they were prompt to defend one another from attack; and the majority in the House of Commons was arrayed in good order under the leadership of the ministry. Neither the king nor his most enlightened advisers fully understood the nature and importance of this noiseless revolution. It was "the work, partly of mere chance, and partly of wisdom; not however of that highest wisdom which is conversant with great principles of political philosophy, but of that lower wisdom which meets daily exigencies by daily expedients."[2] Macaulay also portrayed the termination of villeinage in the fourteenth century and the elimination of the distinction between Norman and Saxon in the thirteenth as noiseless but beneficent revolutions. Both these developments were "silently and imperceptibly effected. They struck contemporary observers with no surprise, and have received from historians a very scanty measure of attention. They were brought about neither by legislative regulation nor by physical force."[3]

Often, however, noiseless revolutions created dislocations and discontents that undermined the political and social order. They could do this even when the changes themselves were welcome. For example, the growth of literacy, a change in the intensity of religious enthusiasm, the redistribution of wealth, or a shift in population could have this effect. As a result of such usually uncoordinated changes there was a disproportion between political and other institutions; for the political institutions remained comparatively unchanged, while the other institutions were transformed noiselessly. For a long time the changes went unnoticed, but they were accompanied by the growth of discontents; and when these grievances became sufficiently intense, a crisis existed, as it did in 1640 and in 1831. Such crises were the result of inevitable change: "while the natural growth of society went on, the artificial polity continued unchanged.... Then came that pressure almost to bursting, the new wine in the old bottles, the new society under the old institutions."[4]

This was not a parochial problem for Englishmen of the seventeenth or nineteenth centuries. In the seventeenth century it was a reflection of "a law, beyond the control of human wisdom, [which] decreed that there should no longer be governments of that peculiar class which, in the fourteenth and fifteenth centuries had been common throughout Europe. The question, therefore, was not whether our polity should undergo a change, but what the nature of the change would be."[5] Macaulay, speaking of his own time, thought that "over the great changes of the moral world we possess as little power as over the great changes of the physical world. We can no more prevent time from changing the distribution of property and of intelligence, we can no more prevent property and intelligence from aspiring to political power, than we can change the courses of the seasons and of the tides." This had always been true and always would be. It was true in ancient as well as modern times. "In all ages a chief cause of the intestine disorders of states has been that the natural distribution of power and the legal distribution of power have not corresponded with each other."[6]

Macaulay believed there was a close analogy between the seventeenth century and his own time. During both periods there were at least threats of insurrection arising from differences between the governing classes and large segments of the populace regarding the way political power was exercised and regarding the proper composition of the governing classes. Of course there were differences between the two periods — in the issues that divided the nation, in the rhetoric used to express grievances and the philosophies and aspirations that nourished them, and in the historical circumstances that provided opportunities for, and limitations on, the adoption of political remedies. Yet there were fundamental similarities as well; in each case social, economic, and religious developments had altered the society and stimulated the development of political passions in an irrevocable manner, creating the necessity of change in political institutions:

> Time is bringing round another crisis analogous to that which occurred in the seventeenth century. We stand in a situation similar to that in which our ancestors stood under the reign of James the First. It will soon again be necessary to reform that we may preserve; to save the fundamental principles of the constitution by alterations in the subordinate parts.[7]

In his own day, as in the early seventeenth century, noiseless revolutions had brought about changes in opinion and belief and changes in social and economic institutions; all this required adjustments in the political arrangements. Charles I was faced with "a change in the public mind" which might have been regrettable but which could not have been reversed. "You cannot transform the Englishmen of 1640 into the Englishmen of 1560," even though it "may be that the simple loyalty of [their] fathers was preferable to that inquiring, censuring, resisting spirit" that replaced it. An adjustment in political arrangements became a necessity. But Charles I "would govern the men of the seventeenth century as if they had been the men of the sixteenth century." These things, Macaulay said in 1831, "are written for our instruction. Another great intellectual revolution has taken place; our lot has been cast on a time analogous, in many respects, to the time which immediately preceded the meeting of the Long Parliament. There is a change in society. There must be a corresponding change in the government."[8] Thus his analysis of the difficulties and his conception of the appropriate remedies for the seventeenth century and for the nineteenth were quite similar.

The character of a genuine political crisis becomes evident only when the risks become great and the dangers difficult to avoid. Such risks could be greatly reduced by discerning the noiseless changes at an early stage and making institutional adjustments. This was Macaulay's rationale for reform. If reform were not made, societies moved on to crises, as they did during the reigns of James I and Charles I and again later in the seventeenth century, and as they appeared to be doing during the years before 1832. Despite the differences, Macaulay invoked the example of the seventeenth century when he analyzed the approaching crisis of 1832, and he alluded to the events of 1832 when he analyzed the seventeenth century:

> Those are terrible conjunctures [he wrote in 1838], when the discontents of a nation—not light and capricious discontents, but discontents which have been steadily increasing during a long series of years—have attained their full maturity . . . . Society which, but a short time before, was in a state of perfect repose, is on a sudden agitated with the most fearful convulsions, and seems to be on the verge of dissolution; and the rulers who, till the mischief was beyond the reach of all ordinary remedies, had never bestowed one thought on its existence, stand bewildered and panic-stricken, without hope or resource, in the midst of the confusion. One such conjuncture this generation has seen. . . . At such a conjuncture it was that Temple landed on English ground in the beginning of 1679.[9]

Thus 1832 was a date as notable and historically as significant as 1688. Not that the contestants, issues, or outcomes were the same. Whereas 1688 was "the Revolution which brought the Crown into harmony with the Parliament," 1832 was "the Revolution which brought the Parliament into harmony with the nation." The two events were comparable, and in a sense the achievements of 1832 were an enlargment of 1688. In each case consent had been withdrawn by a significant part of the nation, thus impairing the constitutional order; and in each case consent had been restored, allowing for a period of comparative tranquillity. These two turning points were so significant in Macaulay's view that in his initial conception of the *History* they defined the period he intended to cover.[10]

One can discern an implied cyclicalism in Macaulay's observations on historical change and even in the language he uses. An era is characterized either by tumult, conflict, sedition, turmoil, and sectarian zeal or by indifference, tranquillity, drowsiness, and apathy. Thus the eighteenth century was seen as a period of repose between periods of conflict and even revolution. At the time of George III's accession, "factions had sunk into a lethargy, such as had never been known since the great religious schism of the sixteenth century had roused the public mind from repose."[11] Parliamentary politics were calm. "The old party-distinctions were almost effaced.... A new generation of country-squires and rectors had arisen who knew not the Stuarts." In addition, religious passions were greatly attenuated. "The Dissenters were tolerated; the Catholics not cruelly persecuted. The Church was drowsy and indulgent." The aversion with which the monarchy was regarded disappeared (though affection for the royal house had not yet developed). Most of the conflicts that had plagued the seventeenth and early eighteenth centuries had diminished. "Whigs and Tories, Churchmen and Puritans, spoke with equal reverence of the constitution." The previous "dark" era of revolution was succeeded by a "bright and tranquil century" that brought "domestic peace."[12]

Macaulay generalized about this kind of development, and in doing so he may have had in mind his hopes for (and later his observations of) the mid-nineteenth century. "In the body politic, as in the natural body, morbid languor generally succeeds to morbid excitement.... The natural consequences followed. To frantic zeal succeeded sullen indifference.... The hot fit was over: the cold fit had begun: and it was long before seditious arts, or even real grievances, could bring back the fiery paroxysm which had run its course, and reached its termination."[13] Similarly he thought the mid-nineteenth century could be more tranquil than its early decades. This expectation was part of his rationale for the constitutional settlement of 1832. By 1846 he thought he was living at "a time when the prospect of good government and repose was opening before us, — a time when, after so long a period of gloom and tempest, the dawn of a bright and tranquil day seemed to be breaking upon Ireland, — when, throughout Great Britain, all passions seemed to be strangely lulled."[14]

Macaulay saw history (or at least English history) as an unending series of crises, each one unique, yet all comparable in certain respects. For one thing, they were similar in origin, for each one grew out of the resolution of a previous crisis. The remedies adopted at one period became part of the institutions that required reform at a future time. Old remedies thus became associated with new grievances and discontents. For example, "the revolution [of 1688] had saved the nation from one class of evils, but had at the same time—such is the imperfection of all things human—engendered or aggravated another class of evils which required new remedies."[15] The achievements of the Revolution—securing liberty and property against prerogative and establishing at least a measure of toleration—were gained by strengthening the House of Commons, and this created conditions that allowed for the development of what in the eighteenth century was labeled corruption and faction by the newly emerging class of discontented subjects. "Scarcely had the executive government become really responsible to the House of Commons, when it began to appear that the House of Commons was not really responsible to the nation." Many of the constituent bodies were controlled by individuals; often their votes were sold to the highest bidder; the public had no certain means of knowing, nor a right to know, what took place in Parliament; and in these circumstances some members allowed themselves to be bribed and formed themselves "into combinations for the purpose of raising the price of their votes." Thus, Macaulay explains, "while the ministry was accountable to the Parliament, the majority of the Parliament was accountable to nobody." These conditions, which had grown out of the remedies for the problems of Stuart times, opened the door for the movement seeking parliamentary reform.[16]

Noiseless revolutions, such as population shifts, the creation of new kinds of property, and the transformation of small towns into large cities, were irrevocable and made political change necessary. They created a disproportion between the natural, nonpolitical institutions and the artificial polity, and this was the primary source of that discontent which, if unattended, led to the withdrawal of consent and the long-term risk of revolution. Therefore, it was the main strategic task of politicians prudently to direct policy so as to eliminate abuses, preferably before grievances became acute. If this was postponed so long that discontents reached critical levels, it was the politicians' responsibility to make even radical changes, including the alteration of political institutions. At the time of the Reform Bill the greatest danger was the possibility of "a complete alienation of the people from their rulers." Thus Macaulay's immediate purpose was "to soothe the public mind," to "avert civil discord, and to uphold the authority of law." The long-term purpose of the Reform Bill was for "the healing of great distempers, for the securing at once of the public liberties and of the public repose, and for the reconciling and knitting together of all the orders of the State." Reconciliation was the most prominent theme in his rationale for reform, for it prevented the kind of conflict that undermined consent and legitimacy.[17]

It was not only necessary to appease discontent; it was also necessary to persuade those who feared change to agree to the adjustments in the constitution that were being proposed. Some sort of change was unavoidable; for once the public mind was severely agitated, the only question was what kind of change would take place — whether it would be change that was congenial to the social and political system as it had existed, or whether it would be radically discontinuous with the past. By making concessions that were compatible with the existing system and yet calculated to reduce grievances, the system, though changed, could be saved.

> It will soon again be necessary [he wrote in 1828] to reform that
> we may preserve; to save the fundamental principles of the con-
> stitution by alterations in the subordinate parts. It will then be
> possible, as it was possible two hundred years ago, to protect
> vested rights, to secure every useful institution — every insti-
> tution endeared by antiquity and noble associations; and, at
> the same time, to introduce into the system improvements
> harmonizing with the original plan.[18]

Reform had a conservative purpose; therefore conservatives ought to be willing to change. There was to be a blend of old and new. Macaulay thus met the conventional Tory-conservative position by urging that the country "pay a decent, a rational, a manly reverence to our ancestors, not by superstitiously adhering to what they, in other circumstances, did, but by doing what they, in our circumstances, would have done."[19]

The appropriate remedies could be prescribed only if the politician understood the origin of discontents in the uncoordi-nated changes that had taken place in social and economic institutions. He had to discern the noiseless revolutions and the way they developed. Correct (and this meant "early") diagnosis and treatment depended on historical analysis, and this gave practical utility to the study of history. "No past event has any intrinsic importance. The knowledge of it is valuable only as it leads us to form just calculations with respect to the future." It was the function of history "to supply statesmen with examples and warnings."[20]

With this as their purpose, most historians, in Macaulay's judgment, were strangely narrow and even irrelevant in their focus on the great and apparently decisive event. Instead of confining their attention to battles and courts and cabinet councils, it would have been more appropriate for them to study "the under current of human life" which flows on "unruffled by the storms which agitate the surface. The happiness of the many commonly depends on causes independent of victories or defeats, of revolutions or restorations, — causes which can be regulated by no laws, and which are recorded in no archives." These causes were the things to be understood. "History, without these, is a shell without a kernel." The historian must be like the intelligent traveler who tries to observe ordinary men as they appear in daily business and daily pleasure; who mingles in crowds, visits coffee-houses, obtains admittance to the domestic hearth; who bears with vulgar expressions and does not shrink from exploring even the retreats of misery. Yet historians "rarely descend to those details from which alone the real state of a community can be collected." Posterity is deceived by evidence from those "who mistake the splendour of a court for the happiness of a people."[21]

In making this plea for social history Macaulay was not asking that historians indiscriminately present all the facts bearing on man's daily life. They were to focus on the accumulation of small changes that led to noiseless revolutions. It was patterns that could be discerned by examining a long period of time that would be most significant; history "in small fragments, proves anything, or nothing, so I believe that it is full of useful and precious instruction when we contemplate it in large portions."[22]

Social history was politically relevant. The history of the people and the history of government were to be presented "in insep-arable conjunction and intermixture." Its justification was its usefulness to the politician. The main purpose of including in history the analysis of noiseless revolutions was to provide the politician with an intellectual tool that would permit him to preserve the constitution by making changes in it that restored its harmonious relationship to social and economic institutions:

> The instruction derived from history thus written, would be of a vivid and practical character.... As the history of states is generally written, the greatest and most momentous revolutions seem to come upon them like supernatural inflictions, without warning or cause. But the fact is, that such revolutions are almost always the consequences of moral changes, which have gradually passed on the mass of the community, and which ordinarily proceed far, before their progress is indicated by any public measure. An intimate knowledge of the domestic history of nations is therefore absolutely necessary to the prognosis of political events. A narrative, defective in this respect, is as useless as a medical treatise which should pass by all the symptoms attendant on the early stage of a disease and mention only what occurs when the patient is beyond the reach of remedies.

The proper kind of history would allow one to "see those opinions and feelings which produced the great struggle against the house of Stuart slowly growing up in the bosom of private families, before they manifested themselves in parliamentary debates."[23]

Revolution, then, could be avoided if concessions were made. But concessions had to be timely. Postponed too long, their only effect would be to exacerbate angry passions. Since their purpose was to maintain consent, which involved at least minimal attachment to the institutional order, concessions should be made "while old feelings and old associations retain a power and a charm which may too soon pass away." Thus it was important to concede early, while discontents and resentments were still muted, before political feeling was mobilized by an overtly hostile, subversive political movement. Macaulay thus concluded that there was "no great revolution which might not have been prevented by compromise early and graciously made...; in all movements of the human mind which tend to great revolution, there is a crisis at which moderate concession may amend, conciliate, and preserve."[24]

As an example of a concession postponed too long, which did not appease but stimulated discontent, Macaulay cited Catholic emancipation. "Remember how, in [Ireland], concessions too long delayed were at last received. That great boon which in 1801, in 1813, in 1825, would have won the hearts of millions, given too late, and given from fear, only produced new clamours and new dangers."[25] On the other hand, Elizabeth, whose conduct was "an admirable study for politicians who lived in unquiet times," exemplified the prudence of timeliness. "What she held, she held firmly. What she gave, she gave graciously. She saw that it was necessary to make a concession to the nation; and she made it, not grudgingly, not tardily, not as a matter of bargain and sale, not, in a word, as Charles the First would have made it, but promptly and cordially."[26] By contrast there was James I, "one of those kings whom God seems to send for the express purpose of hastening revolutions." He resembled the man who assists at a bullfight, who "goads the torpid savage to fury, by shaking a red rag in the air, and now and then throwing a dart, sharp enough to sting, but too small to injure."[27] In another example, Macaulay saw the intensity of vengeance during the French Revolution as a consequence of the delay with which concession was made. The French people were like the imprisoned genie who promised rewards to his liberator but in the end, after waiting too long, vowed to destroy him. "Such is the gratitude of nations exasperated by misgovernment to rulers who are slow to concede. The first use which they make of freedom is to avenge themselves on those who have been so slow to grant it."[28]

While urging timely concession, Macaulay did not recommend that a government treat every sign of dissatisfaction as a symptom of incipient revolution. He was in favor of firm repression of insignificant outbreaks, such as the Gordon Riots, that reflected a controllable local grievance. On the other hand, he certainly was not opposed to agitation. "I hold agitation to be essential, not only to the obtaining of good and just measures, but to the existence of a free Government itself . . .; the Slave-trade would never have been abolished without agitation . . .; what is agitation when it is examined, but the mode in which the people in the great outer assembly debate?" On the other hand, if agitation, even in a worthy cause, led to violation of the law, the transgressors were to be punished: "while the grievances should be remedied, the violation of the law should be punished." Or, as he put it on another occasion, "I altogether deny that assertion or insinuation . . . that a government which countenances, or does not discountenance, agitation will not punish rebellion."[29] It was a matter of judgment. The government, keeping in mind both libertarian values and its duty to enforce the law, would have to decide. Although he welcomed the agitation for parliamentary reform and against the slave trade, he approved of punishments for the rick-burners and the Bristol rioters; he wished to suppress Chartist rioting; and in 1848 he would have made an example of the rabble of the Faubourg St. Antoine.[30] He even defended the temporary suspension of habeas corpus and trial by jury as a way of controlling disturbances in Ireland; indeed, he "would rather err on the side of vigour than of lenity."[31]

The most vital question was whether popular agitation required concession. "Conspiracies and insurrections in which small minorities are engaged, the outbreakings of popular violence unconnected with any extensive project or any durable principle, are best repressed by vigour and decision. To shrink from them is to make them formidable." On the other hand, "no wise ruler will confound the pervading taint with the slight local irritation. No wise ruler will treat the deeply-seated discontents of a great party, as he treats the conduct of a mob which destroys mills and power-looms." It is necessary to "distinguish between a nation and a mob. Woe to the Government which thinks that a great, a steady, a long continued movement of the public mind is to be stopped like a street riot!"[32] Elizabeth made this distinction. In her day the monopoly question had provoked much anger:

> The language of the discontented party was high and menacing, and was echoed by the voice of the whole nation...; an indignant populace ... cursed the monopolies. There seemed for a moment to be some danger that the long and glorious reign of Elizabeth would have a shameful and disastrous end. She, however, with admirable judgment and temper, declined the contest, put herself at the head of the reforming party, redressed the grievance, ... brought back to herself the hearts of the people, and left to her successors a memorable example of the way in which it behoves a ruler to deal with public movements which he has not the means of resisting.[33]

To yield to the mob from fear would undermine the government; but a concession made before a large segment of the populace is alienated from the constitution is not intimidation but "honourable fear."[34]

In Macaulay's judgment the nation in 1831 could still be saved from revolution. The country was in a condition analogous to that of France under Turgot. There was still time to reform; indeed, a comparatively mild reform would be sufficient. But a time would come when this would do no good. Whereas many argued that the Reform Bill should be passed in order to ward off the threat of imminent revolution, Macaulay, despite moments of nervousness about the immediacy of the threat of revolution, on the whole felt that the nation was quite secure. The danger lay not in an explosive overthrow but in slow deterioration accompanied by petty but endemic attacks on public authority, such as existed in Ireland, where there was "a silent, but extensive and persevering war against the law" and "agitators stronger than the magistrate, associations stronger than the law, a Government powerful enough to be hated, and not powerful enough to be feared."[35]

Macaulay therefore justified the reforms proposed in 1831 as an early concession that would provide the reconciliation necessary to prevent revolution a decade or a generation later. Consequently, the events of 1848 later had special significance for him, for, after a moment of nervousness, and once the dust had settled, he saw the seeming immunity of Britain from the epidemic of revolution as the result of a policy of concession implemented in 1832.

> All around us [Macaulay wrote in November 1848] the world is convulsed by the agonies of great nations. Governments which lately seemed likely to stand during ages have been on a sudden shaken and overthrown. The proudest capitals of Western Europe have streamed with civil blood. All evil passions, the thirst of gain and the thirst of vengeance, the antipathy of class to class, the antipathy of race to race, have broken loose from the control of divine and human laws. Fear and anxiety have clouded the faces and depressed the hearts of millions. Trade has been suspended, and industry paralysed. The rich have become poorer; and the poor have become poorer.

In contrast to the Continent, "in our island the regular course of government has never been for a day interrupted. The few bad men who longed for license and plunder have not had the courage to confront for one moment the strength of a loyal nation, rallied in firm array round a parental throne."[36]

Macaulay celebrated the contrast between the tumultuous Continent and free yet orderly England. "The hurricane, which has recently overthrown so much that was great and that seemed durable, has only proved their [the institutions of Great Britain] solidity." The explanation for this contrast lay in the policy of timely concession, particularly as it was used in 1832. The resistance to revolution in 1848 was the result of "a policy of which the principle is to preserve what is good by reforming in time what is evil." The policy adopted in 1832 was not, however, a modern discovery. The English had a "history of a succession of timely reforms." The year 1688, for example, was so mild compared to 1848 that it seemed an abuse of language to call it a revolution. It helped to establish the belief that reforms could be achieved by appealing to the force of reason and public opinion, as had been done in 1846, when the Corn Laws were repealed. What was achieved on these earlier occasions "carried us safely through the year of revolutions and through the year of counterrevolutions."[37]

Macaulay's rationale for reform, that is, for concession, is in negative terms: it is formulated as a statement of the consequences of not reforming. Failure to reform would lead to conflict between irreconcilable sectarian parties, and perhaps revolution, if the discontented faction were strong enough, and to civil war as well, if the privileged classes were not too weak. On the other hand, if one does reform, all that is gained is a continuation of the old constitutional order. Social and economic changes would, of course, have taken place, some of them quite substantial; indeed, improvement, "progress," was to take place in this realm. But the emphasis is on continuity. Macaulay's outlook assumed that the institutional character of the historical polity was at least satisfactory and not easily to be improved.

Since Macaulay's argument emphasized the dreadful consequences of not making those timely concessions that would allow for continuity, one of its main components was an account of the process of deterioration that could take place if reforms were not made. Such deterioration was hastened by those who, by their rhetoric and their organizational efforts, were responsible for a push to the extremes. They could be either those who were eager for fundamental change or those who wanted no change at all. It was doctrinaires, whatever side they were on, who were objectionable, for they were obstacles to the practice of conciliatory politics. The timeliness of concession was necessary in order to deny doctrinaires an opportunity to exploit and mobilize grievances in a way that would have a destructive effect on the political system.

Distaste for, and disapproval of, doctrinaires, whether in politics or religion, is a pervasive theme in all of Macaulay's writings and speeches. It is as prominent in the *History* as in the essays. Of course the seventeenth century provided an amplitude of examples, whether among the Puritans or Jesuits, doctrinaire royalists or zealous republicans, as it threw up demagogic leaders and filled the ranks of the sects and factions that delayed the emergence of a stable and tolerant political order. Indeed, doctrinaires and fanatics are the villains of the *History*.

Doctrinaires were objectionable to Macaulay because they encouraged the development of separatist sects and factions by providing them with arguments and sometimes with leadership. Doctrinaire leaders introduced dogma into the political system — either the dogma of logic or the dogma of religion. They also articulated grievances and often sought political remedies for grievances that could be left apolitical. Furthermore, they mobilized the populace and committed their followers to irreconcilable positions. Once the doctrinaire spirit enters public debate, fragmentation develops; what once had been cleavages are turned into open conflicts.[38]

Doctrinaire leaders are zealous, with "all the strong lineaments which distinguish the men who produce revolutions from the men whom revolutions produce." Such leaders may have qualities that call for admiration — for example, Hampden, Pym, and Cromwell; but they can also be dangerous — for example, Caesar, Mahomet, and Robespierre. In either case, their distinguishing characteristic is their zeal, their "fixedness of purpose, intensity of will, enthusiasm which is not the less fierce or persevering because it is sometimes disguised under the semblance of composure."[39] Macaulay probably would have placed Cobbett in this category. He read through several volumes of Cobbett's writings during the late 1850s; and while he was fascinated by Cobbett's style, he could not restrain himself from recording his view that Cobbett was a "hateful fellow," indeed "an odious fellow on whichever side he fought — I hardly know a worse man."[40] In addition to the zealous men, there are those who join them, "common barrators in politics, dregs of society which, in times of violent agitation, are tossed up from the bottom to the top, and which, in quiet times, sink again from the top to their natural place at the bottom. To these men nothing is so hateful as the prospect of a reconciliation between the orders of the State."[41] Here he had in mind such men as Robert Ferguson, Titus Oates, Barère, and "that stupid worthless drunken dirty beast Tom Paine."[42] Whereas the zealots are driven to an irreconcilable position from conviction, the demagogue adopts the same posture but combines a certain amount of self-seeking with his misguided convictions.

Macaulay's disapproval of zealots, fanatics, and demagogues was enhanced by his belief that a large part of the populace was inclined to irrational, impassioned outbursts and was easily misled by leaders who appealed to its prejudices. The *History* often referred to the prejudices and passions, the ignorance and gullibility, of the vulgar multitude.[43] The period immediately after James II took flight provided an example of this mentality:

> All those evil passions which it is the office of government to restrain, and which the best governments restrain but imperfectly, were on a sudden emancipated from control; avarice, licentiousness, revenge, the hatred of sect to sect, the hatred of nation to nation. On such occasions it will ever be found that the human vermin, which, neglected by ministers of state and ministers of religion, barbarous in the midst of civilization, heathen in the midst of Christianity, burrows, among all physical and all moral pollution, in the cellars and garrets of great cities, will at once rise into a terrible importance.[44]

This was by no means a matter of historical interest only. The assumption that many wild passions lay barely dormant, always ready to burst out, perhaps explains why Macaulay was willing to allow some severity in the enforcement of the criminal law.[45] During the Indian Mutiny he was shocked by the emergence of ugly passions that were brought to the surface by accounts of atrocities. The nation was inflamed; even he was not immune. There was "one terrible cry for revenge." The account of the executions at Peshawar—forty men blown from the mouths of cannons—"was read with delight by people who three weeks ago were against all capital punishment." Until this year (1857), he said, "I did not know what real vindictive hatred meant."[46]

The great passions of the multitude were easily inflamed by

demagogues. There were natural agitators, exemplified by Robert Ferguson:

> Long habit had developed in him a moral disease from which
> people who have made political agitation their calling are
> seldom wholly free. He could not be quiet. Sedition, from being
> his business, had become his pleasure.... His hostility was
> not to Popery or to Protestantism, to monarchical or to
> republican government, ... but to whatever was at the time
> established.[47]

There were also the self-seekers and the fanatics; all played the
same role of exacerbating hostile feelings. The relation of agitator
to populace was exemplified by the popular response to the
accusations made in 1678 by Titus Oates. Oates imagined and
spread rumors about a Catholic conspiracy; he "constructed a
hideous romance, resembling rather the dream of a sick man
rather than any transaction which ever took place in the real
world." Bizarre though his accusations were, "the public mind was
so sore and excitable that these lies readily found credit with the
vulgar," and even reflecting men gave them some credence. "The
capital and the whole nation went mad with hatred and fear."
Oates's crime was not unique. The populace was vulnerable to this
kind of exploitation of their fears. There were other Popish plots;
there were Whig plots; and then there were Jacobite plots. Titus
Oates "was the founder of a school. His success proved that no
romance is too wild to be received with faith by understandings
which fear and hatred have disordered. His slanders were mon-
strous: but they were well timed: he spoke to a people made
credulous by their passions." No story, Macaulay said in another
context, "is too absurd to be imposed on minds blinded by
religious and political fanaticism."[48]

The image of great passions in the subterranean depths of
society, as in a dormant volcano, was part of Macaulay's outlook.
Even when the passions were not angry or violent, he felt uneasy
about them. Love of church and love of freedom, in themselves
commendable, were able, if excited, to "convulse the state." And
patriotism, "a most useful sentiment ... has given a character of
peculiar atrocity to war, and has generated that worst of all
political evils, the tyranny of nations over nations."[49]

Since the populace is vulnerable to the influence of the
demagogue or the zealot, particularly when it has genuine

grievances, concessions must be made before it is driven to support extreme parties. Thus the mere proposal of the Reform Bill "took away the power of interested agitators." It was a mistake merely "to oppose agitation and multiply the grievances by which agitation is alone supported, and by which it was originated."[50] There are two alternatives in times of change and agitation—the counsels of moderate reformers or the counsels of extremists. On the one hand, there is "true statesmanship, which, at once animating and gently curbing the honest enthusiasm of millions, guides it safely and steadily to a happy goal." On the other hand, "when men are refused what is reasonable, they ... demand what is unreasonable. It is not strange that, when they find that their opinion is condemned and neglected by the Legislature, they ... lend a too favourable ear to worthless agitators." Macaulay concluded that "the true source of the power of demagogues is the obstinacy of rulers and that a liberal Government makes a conservative people."[51]

While Macaulay clearly had religious and political Radicals in mind when he discussed extremists, he did not exclude the Tories from this description. By denying the need for concession (or by conceding too little or conceding too late), they prevented reform and thus facilitated the rise of the zealots and the demagogues. In this way they intensified conflict and made parties and classes irreconcilable. To Macaulay the Tories were in their own way doctrinaire, even fanatical. They had an image of the past that was a standard by which they judged the needs of the present. They, like some Radicals, had "general doctrines" to which they sacrificed practical considerations.[52] Such Tories were exemplified by Southey and Sidmouth and Eldon and Croker and by the ultras, all of whom were seen as uncompromising. This image prevailed even when Peel was their leader. He was regarded (in 1840) as a calm and moderate leader unable to control his party. He was "free from the fanaticism which is found in so large a measure among his followers...; the party which follows him ... has become fiercer and more intolerant even than in days gone by." Thus Macaulay visualized the Tory party as attempting to perpetuate or even restore the conditions of a past time. For example, in 1840 he suspected that the repeal of the Catholic Emancipation Act was the chief object of the great majority of that party and that they even wanted to undo 1832.[53]

To him the Tory creed consisted of antiquated views that were the subject of toasts by squires and rectors of Pitt clubs—for example, the favoring of restrictions on worship and trade.[54] With regard to the Corn Laws, Macaulay asserted that nine-tenths of Peel's followers were opposed to all change. They were a formidable obstacle to the implementation of the policy of timely concession.[55]

Macaulay's judgment of Tories as insensitive to the importance of timely concession is also revealed in his condemnation of Sir Robert Peel's stand on Catholic emancipation. The way in which Peel dealt with that question was a model of imprudence. The concession would have removed grievances and avoided indignation, had it been made earlier; but in the end this concession was made for the wrong reason and long after it would have had a healing effect. To the Irish Catholics the association with England meant penal codes and religious disabilities:

> [It] became an emblem of disappointed hopes and violated pledges. Nevertheless, it was not even then too late. It was not too late in 1813; it was not too late in 1821; it was not too late even in 1825; if the same men who were then, as they are now, high in the service of the Crown, would have made up their minds to say that which they were forced to say four years later; even then the benefits . . . might have been realized. The apparatus of agitation was not then organized, the Government was under no coercion; that which was afterwards given in 1829 might have been given with honour and advantage, and might, most probably would, have secured the gratitude of the Irish Catholic people. But in 1829 concession was made, and largely made . . . but still made reluctantly, and with obvious dislike . . . while the Government was in a state of duresse, and made from the dread of civil war.[56]

Macaulay acknowledged that Peel was correct in stating in 1829 that the state would have been in danger if the concession had not been made; but he held that there would have been no danger had concession been made at an earlier date:

> What we blamed was his conduct in 1825 and still more in 1827. We said—either you were blind not to foresee what was coming; or you acted culpably in not settling the question when it might have been settled without the disgrace of yielding to agitation and to the fear of insurrection.[57]

This conduct was a reflection of Peel's general insensitivity to the dangers of stimulating and disappointing the passions of party men and the populace. Although Macaulay, after years of being severely critical of Peel, finally softened and even celebrated his 1846 achievement as that of a great commercial reformer, he never forgot or forgave the way Peel had dealt with the Catholic question. It was this that made the Tories for him a party that would conduct "a pertinacious, vehement, provoking opposition to safe and reasonable change, and that [would] then, in some moment of fear or caprice . . . bring in, and fling on the table, in a fit of desperation or levity, some plan which will loosen the very foundations of society."[58]

The Tory resistance to change would alienate even the middle classes, among whom there was hope for moderate reform as well as an interest in property and tranquillity. This class could be made more radical, and it might be driven to combine with the working classes. An Eldonine government would provoke even moderate reformers into becoming revolutionaries. Macaulay genuinely believed that such a government might lead to "a revolution, a bloody and unsparing revolution."[59] In addition, the Tory disposition to repress would have the same effect. Recalling the "Six Acts" of 1819 and the press prosecutions, he saw the Tory policy of suppression as a way of stimulating, not removing, grievances.[60]

The consequences of extremism were the same whichever side of the political spectrum it was on. "Fanatics of one kind might anticipate a golden age, in which men should live under the simple dominion of reason, in perfect equality and perfect amity, without property, or marriage, or king, or God. A fanatic of another kind might see nothing in the doctrines of the philosophers but anarchy and atheism, might cling more closely to every old abuse, and might regret the good of old days. . . ."[61] Each kind, by adopting a posture that provoked opposition from both the center and its own ideological opposite, made conciliation impossible. However, with the postponement of concession, the center might diminish as those located there moved toward the extremes. Consequently, the extremes would flourish, and there was a risk that they would dominate the political arena. They had a mutually stimulating effect: "each extreme necessarily engenders its opposite." For example, "imprudent and obstinate opposition to reasonable demands had brought on anarchy; and as soon as men had a near view of anarchy they fled in terror to crouch at the feet of despotism."[62] Each thrived on conflict with the other, as might be expected, for each addressed itself to the same issues. Indeed, there seemed to be "a real alliance between the two extreme parties," whose conduct jointly frustrated attempts at conciliation. Thus there was a "coalition between those who hate all liberty and those who hate all order." Both parties were made up of malcontents, and they were to "be divided into two classes, the friends of corruption and the sowers of sedition." This classification was not applicable to the early nineteenth century alone. In Stuart, indeed in all times, there would be extremists — on one side "bigoted dotards," and "shallow and reckless empirics" on the other.[63]

This kind of situation was frustrating to moderate men, who found themselves driven to adopt extreme postures. Even those leaders who had attempted to seek compromise were led to see only two extreme alternatives. For example, Hampden, whose "influence had hitherto been exerted rather to restrain than to animate the zeal of his party," finally, in the face of the king's severity and intransigence, concluded that the situation "left no hope of a peaceable adjustment." Consequently "nothing remained but to try the chances of war."[64] In the end "all accommodation had become impossible." Even the moderate "constitutional Royalists [Hyde, Falkland, Colepepper] were forced to make their choice between two dangers." Charles "had made his old enemies irreconcilable, had driven back into the ranks of the disaffected a crowd of moderate men who were in the very act of coming over to his side . . .; the sword was at length drawn . . .; two hostile factions appeared in arms against each other."[65]

Once a society became fragmented and passions were aroused, even a political genius such as Cromwell could hardly be expected to reestablish a stable, libertarian order acceptable to the conflicting sects and factions. The political and religious passions, not only of his followers but of his enemies, were too varied and too intense. Macaulay therefore concluded that "the violence of religious and political enmities rendered a stable and happy settlement next to impossible."[66] In Macaulay's view, Cromwell was forced by his followers to become a regicide; he sought to heal the wounds left by civil war and "to restore, in all essentials, that ancient constitution which the majority of the people had always loved, and for which they now [in the 1650s] pined." But this was beyond the power even of Cromwell, "the most profound politician of that age."[67]

The literature of antiquity must also have encouraged Macaulay to think about seventeenth-century events in relation to a theory of history in which despotism and anarchy were the most important categories. However, during the period when his political outlook took shape, the French Revolution was an event he could not ignore; and he was able to comprehend it with the historical theory that was so prominent a part of the 1822 essay on William III. He had no difficulty in seeing French history as alternating between regimes that were oppressive and even despotic and regimes that were destructive and sometimes anarchic; indeed, this was the conventional way of understanding modern French history. In this view, revolution, including the prototype event of 1789, was not a permanent remedy; rather, it was a prelude to counterrevolution (and therefore a return to despotism) if not to civil war.[68] This is borne out by Macaulay's analysis of the Napoleonic period in his unfinished "History of France from the Restoration of the Bourbons to the Accession of Louis Philippe" (written in 1830–31), in which the Napoleonic regime is described as a military despotism that replaced the "calamities of anarchy" prevailing during the Revolution, in which there had been "an utter dissolution, a chaos, a new creation" produced by "jacobinical fanaticism."[69] Napoleon, however, like all despots, brought order but not true stability, as was revealed in 1814, when, because of defeat on the battlefield, he retired to Elba. Feeling neither veneration nor loyalty, the extremist groups into which the nation was divided demonstrated that the foundations for a regime enjoying genuine consent did not exist. On one side the ultra-royalists wanted restoration; on the other were the "zealous republicans," so animated by the ideals of the Revolution that they could not accept the monarchy of Louis XVIII.[70] Facing such divisions, compromise, if not reconciliation, was necessary. Unfortunately, Talleyrand, "who was fitted beyond any man in France, by his talents and by his situation, to act the part of mediator between the old dynasty and the new people," was about to depart for the Congress of Vienna.

In his absence, Louis XVIII offered concessions and attempted to arrange a compromise, but the divisions were too deep and the passions too powerful.[71] The nation (to use the language of the 1822 essay on William III) was not in "that happy central point in which alone it can repose"; on the contrary, it continued "to oscillate between . . . extremes." Thus, within the year, Napoleon was restored. Although the regime again fell because of military defeat, the succession of regimes in France allowed Macaulay to believe that his expectation of alternating periods of anarchy and despotism was based on a true understanding of history.

Macaulay of course approved of neither extreme; but in making historical judgments, he had, while condemning violence, an understanding for the grievances of the revolutionaries. Although he never failed to point to the excesses of the Jacobins, he also "acknowledged that the subjects of Louis the Fifteenth had every excuse which men could have for being eager to pull down." Furthermore, he held that "the evil was temporary, and the good durable." He felt that revolutions had to be judged, not episodically, but with their long-term consequences in mind. While he understood the response of liberal-minded men who condemned the Revolution, he thought they judged too quickly, without evidence of the long-term results. With his larger perspective, he announced his "deliberate opinion that the French Revolution, in spite of all its crimes and follies, was a great blessing to mankind."[72] This kind of judgment was not confined to the French Revolution. "Many evils, no doubt, *were* produced by the [English] civil war. They were the price of our liberty." He deplored the high price (and specifically condemned the regicides), but attributed it to the magnitude of the evil that was even more unacceptable.[73] Indeed, revolutionary violence was to be understood in terms of a sociological law; it was "a rule without exception, that the violence of a revolution corresponds to the degree of misgovernment which has produced that revolution." This explained the variations in the amount of violence accompanying 1641 and 1688, 1776 and 1789, and the rebellions in 1688–89 in England and in Scotland.[74]

Although he acknowledged the good results, even when combined with great human cost, of certain historical revolutions, he responded to all contemporary revolutionary situations at least with great caution and usually with alarm. There is a bold statement in a letter to his father from Cambridge: "I am impatient for what, I fear, can alone terminate this [the slave trade] and innumerable other abuses, an explosion in France, which may at once overthrow a family on which prosperity and adversity, empire and exile, have in vain been tried, — and whom the tremendous past has not instructed to read the most palpable signs of the more tremendous future."[75] Apart from this statement, Macaulay was severe in his judgments of revolution.

> Revolution [he wrote in 1830] is . . . in itself an evil; — an evil, indeed, which ought sometimes to be incurred for the purpose of averting or removing greater evils, but always an evil. The burden of the proof lies heavy on those who oppose existing governments; nor is it enough for them to show that the government which they purpose to establish is better than that which they purpose to destroy. The difference between the two systems must be great, indeed, if it justifies men in substituting the empire of force for that of law; in resolving society back into its original elements; in breaking all those associations which are the safeguards of property and order.[76]

He evaluated actual revolutions with the example of 1789 in mind. Although he regarded the events of July 1830 as benign, he also sensed the dangers. The spirit of 1789 "revived with all its original energy, but with an energy moderated by wisdom and humanity." In Paris, six weeks after the revolution was accomplished, he acknowledged that in general the working class was not disorderly. Yet he also reported that "there have been little signs," such as strikes, attacks on machinery, and the distribution of inflammatory handbills. "At present every thing is quiet.... Still the thing may happen . . . the multitude may become discontented. Such a crisis . . . might bring back the worst scenes of the former revolution."[77] When the revolutions in 1848 broke out, he was even more severe. And when French visitors broached the question of resistance to the regime of Napoleon III, he was dubious. In talking to a German visitor, he "argued strongly against the notion that much good was likely to be done by insurrection against even the bad govts of the Continent. What good have the revolutions of 1848 done? Or rather what harm have they not done? Here is France worse than in 1788 after seventy years of revolutions."[78]

Macaulay speculated about how he might have felt about the Revolution of 1789. He thought that Bentham, Dumont, and Mackintosh were reasonable in initially welcoming the French Revolution; but he admitted that, had he lived at the time, he too might have reacted against it as they did. "We cannot be sure that, if our lot had been cast in their times, we should not, like them . . . have seen, in that great victory of the French people, only insanity and crime."[79] And in the "History of France," while acknowledging that there had been benefits from the Revolution, he held that,

> If, in 1789, a wise and good man could have foreseen all the calamities through which the existing generation was about to pass, he would have thought it better to accept those concessions which the king and the aristocracy were disposed to offer, and to trust the rest to time and the progress of the human mind, than to make society pass through the agonies and convulsions of an utter dissolution, for the purpose of effecting a complete purification in a few years.[80]

He even thought Voltaire "would have been very much against the Revolution."[81]

The only kind of revolutions that Macaulay unequivocally approved were those he called "defensive." Although revolutions, they were not marked by vindictive hatred and great destruction, and the changes that accompanied them did not require the sacrifice of historical continuity; indeed, they were defensive because they preserved some essential feature of the polity that experienced the revolution. The attraction of defensive revolutions was their moderation—passions were restrained, conflicts were attenuated. They were managed by men who were neither visionaries desperately anxious to destroy the existing social order, nor conservatives, rigidly attached to that order. These "revolutionaries" were willing to make changes in order to reestablish consent for the essential features of the existing order—for the institution of private property or for the rule of law. Thus they were engaged in political battle on two fronts: against those who would, in a sense, change everything in order to establish a new regime, and those who would change nothing in order to preserve the existing regime. For example, Macaulay saw the revolution in France in 1830 as being supported by the middle classes against "an exclusive and oppressive aristocracy" and against the working class, which, though still quiet, showed in its conduct signs that were potentially dangerous.[82] The Revolution of 1688 was celebrated as a defensive revolution in the *History,* and this had been his view as early as 1822 (although he did not then use the phrase), when he emphasized that it was a revolution that supported social order and the rule of law. And this remained his view, for in 1858 he observed that "the only revolutions which have turned out well have been defensive revolutions—ours of 1688—the French of 1830—the American [which] was, to a great extent, of the same kind."[83]

The benefits of having experienced a defensive revolution were not necessarily permanent. Inevitably there would be social dislocations and discontents which political skill would not remedy. Consequently, it was not impossible that another (and not a defensive) revolution might take place. It was unlikely, but it was not impossible; and over a long period of time this was Macaulay's nightmare. His belief that it was not unlikely came to the surface in 1827, when he forecast that "this country could not be governed for a single generation by such men as Lord Westmoreland and Lord Eldon, without extreme risk of revolution." The risk of foreseeable if not immediate revolution justified reform in 1832. Even at mid-century, when he was less alarmist, Macaulay still was fearful that apparent calm might conceal imminent danger. Remembering the Continent before 1848, he noted the "outward show of tranquillity; and there were few, even of the wisest among us, who imagined what wild passions, what wild theories, were fermenting under that peaceful exterior." This uneasiness about the real condition of the foundations made him alert, even hypersensitive, to symptoms of disorder. He was quick to recall examples of riots—the Gordon Riots, machine-breaking, Peterloo, and rick-burning; riots at Nottingham, Bristol, and Newport; the Luddites, Swing, Cold Bath Fields, and Rebecca. It is often pointed out that Macaulay was exultant over the failure of the threat to public order in England in April 1848; but at the time, and before the threat passed, he felt quite uneasy. "I did for one moment doubt," he said, "whether the progress of society was not about to be arrested, nay, to be suddenly and violently turned back."[84] Even as late as 1850 he confessed being "more inclined to be an alarmist in politics than is usual with me":

All is quiet in appearance; and yet there is a look about things which alarms me. I see nothing, man or institution, that seems to be of force to stand against a storm; and a storm must come, God knows whence or when, but from some quarter or other and in no long time. I try to comfort myself by saying that such a storm will of itself call out a force of character which seems wanting and will dispel many pernicious illusions. All this is probably true. But yet, I feel, I fear.[85]

In view of these apprehensions, it is surprising that so many of Macaulay's critics have accused him of complacency about the condition of society and optimism about its future. In some moods and on many occasions he did display confidence, but it was usually a comparative confidence, based on a historian's awareness of what the level of achievement had been in a previous age. Regardless of the confidence that was a product of historical perspective, he was never without an undercurrent of anxiety about the durability and foundation of apparently stable societies.

Fear of revolution was, to be sure, a part of the conventional outlook of Macaulay's educated, propertied contemporaries, but Macaulay's image of the problem of revolution as it was found in his country in his time was not typical. Whereas many of his contemporaries feared a cataclysmic explosion, Macaulay pictured revolution developing from the slow erosion of consent and the accumulation of grievances that made violent revolution a long-term danger. Whereas his contemporaries seemed to associate revolution solely with Jacobinism, Macaulay formed his image of revolution on a more varied historical experience, in which the events of the seventeenth century in England, the political dimensions of the Reformation, as well as the discussions of historical change in the literature of antiquity all played a part. Furthermore, whereas Macaulay's contemporaries typically thought of revolution in economic and class terms, he was sensitive to the way religious enthusiasm, doctrinaire politics, and traditionalism that causes resistance to change could combine with the resentments of an economically deprived class to create revolutionary situations. Moreover, unlike many of his contemporaries, Macaulay did not have a simple bourgeois concern with the threat to private property; he was also worried by the threat of a counterrevolution that would bring despotism in its train, and here his image of the danger was shaped by the theory of historical cycles found in his

1822 prize essay on William III. Thus he was not only worried by Radicals, who created the appearance of anarchy and revolution, thereby stimulating the fears of the governing class; he was also worried by a ruling class that failed to relieve distress and reduce grievances and that became insensitive, unyielding, and repressive through an exaggerated fear of violent revolution. Each contributed its own threat — anarchy and perhaps revolution from one, and the undermining of the constitution and perhaps despotism from the other. Together they held out the danger of civil war.

For Macaulay there were two main intellectual sources of erroneous political judgment. One lay in attempts to achieve a precision of definition and rigorous certainty through a form of deductive thinking that was inappropriate to politics. This was exemplified by James Mill. The other lay in an inappropriate attitude to the past, an attitude which assumed that what was established in the past should be a model for the present. Both outlooks were dangerous because they encouraged an inflexible mode of political conduct; both prevented the politician from playing the role of conciliator. The one error might be called the fault of the Radical, the other the fault of the Tory.

The Tory's — or perhaps we should say the ultra-Tory's — error arose from a tendency to revere whatever was old. This error, said Macaulay, "may perpetually be observed in the reasonings of conservative politicians on the questions of their own day." They assumed that what was established in the past represented the achievement of good and wise men whose judgment ought not to be questioned. They made the mistake of "judging the present by the past." For example, on the issue of Catholic disqualifications from public office, some politicians, "starting from the true proposition that the Revolution had been a great blessing to our country, arrived at the false conclusion that no test which the statesmen of the Revolution had thought necessary for the protection of our religion and our freedom could be safely abolished." This fallacy could be found in the speeches of "the acute and learned Eldon" and was also exemplified by Charles I, who sought to govern as if society were still in the condition it had been under

Elizabeth.[1] Such a politician became a "bigot who pleads the wisdom of our ancestors as a reason for not doing what they in our place, would be the first to do." Although Macaulay entertained the thought that some conservatives "profess to hold in reverence the great names and great actions of former times . . . in order to find in them some excuse for existing abuses," he also acknowledged that their outlook arose from honest though misguided conviction, shaped more by ideology than by cynical calculation. But whatever its origin, the "error bears directly on practical questions, and obstructs useful reforms."[2]

Macaulay admired Bacon and advocated the inductive method, and in this connection he often criticized those who were guilty of another intellectual error — that of manipulating abstractions through deductive reasoning, which led to erroneous and perhaps dangerous conclusions. Macaulay formed his judgment about these matters by considering their relations to politics and not as one deeply concerned with epistemology. His sole concern was to identify the way of discovering the principles of what he called "civil prudence."

Those who used the deductive method performed discrete intellectual operations: first, the arbitrary selection of assumptions about reality; second, the process of drawing inferences from them. The making of assumptions is inherently arbitrary and necessary to logical and mathematical inquiries, but Macaulay questioned whether the deductive method was appropriate to the investigation of politics or any kind of problem for which the data were human conduct and individual psychology. There were great variations in conduct and in the social manifestations of individual motivation; in addition, there was a variety of ways in which motivation could be understood, either by the actor or by the observer. Because of this variation, any arbitrary assumption about motivation or behavior, if then made the source of deductions, would lead to a distorted understanding. It is by making definitions, which give only an "affectation of precision," that arbitrariness enters into the understanding of those responsible for this intellectual error. "The fact is, that when men, in treating of things which cannot be circumscribed by precise definitions, adopt this mode of reasoning, when once they begin to talk of power, happiness, misery, pain, pleasure, motives, objects of desire, as they talk of lines and numbers, there is no end to the contradictions and absurdities into which they fall."[3]

In Macaulay's view, James Mill exemplified this type of erroneous thinking in his "Essay on Government." Using a Hobbesian model, Mill assumed that all men are rapacious in their efforts to maximize pleasure and minimize pain and that, if not restrained by government, they will do injury to their neighbors. Mill "proceeds to reason as if men had no desires but those which can be gratified only by spoliation and oppression." Macaulay insisted that Mill was being arbitrary in face of the fact that men vary in this respect. Mill "has chosen to look only at one-half of human nature, and to reason on the motives which impel men to oppress and despoil others, as if they were the only motives by which men could possibly be influenced." Admittedly some—indeed, all men—have some desires that impel them to injure their neighbors; occasionally, however, such desires are restrained by a wish to avoid the disapproval of others. To want their approval is a different kind of desire, and it does not require spoliation in order to be gratified.[4] Acknowledging that men desire gratification and that they "always act from self-interest," Macaulay also insisted that these propositions, though universally and absolutely true, are useless, for they conceal the great variation in the ways men define gratification and self-interest. Mill gained assent for the general proposition that men act from self-interest, but he then assumed that self-interest consisted of the gratification of only certain desires, whereas desires in fact vary: "Man differs from man; generation from generation; nation from nation. Education, station, sex, age, accidental associations, produce infinite shades of variety."[5]

The making of arbitrary assumptions, Macaulay held, is but the first step in the process of reasoning deductively. Because the necessarily arbitrary assumptions remove from consideration much of the empirical basis for sound understanding of any political or social phenomenon, they provide a false foundation for the ensuing deductions. Consequently, deductive reasoning, in this kind of inquiry, only compounds the fallacy established by the selective, biased assumptions. It is "easy to deduce doctrines of vast importance from the original axiom." However, because of the arbitrariness and narrowness of the assumptions, "the axiom becomes false, and all the doctrines consequent upon it are false likewise." Thus "logic has its illusions."[6] Its practitioners, who misapply it in social and political investigations, are misled "by a fondness for neat and precise forms of demonstration"; they consider politics "as a science of which all the difficulties may be resolved by short synthetical arguments," but their only achievement is a "pretended demonstration."[7]

It was this method of reasoning that had misled James Mill. Mill held that there were no adequate checks on the rapacity of the government; but this conclusion, the fruit of logic, ignored the way constitutional restraints and public opinion in fact prevented the outcome he foresaw. Mill held that there was an inevitable tendency for power to concentrate in the aristocracy; he thus held that mixed government was impossible. But these inferences from his assumption about human nature and his formal definition of power prevented him from observing that power is shared, that there is a "real distribution of power" that does not coincide with his labels and definitions of social classes.[8] Finally, as a remedy for aristocratic control of government and, what went with it, exploitation of the populace, Mill prescribed popular control, that is, democracy; but Macaulay thought him blind to informal but nonetheless real controls of the government by the people.[9]

Macaulay thought that James Mill visualized political problems in overly simple ways and that this was the result of his use of the a priori method. Macaulay recognized, however, that the temperament of the zealot could produce the same result. In either case, oversimplification prevented a correct understanding of the problems, since it did not take into account all the gradations and variations that cannot be summarized, either by the arbitrary assumptions with which such investigators begin or by the inferences they draw from them. "The subtilty [sic] of nature, in the moral as in the physical world, triumphs over the subtilty of syllogism." Macaulay concluded that "the a priori method is altogether unfit for investigations of this kind" and that "it is utterly impossible to deduce the science of government from the principles of human nature."[10]

Although Macaulay often objected to the a priori method on the ground that it leads to fallacious conclusions, he was primarily concerned with the political consequences of such judgments. Such judgments, he argued, are inflexible, and their inflexibility has an intellectual origin. Insofar as the intellectual process on which they rest begins with arbitrary assumptions, the eye is closed to all the variations in motivation and conduct that are not incorporated in the assumptions. In addition, the drawing of logically necessary conclusions from this overly narrow foundation has the effect of closing the mind to alternative understandings. This lack of flexibility would hardly be useful to a politician who sought to gain consent for a policy among men and parties of diverse outlooks and interests. "Logic admits of no compromise. The essence of politics is compromise. It is therefore not strange that some of the most important and most useful political instruments in the world should be among the most illogical compositions that were ever penned."

In connection with the resolution of January 1689, declaring the throne vacant, Macaulay noted that many of those taking part in the deliberations were committed to theoretical understandings derived from assumptions about the obligations of the subject to the sovereign and about the nature of sovereignty. Some of these positions were associated with Sidney, others with Harrington, some with Anglicanism, others with the Puritans. Some pointed to the necessity for toleration, some to the necessity of its opposite. Propositions fully satisfactory to any one of these contestants would have antagonized the others; Macaulay contrasted them all to the "real statesmen" (Somers, Maynard), who were indifferent to logic. For them, words, "if they effect that which they are intended to effect, they are rational though they may be contra-dictory. If they fail of attaining their end, they are absurd, though they carry demonstration with them." Thus the real statesmen used "language which, in a philosophical treatise, would justly be reprehended as inexact and confused. They cared little whether their major agreed with their conclusion, if the major secured two hundred votes, and the conclusion two hundred more. In fact the one beauty of the resolution is its inconsistency."[11]

The rigidity associated with a priori reasoning in politics was of course not solely intellectual in origin. Rigidity and dogmatism can also come from zeal and fanaticism. And, as already men-tioned, there is no character that Macaulay condemns more consistently than the fanatic, whether in religion or politics, among historical figures or contemporaries, and regardless of political outlook. Titus Oates, Loyola, Ferguson, Paine, Barère,

Father Petre, Robespierre — all are condemned. In some of these men Macaulay sees the visionary whose moral certainty and millennial fantasies justify the most hideous crimes. But he is hardly less harsh on the ideologue, "those people who, in their speculations on politics, are not reasoners but fanciers; whose opinions, even when sincere, are not produced, according to the ordinary law of intellectual births, by induction and inference, but are equivocally generated by the heat of fervid tempers out of the overflowings of tumid imaginations. A man of this class," Macaulay continued, "is always in extremes. . . . His admiration oscillates between the most worthless of rebels and the most worthless of oppressors. . . . He can forgive anything but temperance and impartiality."[12]

This kind of outlook was equally objectionable in religion or politics. Indeed, Macaulay's objection originated in the realization that it flourished among those for whom religion and politics were hardly distinguishable and whose success would merge these two realms. While some might object that considerations of power corrupted religion, this was no great concern for Macaulay; what he objected to was the infusion of the religious spirit into politics. Religious faith mixed with politics made men dogmatic, tendentious, and irreconcilable. In 1688–89 it was "the bigots who still clung to the doctrines of Filmer" and "the enthusiasts who still dreamed the dreams of Harrington" who blocked a settlement. The nonjurors were willing to give up both order and liberty from devotion "to a superstition as stupid and degrading as the Egyptian worship of cats and onions."[13] In his own time, of course, those who betrayed a religious dimension in their politics were usually not, in the strict sense of the word, religious. They were, however, advocates of ideologies and were rigid and dogmatic; in a sense, they were spokesmen for political religions. So Macaulay called them enthusiasts and, collectively, sectarians. At the horizon of his vision loomed the ultimate threat posed by zealots: "zeal makes revolutions"; but his more immediate and typical concern was with the way that ideologies, like religious doctrines in the past, would mislead politicians, causing them to attend only to the symbols and mythological fables with which every political sect was preoccupied. There were the squires and rectors at the Pitt clubs and the honest Radicals who enthusiastically toasted the cause of Hampden and Sidney.[14] Such persons, blind to the underlying realities, could not practice conciliatory politics.

James Mill and his disciples were irreconcilable, doctrinaire, and sectarian both by their adoption of the a priori method and by their dogmatic temperaments. Their argument and their fervor combined to make them particularly objectionable to Macaulay. The *Westminster* reviewer was a "zealot of a sect." The religiosity that flavored the politics of Mill's disciples attracted Macaulay's criticism. "By the members of his sect . . . [James Mill's "Essay on Government"] is considered as perfect and unanswerable. Every part of it is an article of their faith; and the damnatory clauses in which their creed abounds far beyond any theological symbol with which we are acquainted, are strong and full against all who reject any portion of what is so irrefragably established."[15] Macaulay was not alone in observing the sectarian character of James Mill's disciples. John Stuart Mill in his *Autobiography* confessed that he and his friends eagerly adopted his father's opinions with "youthful fanaticism."[16]

In part Macaulay found the disciples of James Mill an embarrassment. Like them, he thought of himself as a reformer, yet as political allies they drove away support. They used "Benthamese" jargon, "a new sleight of tongue." They had "narrow understandings, and little information"; "they surrender their understandings . . . to the meanest and most abject sophisms, provided these sophisms come before them disguised with the externals of demonstration." To read their works, Macaulay said, "is the most soporific employment that we know." They deserved "the derision of mankind." For these reasons they were poor allies:

> We dread the odium and discredit of their alliance. We wish to see a broad and clear line drawn between the judicious friends of practical reform, and a sect. . . . There is not . . . in this country, a party so unpopular. They have already made the science of Political Economy . . . an object of disgust to the majority of the community. The question of Parliamentary Reform will share the same fate, if once an association be formed in the public mind between Reform and Utilitarianism.[17]

There was more than embarrassment, however, in Macaulay's criticisms of the young Benthamites. In some circumstances they would be a dangerous menace. In what was certainly an allusion to them, written at a time when Macaulay had become acquainted with John Stuart Mill and his friends, he described them as a republican sect, comparable in certain respects to the Jacobins and the Puritans, whose members "profess to derive their opinions from demonstration alone." Their arrogance, intolerance, and "philosophic pride" invited derision, at least in normal times, that is, as long as there was no serious discontent. However, he could visualize circumstances—if an extreme Tory government gained power—in which they could be dangerous. "Under an ignorant and tyrannical ministry, obstinately opposed to the most moderate and judicious innovations, their principles would spread.... A strong democratic party would be formed in the educated class." This would give radical middle-class leadership to a revolutionary movement composed of both middle and working classes, and the stage would be set for civil conflict.[18]

It is not surprising that, with concerns like these, Macaulay tried to discredit the aspects of Utilitarianism that fostered doctrinaire and sectarian politics. He may well have seen Mill's "Essay on Government" as a symbol of intellectualized Radicalism.[19] At Cambridge he had observed its pervasive influence on some of his contemporaries. There he had known Charles Austin, who was a bearer of James Mill's influence among the students.[20] Both had taken part in the Union debates in which Mill's doctrine was disputed; and he had "disputed with Charles Austin till four in the morning over the comparative merits of the Inductive and the *apriori* method in politics."[21] Macaulay might also have observed that James Mill was the source of the main doctrines regularly disputed in the London Debating Society, where the "Essay" was "almost a textbook to many of those who may be termed the Philosophic Radicals."[22]

Macaulay emphasized that it was to Mill's method of reasoning that he objected:

> Our object at present is, not so much to attack or defend any particular system of polity, as to expose the vices of a kind of reasoning utterly unfit for moral and political discussions; of a kind of reasoning which may so readily be turned to purposes of falsehood, that it ought to receive no quarter, even when by accident it may be employed on the side of truth.[23]

This claim gains some credence when we consider Macaulay's views on democracy at this period. In the contest with Mill and the *Westminster Review* he denied that he was advocating an alternative theory of government or that he held democracy to be undesirable.[24] This is borne out by his statement five years earlier (in 1824), when he evaluated democracy in a qualified but by no means hostile way. One of the essential conditions of the best government is the inclination to make the people happy, and it is only "pure democracy" that provides this. Using language that would have been congenial to James Mill, Macaulay argued that, given the opportunity, governments would exploit the populace, and this evil would be eliminated only if there was a coincidence of interests between governors and governed—a coincidence that would exist only when the subjects themselves became the rulers. His formulation is so similar to James Mill's that one may suspect that Macaulay was influenced by the "Essay on Government"; that he had been exposed to it is almost certain.[25]

To be sure, this was not Macaulay's whole view of democracy, nor was it his final assessment. Democratic control assured that the governors would be inclined to serve the people; but to have the best government, it was also necessary that they know how to do so. Therefore, before the people were allowed to take part in government, it was necessary that they be educated. Macaulay thus concluded that "he alone deserves the name of a great statesman, whose principle it is to extend the power of the people in proportion to the extent of their knowledge, and to give them every facility for obtaining such a degree of knowledge as may render it safe to trust them with absolute power." Meanwhile, Macaulay said, "it is dangerous to praise or condemn constitutions in the abstract." In keeping with this, he was as critical of doctrinaire opponents to democracy (e.g., Mitford) as of its doctrinaire defenders. Both sides suffer from "an ignorance or a neglect of the fundamental principles of political science."[26]

Macaulay's assessment of democracy was not simple or dogmatic, and over the years it may have changed somewhat. The differences between his view and Mill's on this question are not sufficiently great to cast doubt on Macaulay's statement that the object of his criticism was Mill's method of reasoning and not the substance of Mill's views. Apart from the theory of government, there were other questions on which there was even less disagreement. Macaulay shared Mill's belief in the importance of political economy as a means of promoting human welfare. In India during the next decade he demonstrated how much he deserved the approbation of the Benthamite law-reformers.[27] And for Bentham himself he was almost never sparing of genuine esteem, at least where jurisprudence, political economy, legislation, prison reform, and rhetoric were concerned. He distinguished between all this and Bentham's political speculations, which presumably meant his unqualified advocacy of universal manhood suffrage. Otherwise Bentham was "a truly great man"; "the father of the philosophy of Jurisprudence ... a great inventor"; "a great original thinker" — in the same rank as Galileo and Locke; "the man who found jurisprudence a gibberish, and left it a science."[28] Many of the views held by James Mill and his followers were shared by Macaulay. It was not their opinions that made the young Benthamites objectionable but their formulation and their reasoning, which gave intellectual nourishment to doctrinaire and sectarian politics.

In the course of defining his alternative to the deductive method, Macaulay endorsed induction as the means of contributing to the development of experimental science, including a science of politics. "Our creed is, that the science of government is an experimental science, and that, like all other experimental sciences, it is generally in a state of progression."[29] This belief was historically associated with Bacon, and Macaulay traced it back to him and to the scientific revolution of the sixteenth and seventeenth centuries. "The English genius was effecting in science a revolution which will, to the end of time, be reckoned among the highest achievements of the human intellect. Bacon had sown the good seed in a sluggish soil and an ungenial season.... During a whole generation his philosophy had ... been slowly ripening in a few well constituted minds." After diversions and delays, Bacon's outlook finally began to flourish at the time of the Restoration. With the founding of the Royal Society in 1660 one can discern "the ascendancy of the new philosophy."[30]

Bacon's achievement, according to Macaulay, was not philosophical but historical. Macaulay denied that Bacon had invented a new method of arriving at the truth; this was the vulgar notion. On the contrary, the inductive method had always been practiced; it was a matter of common sense. Bacon codified the practices that had always been in use. In addition, he was the first person who directed the attention of speculative men, who had been too long occupied in meaningless disputes, to the discovery of new and useful truth; and by doing so he gave to the inductive method an importance which had never before belonged to it. "He was not the maker of that road.... But he was the person who first called the public attention to an inexhaustible mine of wealth, which had been utterly neglected, and which was accessible by that road alone."[31]

Macaulay's eulogy of Bacon and experimental science was part of his general celebration of modernity and progress. Consequently, he tended to depreciate antiquity, though this did not spoil his life-long pleasure in reading ancient literature. These attitudes are best revealed in his comparison of Bacon with Plato. Plato was selected for the comparison because "he did more than any other person towards giving to the minds of speculative men that bent which they retained till they received from Bacon a new impulse in a diametrically opposite direction." The two were contrasted mainly with regard to their understandings of the purpose for which the sciences were to be cultivated. Whereas for Plato the study of the properties of numbers "habituates the mind to the contemplation of pure truth, and raises it above the material universe," Bacon "valued this branch of knowledge only on account of its uses with reference to that visible and tangible world which Plato so much despised." Similarly with geometry, Plato saw it as a way of leading men to the knowledge of abstract, eternal truth; and despite its potential utility to craftsmen, he thought its purpose "was to discipline the mind, not to minister to the base wants of the body." Bacon, on the other hand, "valued geometry chiefly, if not solely, on account of those uses which to Plato appeared so base." Turning to legislation, Macaulay contrasts Plato's belief that the end of legislation is to make men virtuous with Bacon's that "the end is the well-being of the people."[32]

Macaulay emphasized the utopian dimension in Plato and contrasted this to the more modest, worldly character of Bacon's goals. "To make men perfect was no part of Bacon's plan. His humble aim was to make imperfect men comfortable.... In Plato's opinion man was made for philosophy; in Bacon's opinion philosophy was made for man; it was a means to an end; and that end was to increase the pleasures and to mitigate the pains of millions who are not and cannot be philosophers."

> To sum up the whole [Macaulay added]: we should say that the aim of the Platonic philosophy was to exalt man into a god. The aim of the Baconian philosophy was to provide man with what he requires while he continues to be man. The aim of the Platonic philosophy was to raise us far above vulgar wants. The aim of the Baconian philosophy was to supply our vulgar wants. The former aim was noble; but the latter was attainable. Plato drew a good bow; but, like Acestes in Virgil, he aimed at the stars; and therefore, though there was no want of strength or skill, the shot was thrown away.[33]

And for Macaulay confirmation was found in what the new philosophy was achieving for mankind.

> It has lengthened life; it has mitigated pain; it has extinguished diseases; it has increased the fertility of the soil; it has given new securities to the mariner; it has furnished new arms to the warrior; it has spanned great rivers and estuaries with bridges of form unknown to our fathers; it has guided the thunderbolt innocuously from heaven to earth; it has lighted up the night with the splendour of the day; it has extended the range of the human vision; it has multiplied the power of the human muscles; it has accelerated motion; it has annihilated distance; it has facilitated intercourse, correspondence, all friendly offices, all dispatch of business; it has enabled men to descend to the depths of the sea, to soar into the air, to penetrate securely into the noxious recesses of the earth, to traverse the land in cars which whirl along without horses, and the ocean in ships which sail against the wind.

"These are but a part of its fruits, and of its first fruits," Macaulay added. "For it is a philosophy which never rests . . . which is never perfect. Its law is progress. A point which yesterday was invisible is its goal today, and will be its starting-post to-morrow."[34]

Included in this prospect was the growth of political science. Although Bacon's illustrations are drawn from physical science, "the principles which those illustrations are intended to explain are just as applicable to ethical and political inquiries as to inquiries into the nature of heat and vegetation." Thus at the culmination of his critique of deduction as found in James Mill's

"Essay on Government," Macaulay gives this account of the science of politics:

> How then are we to arrive at just conclusions on a subject so important to the happiness of mankind? Surely by that method, which, in every experimental science to which it has been applied, has signally increased the power and knowledge of our species . . . ; by the method of Induction; — by observing the present state of the world, — by assiduously studying the history of past ages, — by sifting the evidence of facts, — by carefully combining and contrasting those which are authentic, — by generalising with judgment and diffidence, — by perpetually bringing the theory which we have constructed to the test of new facts, — by correcting, or altogether abandoning it, according as those new facts prove it to be partially or fundamentally unsound. Proceeding thus, — patiently, — diligently, — candidly, — we may hope to form a system as far inferior in pretension to that which we have been examining, and as far superior to it in real utility, as the prescriptions of a great physician, varying with every stage of every malady, and with the constitution of every patient, to the pill of the advertising quack, which is to cure all human beings, in all climates, of all diseases.

This, Macaulay said, is the "noble Science of Politics."[35]

All this suggests that Macaulay's main concern was to establish a science of politics. However, he was really seeking an understanding of politics useful to practitioners. He makes this clear in drawing an analogy between the "science of Politics" and the "science of mechanics." Both were practically oriented; the politician was like the engineer; whereas the latter practiced the science of mechanics, the politician was engaged in the science of politics. In each case the practitioner draws on the principles provided by the men of knowledge, but he must also take into account circumstances that are not incorporated into the propositions of theory. "If the engineer . . . should absolutely rely on the propositions which he finds in treatises on Dynamics, and should make no allowance for the imperfection of his materials, his whole apparatus . . . would soon come down in ruin." The same holds for the politician.

> What the engineer is to the mathematician, the active statesman is to the contemplative statesman. It is indeed most

important that legislators and administrators should be versed
in the philosophy of government. . . . But, as he who has
actually to build must bear in mind many things never noticed
by D'Alembert and Euler, so must he who has actually to govern
be perpetually guided by considerations to which no allusion
can be found in the writings of Adam Smith and Jeremy
Bentham.[36]

The practitioner — the politician — was distinguished from the
man of knowledge (in conventional language, from the scientist).
Yet it was the practitioner who was engaged in the inductive
science of politics. Thus when Macaulay recommended induction
as the method that should be used by those engaged in the science
of politics, he was recommending it to politicians for the benefits
it would confer on practice and not to those who were mainly
seeking to enlarge the body of theoretical knowledge about
politics. This is confirmed if we ignore the eulogies of Baconian
methods and instead examine Macaulay's accounts of how the
inductive method actually works. Amidst the invocations of
empiricism and generalization one finds statements that induction
is the best tool for comparing the evidence as it bears on the choice
of alternative policies. In addition to reasoning from the particular
to the general, induction requires one "to mark slight shades of
difference in quality, or to estimate the comparative effect of two
opposite considerations between which there was no common
measure." For example, how could one determine the way to
establish good government, which was the professed goal of James
Mill in the "Essay"? "The latent principle of good government
ought to be tracked, as it appears to us, in the same manner in
which Lord Bacon proposed to track the principle of Heat."
Bacon proposed that one observe bodies both with and without
heat and search for something found only in hot materials whose
magnitude varies with degrees of heat. "In the same manner, we
ought to examine the constitution of all those communities in
which, under whatever form, the blessings of good government
are enjoyed; and to discover, if possible, in what they resemble
each other, and in what they all differ from those societies in
which the object of government is not attained." This procedure,
Macaulay says, will yield, not a perfect theory of government, but
one of great practical use.[37]

Although Macaulay's most optimistic assertions about the prospects for a science of politics were made during the first decade or so of his career as a writer (until 1837), he continued to think of induction in connection with policy-making. He retained the language of science after the dream of genuine science was abandoned; thus, when the Irish Church question was under consideration in 1845, he appealed to it once again: "There is no sort of experiment described by Lord Bacon which we have not tried. Inductive philosophy is of no value if we cannot trust to the lessons derived from the experience of more than two hundred years." He then presented his summary of that experience, which, in keeping with his understanding of how the inductive method should be used by politicians, required comparison of two related but critically different cases. There were two nations that England attempted to retain within her empire, both less powerful than herself and both different in religion. England attempted to force Anglicanism on both, and both countries rebelled. In the case of Scotland, after observing a long period of oppression, resistance, insurrections, and assassinations, finally "a wise government desisted from the vain attempt to maintain an Episcopal Establishment in a Presbyterian nation. From that moment the connection between England and Scotland became every year closer and closer...; all angry feelings died rapidly away. The union of the nations became complete." However, had they "adhered to the mad scheme of having a religious union with Scotland, [England] never would have had a cordial political union with her." Now compare the case of Ireland: it was still governed as Scotland was before religious toleration was permitted. The result was that Ireland was a source of weakness, discontent, and potential danger.

Having compared the two cases in their historical contexts, Macaulay pointed to the lesson for policy. "Can you," he asked, addressing his parliamentary colleagues, "with such facts before you, doubt about the course which you ought to take?" He considered the analogy of a physician with two patients, both afflicted with the same disease. Under the same remedy both became worse; but when the treatment is changed for one of the patients, he improves and is finally restored to health, while the other patient, still subjected to the old treatment, becomes worse.

"How would a physician act in such a case? And are not the principles of experimental philosophy the same in politics as in medicine?"[38]

Macaulay argued in similar fashion when he defended state responsibility for the education of the people. "I doubt whether it be possible to find, if there be any meaning in the science of induction as applied to politics, any instance of an experiment tried so fully and so fairly, tried with all the conditions which Lord Bacon has laid down in his *Novum Organon* [*sic*], and of which the result was so evident." Scotland and England, similar in so many ways, differed with regard to education. In Scotland there was state education, whereas in England it was left to free competition, that is, there was no legal obligation to provide formal education to children and no prescribed educational experience for those that were sent to school. Macaulay compared the educational consequences. Whereas initially England had been the most opulent and civilized of nations, Scotland had been poor and half-barbarous. Yet, after a century and a half, the common people of Scotland were better educated than the common people of England. The system of free competition had produced results about which England should be ashamed, whereas state education had brought unparalleled improvement to Scotland. "If this had been the case in surgery or chymistry [*sic*], and such experiments and results had been laid before you, would it be possible for you not to see which was the wrong course and which was the right?"[39]

These references to the experimental science of politics indicate that, when Macaulay discussed the application of Baconian methods to politics, he really had in mind practical political decisions and not a genuine science of politics. It is noteworthy that he often emphasized the practicality of the scientific conclusions yielded by this method. Furthermore, when he indicated the way inductive method had proved useful in other fields, he usually referred to other practitioners, particularly physicians. The body politic was like the patient. Both statesman and physician interpreted symptoms and treated maladies. They both engaged in induction—that is, observation of present circumstances, the study of past conditions, and tentative generalization. He explicitly states that by using the method of induction one can develop an understanding of politics as useful as the prescriptions of a great physician. This conception of the statesman's activity was described as if it were part of a science of politics; yet his examples indicate that the statesmen's activity, even when most "scientific," involved sustaining and healing, and these, if well performed, required him to know all the circumstances of the particular case. The discrepancy between the use of the language of science and the actual activities of those using the method of induction, as Macaulay thought of it, justifies the observation that his appeal to the inductive method of science and the tradition of Bacon "was something of a façade."[40]

Clearly, historical analysis played an important part in inductive operations as Macaulay conceived them. He wanted to establish generalizations that would facilitate the making of political judgments. On the one hand, he wanted to avoid generalizations that were not really useful because not based on sufficient experience. James Mill's general propositions, based on arbitrary assumptions about human conduct, were hardly to be the model. On the other hand, Macaulay wanted to establish some kind of generalization, for he did not recommend that judgment be based on intuitive responses to particular circumstances. Not that he did not admire this—for example, the Mohawk's "far-sightedness and penetration . . . in concerting his stratagems, or in discerning those of his enemies"; or "that peculiar ability which is required in constructing ingenious schemes, and for obviating remote difficulites," which is possessed by "thieves and thief-takers" (police) in England; or "the penetration, the exquisite tact, the almost instinctive presentiment of approaching events which gave so much authority to the counsel of Shaftesbury." Such insight was admirable; but its usefulness was limited, for such judgments were useful only in a single transaction. Furthermore, there was a risk that one might confuse accidental circumstances with generally valid causes. It was necessary to find a way "to correct those errors into which the most acute men must fall when they reason from a single species to a genus."[41]

The problem was to strike a balance between these two modes of forming political judgments. "The perfect lawgiver is a just temper between the mere man of theory, who can see nothing but general principles, and the mere man of business, who can see nothing but particular circumstances."[42] And it was historical analysis involving the comparison of many cases, called induction by Macaulay, that allowed the politician to avoid both particularity and irrelevant general propositions. This analysis was the fruit of "scientific" investigation of historical cases as they bore on a particular problem of policy. It was neither abstract nor fully general, like the conclusions of deductive reasoning or the propositions of much political philosophy; nor was it the result of an intuitive judgment. This balance was achieved only by making historical comparisons. The historical character of the evidence gave immediacy and applicability; the comparative aspect gave a measure of generality. Thus Macaulay decided that "a single experiment is not sufficient to establish a general rule even in sciences much less complicated than the science of government; that, since the beginning of the world, no two political experiments were ever made of which all the conditions were exactly alike; and that the only way to learn civil prudence from history is to examine and compare an immense number of cases."[43]

Macaulay's writings and speeches include frequent reference to what he often, and rather pretentiously, called "general laws," which were supposed to have been the fruit of this kind of inquiry. One of them, for example, concerned the extent of the violence that accompanies revolution. "We believe it to be a rule without an exception, that the violence of a revolution corresponds to the degree of misgovernment which has produced that revolution." This proposition was made plausible by comparing the events associated with 1789, 1641, 1688, 1776, 1830, and 1832. The greater the oppression, the more bloody and destructive the revolution. "The reaction was exactly proportioned to the pressure, — the vengeance to the provocation."[44] To take another example, Macaulay explained the dissension in William's camp that followed initial success by referring to a "general law which governs human affairs, [whereby] prosperity began to produce disunion."[45] Many of his general laws were variations on a theme of action and reaction. Thus "public opinion has its natural flux and reflux. After a violent burst, there is commonly a reaction." Or, "it is a law of our nature that such fits of excitement [as greeted Charles at the time of the Restoration] shall always be followed by remissions."[46]

These proclaimed laws were not the result of systematic or exhaustive inquiry. Far from being inductive, they often appear to have been derived from his assumption that every development provokes its opposite — that action and reaction will define the pattern into which events will fall. This assumption was part of Macaulay's expectation of alternating, even cyclical, episodes through which a nation moves. However, even though they were not genuinely inductive, as Macaulay might have thought them, his maxims were made plausible by historical examples. But sometimes he proclaimed a general law that was based on a particularly parochial interpretation of selected historical episodes, as when (probably thinking of the periods immediately before and after 1688) he announced, "It is the natural, the almost universal law, that the age of insurrections and proscriptions shall precede the age of good government, of temperate liberty, and liberal order."[47] Obviously not strictly scientific, the formulations of Macaulay's general laws reflects his esteem for the achievements of science. He thought political economy was an example of what science could achieve.[48] And he sometimes made the facile assumption that the political realm might be subjected to the same kind of ordering as was achieved by scientists for the physical world.[49] All the same, his use of the language of science does not conceal the character of his intellectual enterprise, which was to extract from the record of history maxims that would be useful to practicing politicians.

The advantage of historical inquiry was that it provided evidence of the great variation in the ways of society and human nature. It was a kind of laboratory that presented the inquirer with the opportunity of conducting, by means of comparisons, a great number of "experiments in moral science." Hence it was "that, in generalization, the writers of modern times have far surpassed those of antiquity," for they had more historical experience available to them. Macaulay pointed to Machiavelli as a writer who combined generality and particularity. "We give the highest and most peculiar praise to the precepts of Machiavelli, when we say that they may frequently be of real use in regulating conduct." Thucydides, too, though one of the ancients, earned Macaulay's commendation; after initially depreciating him for not being a sufficiently "philosophical historian," Macaulay confessed he had been wrong; after again "reading him [1835] with a mind accustomed to historical researches, and to political affairs . . . I am astonished at my own former blindness, and at his greatness."[50]

The maxims or general laws were to be available to the

politician as he made his judgments. Since they were to have this practical use, it is not surprising that almost every one of Macaulay's proposed laws concerned the problem that Macaulay was preoccupied with, both as politician and as man of letters — namely, threats to the equilibrium of a constitutionally ordered society posed by the extremes of anarchy and despotism. Thus an examination of his general laws shows them to concern such things as the level of violence in relation to the amount of oppression. However, he did not assume that the maxims based on historical examples predetermined the statesman's decision, for the decision inevitably dealt with imponderables and required delicate judgment. "Now in all questions of this sort, it is the part of wisdom to weigh, not indeed with minute accuracy, — for questions of civil prudence cannot be subjected to an arithmetical test, — but to weigh the advantages and disadvantages carefully, and then to strike the balance." Such judgments would vary: "Gentlemen will probably judge according to their habits of mind, and according to their opportunities of observation."[51] It was Macaulay's purpose as a historian so to shape his countrymen's "habits of mind" as to make them sensitive to the problem he thought most important and to the remedy he thought most wise.

When we turn to Macaulay's words as he took part in the making of the critical decisions that affected the equilibrium of his own society, we observe him as the practitioner of the art of civil prudence. And as a historian scrutinizing the decisions of others, he sought to explain and eulogize examples of civil prudence so as to keep alive the tradition by which it is perpetuated. For example, his arguments for timely concession as a way of enlarging consent and avoiding resistance — and ultimately conflict between extremes — fit his description of civil prudence. Here was a prescription for policy based on an interpretation of the contemporary situation in the light of comparable events not only in Tudor times but during the period leading to the French Revolution and, most notably, in the Stuart period. Another example of what he meant by civil prudence is his rationale for toleration. It was not simply derived from a doctrine of natural rights or even from Locke's *Letters Concerning Toleration*; rather, it was based on an understanding of the consequences of conflict between groups holding passionate, uncompromising religious opinions, and this understanding was nourished by historical study of developments in France, Scotland, and Germany, as well as in England, during the post-Reformation centuries. "Experience has clearly shown," he says, "that a Calvinistic church, like every other church, is disaffected when it is persecuted, quiet when it is tolerated, and actively loyal when it is favoured and cherished."[52]

These are among the themes that can be found in his *History*. Indeed, the largest theme of the *History*, for which the entire narrative provides support, is the identification of an approach to politics that, in the face of great difficulty, brought security, prosperity, and, above all, internal peace combined with individual liberty. Since domestic peace is essential to prosperity and to success in foreign relations, it is Macaulay's supreme concern. Those who practiced the conciliatory politics that provide for domestic peace in a free and diverse society are the heroes of the *History*—above all Halifax and William III and Somers. Their conduct is analyzed, and their goals and methods are identified. They were the ones who studied history, discerned the noiseless revolutions of their time, and practiced conciliatory politics. They were the ones who in the seventeenth century came closest to understanding what Macaulay meant by "civil prudence." And they were the ones he would have his contemporaries and successors imitate when acting on his recommendation "to pay a decent, a rational, a manly reverence to our ancestors, not by superstitiously adhering to what they, in other circumstances, did, but by doing what they, in our circumstances, would have done."[53] Thus Somers could well have approved of the Reform Bill; and those who, in the late seventeenth century, believed in toleration yet excluded the Catholics might have approved of Catholic emancipation in the nineteenth century.[54] It was not the conduct of the ancestral models that was to be imitated but their approach. Their values and way of solving problems, their prudence and skill and their concern for reconciling diverse and conflicting factions, were to be the model. This outlook entered into the *History*; and it was the *History* which—with its emphasis on the way Macaulay's heroes, while respecting liberty, toleration, and rule of law, sought to establish civil peace in the face of religious passions, class and political resentments, and tyrannical politicians—was to provide a model of the way civil prudence operated. In a sense the *History* attempted to identify and keep alive a tradition in which this approach to politics is highly valued.

In order to achieve this purpose—to identify the rules of civil prudence so that one may oneself use them—it was necessary to understand the past properly. Yet historical inquiry was not often conducted in a way that promoted this purpose. The difficulty arose from the political partisanship of historians. Partisanship was not unexpected in English circumstances, which included a continuing sense of interconnection between past and present. Where there was a sense of continuity with the past, politicians were bound to appeal to precedents. This required that they consult the historical record. Consequently, historical inquiry became politically significant. When politicians looked to history, historians became political. Since England was a country where "statesmen have been so much under the influence of the past, so there is no country where historians have been so much under the influence of the present.... The dearest interests of parties have frequently been staked on the results of the researches of antiquaries. The inevitable consequence was that our antiquaries conducted their researches in the spirit of partisans." There was so much at stake that "the motive to falsification becomes almost irresistible." Indeed, historical writing was "poisoned by party spirit." (This critique has special interest in view of the almost universal condemnation of his own partisanship by critics of his *History*.) He found illustrations for this kind of biased history among Whigs as well as Tories and in the present as well as the past. During the seventeenth-century contest between Parliament and the Stuarts, "few questions were practically more important than the question whether the administration of that family had or had not been in accordance with the ancient constitution of the kingdom." Therefore Bracton and Fleta, the Mirror of Justice and the Rolls of Parliament, were "ransacked" to find precedents for both sides. Consequently, these partisan historians displayed "the temper, not of judges, but of angry and uncandid advocates. For they were discussing, not a speculative matter, but a matter which had a direct and practical connection with the most momentous and exciting disputes of their own day." Both sides sacrificed historical truth to party ends. "During a long course of years every Whig historian was anxious to prove that the old English government was all but republican, every Tory historian to prove that it was all but despotic.[55]

There were also more recent examples: Hume was "an accomplished advocate":

> Without positively asserting much more than he can prove, he
> gives prominence to all the circumstances which support his
> case; he glides lightly over those which are unfavourable to it;
> his own witnesses are applauded and encouraged; the statements
> which seem to throw discredit on them are controverted; the
> contradictions into which they fall are explained away; a clear
> and connected abstract of their evidence is given. Everything
> that is offered on the other side is scrutinized with the utmost
> severity.... [56]

And about the work of another Tory, Mitford, who was an older contemporary, Macaulay asked, "Is this history, or a party-pamphlet?"

> His passion for a theory ... led him substantially to violate
> truth in every page. Statements unfavourable to democracy are
> made with unhesitating confidence, and with the utmost bitter-
> ness of language. Every charge brought against a monarch, or
> an aristocracy, is sifted with the utmost care....   Two events
> are reported by the same author in the same sentence; their
> truth rests on the same testimony; but the one supports the
> darling hypothesis, and the other seems inconsistent with it.
> The one is taken and the other left.

This was "at present the state of history." Most historians were advocates of "conflicting fallacies."[57]

All these partisan historians allowed considerations arising from the present to intrude upon the past. Mitford's fear of democracy, which was shaped by nineteenth-century experience, although alien to ancient Greece, influenced his analysis of Greek history. Among contemporaries, this tendency was not confined to Tory historians. "The error of judging the past by the present," he said, is the error "of minds readily attracted by whatever is new.... [It] perpetually infects the speculations of writers of the liberal school when they discuss the transactions of an earlier age." Statesmen of the past were criticized because they acted in a way that in the present was no longer appropriate or praiseworthy. For example, "starting from the true proposition that the disabilities imposed on the Roman Catholics had long been productive of nothing but mischief, [they] arrived at the false conclusion that there never could have been a time when those disabilities were useful and necessary."[58] Consequently, "the authors of the Toleration Act are treated as bigots, because they did not go the whole length of Catholic Emancipation." This outlook involves "looking back with contempt on the past," for it fails to take account of all the difficulties encountered by politicians of past ages. "As we would have our descendants judge us, so ought we to judge our fathers. In order to form a correct estimate of their merits, we ought to place ourselves in their situation — to put out of our minds, for a time, all that knowledge which they, however eager in the pursuit of truth, could not have, and which we, however negligent we may have been, could not help having." By failing to visualize all the circumstances of past situations the historian "speaks with scorn of the Great Charter, because it did not reform the Church; of the Reformation, because it did not limit the prerogative; and of the Revolution, because it did not purify the House of Commons."[59]

Historical inquiry should serve politics yet not be partisan. This can only mean that Macaulay thought it could be detached and objective. Yet his concern was not for the integrity of historical inquiry in isolation from other considerations. He was not a professional historian exclusively concerned to understand the past. Historical study was to be an aid to statesmanship. The objection to partisan interpretations was that they prevented historical inquiry from serving the purpose of diagnosis and prescription and the yielding of understanding that would help politicians to implement change while providing for continuity. For Macaulay this was not a partisan goal, for he assumed that all rational men would share in the goal of preserving the constitution, however much they might dispute about lesser matters. In contrast to the situation in which "history is regarded as a repository of titledeeds, on which the rights of governments and nations depend," it might also be "regarded ... as a collection of experiments from which general maxims of civil wisdom may be drawn, [and in this case] a writer lies under no very pressing temptation to misrepresent transactions of ancient date."[60] Thus an understanding of civil prudence was accessible by means of nonpartisan historical inquiry. Unlike partisan history, this was "history proper," and it was exemplified by "the high, grave, impartial summing up of Thucydides."[61]

Macaulay in his *History of England* intended to serve a political purpose but not the partisan purpose that is usually attributed to him. He wanted to extract lessons from the past that would be useful to politicians, regardless of where they might be placed on the spectrum of outlooks and parties. Even the literary dimension of Macaulay's achievement—the vivid and realistic portrayal of scenes from the past—was subservient to his purpose, which was persuasively to impart a particular understanding of politics.

This is revealed in his early writings on history and historians as well as in the *History* itself. History was not merely a record of the past; it should also "extract the philosophy of history,—to direct our judgment of events and men,—to trace the connexion of causes and effects, and to draw from the occurrences of former times general lessons of moral and political wisdom"—what elsewhere he called civil prudence.[1] The historian's task, then, had a philosophic and political component. "Facts are the mere dross of history. It is from the abstract truth which inter-penetrates them, and lies latent among them, like gold in the ore, that the mass derives its whole value."[2]

Clearly, much depended on the selection of facts. Facts in themselves are not significant. If a historian aspired to present a record of everything that took place, the Bodleian Library would not contain the occurrences of a week. By selection, by careful management of foreground and background, the historian, like any good artist, can portray the essential truth. Just as an outline that captures the distinct features of a countenance can give a better idea of it than a bad painting that includes much detail, so the best histories "exhibit such parts of the truth as most nearly produce the effect of the whole. He who is deficient in the art of selection may, by showing nothing but the truth, produce all the effect of the grossest falsehood."[3] The skillful historian will be the one who selects his facts in a way that allows confirmation of useful political principles. The facts do not speak for themselves; it is the creative task of the historian to give them a voice.

But the historian should do more than speak the truth. He should also present the truth persuasively. Ideally, history "impresses general truths on the mind by a vivid representation of particular characters and incidents." In order to do this, the historian should not hesitate to use any relevant detail:

> To make the past present, to bring the distant near, — to place us in the society of a great man, or on the eminence which overlooks the field of a mighty battle, to invest with the reality of human flesh and blood beings whom we are too much inclined to consider as personified qualities in an allegory, to call up our ancestors before us with all their peculiarities of language, manners, and garb, to show us over their houses, to seat us at their tables, to rummage their old-fashioned wardrobes, to explain the uses of their ponderous furniture, — these parts of the duty which properly belongs to the historian have been appropriated by the historical novelist.[4]

Unfortunately, this kind of portrayal of the past is neglected by historians. It is engaged in by Sir Walter Scott but not, for example, by Hallam, even though both were occupied by the same matter. Thus "a truly great historian would reclaim those materials which the novelist has appropriated."[5] All the details of daily life in past ages would be shown in their interrelationships with political developments. Such evidence helps the historian discern noiseless revolutions, but it also serves a rhetorical purpose. "The instruction derived from history thus written would be of a vivid and practical character. It would be received by the imagination as well as by the reason. It would be not merely traced on the mind, but branded into it."[6]

Thinking of the double task of the good historian—to extract useful truths from the great array of facts and to present them persuasively—Macaulay characterized history as consisting of both theory and fiction, philosophy and poetry. There were truth-seeking and rhetoric; the one required reason, the other imagination. Since reason was to provide guidance, he likened its contribution to historical inquiry to a map; and since the rhetorical part was to emphasize the reality and relevance of the past, he likened it to a landscape. Ideally, both realms would be combined by the historian. This need not lead to fictional history or even to distortion. Thucydides, for example, though not faultless, "surpassed all his rivals in the art of historical narration, in the art of producing an effect on the imagination, by skilful selection and disposition, without indulging in the license of invention." Thus, while the talent for writing history has an affinity with the talent of a great dramatist, there is an important difference: "The dramatist creates; the historian only disposes. The difference is not in the mode of execution, but in the mode of conception."[7]

The historian's craft was complex—it included both analysis and rhetoric, both philosophy and a high level of artistic achievement. This allowed Macaulay to say that "to be a really great historian is perhaps the rarest of intellectual distinctions."[8] It is therefore not surprising that he thought it had never been done adequately: "We are acquainted with no history which approaches to our notion of what a History ought to be." The historians of antiquity excelled in narration, especially Herodotus; but, since "philosophy was still in its infancy"—that is, since the ancients were not favored with a knowledge of modern science—they were deficient in analysis. All their rhetorical achievements served no good purpose, for their political understanding was not worth preserving. On the other hand, modern historians were also found wanting. Their analyses suffered from bias—Gibbon's on Christianity, Hume's on party politics, and Mitford's on democracy; and what was even more serious, their rhetorical achievements were nil. They "neglect the art of narration, the art of interesting the affections and presenting pictures to the imagination." Macaulay thus indicates how, when he came to write his *History,* he would think of his task.[9]

When Macaulay undertook to write his *History,* he had two qualifications called for in his recipe for the best historical writing. First of all, his capacity for analysis had grown with his varied experience of the world, which was supplemented by theoretical understanding. He considered the law, trials, and lawyers with an understanding shaped by his own legal training, a full knowledge and appreciation of Bentham's writings, and some administrative experience, including codification. His understanding of economic policy, commerce, currency, and taxation was shaped by serious study of the literature of political economy. His temperament combined with his exposure to modern science to develop his skepticism, and this led him to judge religion as an anthropologist rather than as one concerned with his own salvation. In addition, Macaulay's understanding was shaped by his own administrative and political experience (he had served on the Governor-General's Council in India and in the cabinet under Melbourne and Russell). What he said of Fox and Mackintosh applied also to himself: "They had one eminent qualification for writing history: —they had spoken history, acted history, lived history." Indeed, it has been argued that political experience was the source of the qualities that distinguish his *History*.[10]

And of course Macaulay did not lack rhetorical talent. His great flair as a writer was recognized early in his career, and he consciously cultivated it. As he complacently said, "How little the all important art of making meaning pellucid is studied now. Hardly any popular writer—except myself—thinks of it."[11] His *History* provides a continuing presentation of changing scenes, all of them strikingly vivid to the reader. Whether it be the heroic defenders during the siege at Limerick, or William during the Battle of the Boyne, or the atmosphere of suspicion and treachery at Glencoe, or a scene in Jeffreys' court, or the mood in London at the time of the trial of the Seven Bishops, Macaulay artfully branded it on the mind of the reader. He was equally successful in creating persuasively real pictures of his leading characters—of the cautious Godolphin, of James's immoderation, Jeffreys' ferocity, William's stoicism. These qualities contributed to the *History*'s extraordinary popularity—so great that, as Henry Reeve observed after the appearance of the second installment (volumes three and four) in 1855, "all the world set to work to read the book."[12] Even his severe critics have acknowledged his superb talent as a writer, crediting him with "a rich pictorial imagination, a firm control of tone, a sense of structure." Gladstone, for example, remarked:

> In Macaulay all history is scenic. . . . He did not fetch from
> the depths, nor soar to the heights; but his power upon the
> surface was rare and marvellous, and it is upon the surface that
> an ordinary life is passed, and that its imagery is found. He

mingled, then, like Homer, the functions of the poet and the chronicler; but what Homer did was due to his time, what Macaulay did, to his temperament.... Ease, brilliancy, pellucid clearness, commanding fascination, the effective marshalling of all facts belonging to the external world as if on parade; all these gifts Macaulay has....[13]

It will be noted, however, that Gladstone attributed Macaulay's stylistic preference to his temperament, whereas it should be seen as part of the rhetorical dimension of Macaulay's conception of the historian's enterprise.

The political understanding incorporated in the *History* consisted of what Macaulay sometimes called "civil prudence." Its immediate goal was stability, not as an end in itself but as a means of avoiding political extremes, which alternately produced anarchy and despotism. Toward this end it was, within broad limits, quite flexibly defined. It included certain dogmas of the Whigs, but its rationale was conceived as much in functional as in normative terms. Thus liberty of discussion and consent were desirable as providing means to stability. Those who had this understanding of civil prudence or civil wisdom were Macaulay's heroes; those whose conduct was an obstacle to the practice of civil prudence were his villains. He offered himself as the philosophical historian who, on behalf of posterity, recognized the wisdom of selected ancestors. In this capacity he wrote his *History* to inform the judgments of future politicians, who were to model their conduct on their ancestors by doing what those ancestors would do were they dealing with the circumstances of that future age.[14]

Although this understanding has affinities with Whiggism, it was not conventional early-nineteenth-century Whig doctrine, nor was it part of the tradition of Whig history. Macaulay went beyond the conventions of Whig history, and in doing so he gave his *History* its distinctive character. Perhaps we can see this best if we compare the *History* with Sir James Mackintosh's *A View of the Reign of James II: From His Accession to the Enterprise of the Prince of Orange* (1835);[15] for Mackintosh was part of the Whig tradition, and his views were an orthodox contemporary expression of it.

Mackintosh (1765–1832) in his own time was a prominent Whig intellectual and Member of Parliament. Having begun his career as a Radical defending the French Revolution (in his famous

Vindicae Gallicae) against Burke, he soon moderated his judgment in response to the increasing arbitrariness and terror
unfolding in France. An encounter with Burke completed his
conversion. Following a period of nine years in India, where he
served as a judge, Mackintosh returned to England to engage in
politics and write history. He became an *Edinburgh* reviewer, and
as a Member of Parliament he achieved a reputation as an
advocate of law reform. He also wrote for the *Encyclopaedia
Britannica;* his long article, when reprinted as the *Dissertation on
the Progress of Ethical Philosophy,* gave him his greatest post-
humous fame. Yet these varied achievements did not satisfy his
intellectual ambition, for that could have come only from the
completion of his history, which was to have covered the century
that began with the Glorious Revolution. He thought of himself as
a successor to Charles James Fox, who during his last years busied
himself with the writing of a history of the Revolution that was
meant to be a challenge to the supremacy of Hume. In the end
Mackintosh produced only a fragment, which was published
posthumously. His notes, now amounting to forty bound volumes,
accumulated over many years while he visited private and public
archives both on the Continent and in England, were given to
Macaulay by Mackintosh's son.

To Macaulay, Mackintosh was a famous and estimable man
who was yet something of a failure. There was so much he had
begun but not completed. His great intellectual and political
ambitions had not been satisfied. Macaulay was spurred to
continue his historical labors by Mackintosh's example. While
Mackintosh was still alive, Macaulay already enjoyed the greater
reputation for brilliance as an orator, essayist, and conversational-
ist. It was Macaulay's eloquence that led to their meeting; having
heard about his speech at the Anti-Slavery Society in 1824,
Mackintosh asked Zachary to introduce him to his son. There is
symbolism in an incident that occurred on 5 April 1830, when
both men rose to address the House; Mackintosh, his frustrating
career near its close, yielded the floor to the new Member, about
to make his maiden speech, the first of many notable successes.

The similarities between the two historians are to be expected.
Although they belonged to different generations — Mackintosh
died in 1832, not many years after Macaulay began his career —
both were prominent spokesmen for Whiggism who served their

party in the House of Commons and as contributors to the *Edinburgh Review;* both were important critics of the Utilitarians; and both were intellectual ornaments at Holland House. They both sought to contribute to the shaping of the historical memory of the Revolution of 1688. Both dealt primarily with the reign of James II and the accession of William, and both are considered to be part of the tradition of Whig history. Moreover, though neither completed his work as planned, each had intended to cover a period that began with the reign of James II and the Revolution of 1688 and ended with a comparably momentous occasion that each had experienced as a young man—in Mackintosh's case, the French Revolution, and, in Macaulay's, the Reform Act of 1832.[16] In view of all this it is not surprising that a comparison of their histories reveals little significant disagreement, especially with regard to such issues as liberty and toleration, the Protestant succession, and an independent judiciary and the rule of law.[17] Yet there are significant differences, not in their accounts of events or even in their interpretations of them (though Macaulay's narrative, in keeping with what he had recommended about vividness, is much more lively), but in what Macaulay took to be the purpose of writing history, that is, in drawing from the occurrences of former times lessons of moral and political wisdom useful to present and future politicians. In trying to do this, Macaulay was providing an additional layer of interpretation that had not previously been a part of the tradition of Whig historical writing.

In his *History* Macaulay's understanding of politics was still informed, as it had been as early as 1822, when he wrote the prize essay on William III, by the assumption that centrifugal forces were at work that threatened social and political stability. These forces were embodied in sects and classes and factions each of which was animated by destructive passions. The conflict that emerged was accentuated by irreconcilable doctrines—of Puritanism or Jesuitism, republicanism or belief in divine right or even extreme Whiggism. Since most politicians were merely spokesmen or agents of particular religious and political groups, they blindly played their roles in a sequence of events in which each group alternately became winner and loser, oppressor and oppressed, persecutor and victim. However, there were some few statesmen who, so to speak, stood apart and saw the pattern of endless conflict. These men, who belonged to no party, recognized the need to adopt policies of reconciliation and to establish institutions that would make conflict less destructive. Indeed, their perspective was so great that they adopted a position that ultimately would be justified by the judgment of posterity. Although disdained and misunderstood by their contemporaries, they would be honored by truly philosophical historians.

It was this understanding of seventeenth-century politics, which was a reflection of Macaulay's general political outlook, that provided an extra layer of interpretation to his otherwise conventional account of events. And it was this interpretation that distinguished his *History* from Mackintosh's. Macaulay did not confine himself to an account of what happened. Such facts were "the mere dross of history." He was concerned to present a truth that interpenetrated the facts—that lay latent among them, "like gold in the ore."

One difference between the two Whig historians is the very great prominence Macaulay gave to fanatics and fanaticism. Mackintosh uses the term most sparingly, but for Macaulay the phenomenon is ubiquitous. Fanatics are found in politics as well as religion; some defend the established order, while others are visionaries who attack it. Macaulay saw fanaticism as a weakness of human nature. This outlook affected many of his judgments. For example, Mackintosh had portrayed John Bunyan as a victim of persecution who happened to have embraced the opinions of the Baptists and was a lay preacher. Macaulay, on the other hand, regarded Bunyan's religiosity as a somewhat pathological phenomenon. He noted that Bunyan had severely suffered from the penal laws, and he paid tribute to his genius as "the first of the allegorists"; but the emphasis was on his visions, hallucinations, "mental agony," guilt, terrifying thoughts and fears, and "his experimental knowledge of all the religious passions from despair to ecstasy." He had a "sensibility which amounted to a disease." His excitable mind "was tormented by a succession of fantasies which seemed likely to drive him to suicide or to Bedlam." Indeed, "scarcely any madhouse could produce an instance of delusion so strong, or of misery so acute."[18] In another example, that of Robert Ferguson, the contrast is equally sharp. Mackintosh reports that Ferguson was involved in Jacobite intrigues, but he does not decide why; it was "either from incorrigible habits of conspiracy, or from resentment at the supposed ingratitude of [his] own party, or from the inconstancy natural to men of unbridled passions and distempered minds." To Macaulay, Ferguson was an agitator: "with the malevolent activity and dexterity of an evil spirit, he ran from outlaw to outlaw, chattered in every ear, and stirred up in every bosom savage animosities and wild desires."

> He belonged to the class whose office it is to render in troubled times to exasperated parties those services from which honest men shrink in disgust and prudent men in fear, the class of fanatical knaves. Violent, malignant, regardless of truth, insensible to shame, insatiable of notoriety, delighting in intrigue, in tumult, in mischief for its own sake, he toiled during many years in the darkest mines of faction.[19]

Then there is George Fox, the founder of the Quaker sect. Mackintosh portrays him as a man for whom, "at a time when personal revelation was generally believed, it was a pardonable self-delusion that he should imagine himself to be commissioned by the Divinity to preach a system which could only be objected to as too pure to be practiced by man." This belief and "an ardent temperament" led Fox to seek converts. He intruded in churches; he adopted peculiar modes of language and dress. As a result, he was subjected to the penalties imposed by both law and prejudice. Macaulay, in contrast, described Fox in the language of pathology: Fox suffered from "the constitutional diseases of his mind"; he wandered about "in his paroxysms of fanatical excitement." Penn and Barclay were "among the thousands whom his enthusiasm infected." In view of these contrasting judgments it is perhaps not surprising that Macaulay complained that Mackintosh was too lenient, that he was "full of charity towards individuals."[20]

Macaulay saw the fanaticism of conflicting sects and parties as the cause of the sudden changes in the seventeenth-century polity. The men who were in power—and thus the principles, religious orientations, and policies—changed frequently:

> The strife between the two principles [the popular element and the monarchical element] had been long, fierce, and doubtful. It had lasted through four reigns. It had produced seditions, impeachments, rebellions, battles, sieges, proscriptions, judicial massacres. Sometimes liberty, sometimes royalty, had

seemed to be on the point of perishing. During many years one
half of the energy of England had been employed in counter-
acting the other half.[21]

This statement of course reflects Macaulay's early belief that in
the seventeenth century there were cyclical shifts between anarchy
and despotism. In his *History* the shifts involved less extreme
movements of the pendulum, but the idea is the same.

It is Macaulay's observation and expectation of these alternating
shifts in the political system, each bringing its own danger, that
makes it possible for him to invest some politicians with heroic
status. The severity and duration of the crisis creates an opportunity for a certain kind of politician to put an end to it. And this,
of course, was the role of William. Mackintosh's history, on the
other hand, does not emphasize the alternating or cyclical character of politics. In keeping with this, Mackintosh, although he
admires William, does not attribute to him the enduring importance that Macaulay claims for him. Indeed, for Mackintosh,
William's achievements in England were subordinate to, a by-
product of, his European policy. To check Louis XIV was "the
single object of his high calling," "the sole object of his glorious
life."[22]

Macaulay recognized William's achievement as head of the
alliance against France, but it is above all for his domestic
achievements that Macaulay praises him. William is portrayed as
much more than a highly talented and successful political figure.
He is made responsible for an extraordinary achievement — the
transformation of the political system. Macaulay's interpretation
of William's achievement should be seen in the context of the
understanding of historical development presented in the prize-
winning essay of 1822. There Macaulay had generalized about
how many nations were subjected to an unfortunate cycle of
anarchy and despotism, each provoking the emergence of its
opposite. This was the model with which Macaulay understood
English politics during most of the century preceding the Revolution of 1688. Though he had in mind the checkered and
discontinuous history of much of the century, with its succession of
regimes, each significantly different from its predecessor, he was
especially thinking of the decade immediately preceding 1688 — of
the Exclusion crisis, the Popish Plot, the Rye House Plot,
Monmouth's rebellion, and the reign of James II. Macaulay

characterized this as a period in which a violent opposition "roused the country to transient turbulence and then left it to deeper servitude":

> Such was the fate of the Great Political Faustus of the seventeenth century. Flushed with past success and expected vengeance, he pressed on his desperate schemes with increased boldness. At once the tide of popular madness turned. Remorse and dismay succeeded to fury. The panic created by perjuries of Bedloe and Oates was lost in a different alarm. Civil war, anarchy, regicide were apprehended from the violence of the opposition. The people rallied round the throne, and seemed eager to expiate turbulence by servility. . . . The Whig leaders had recourse to projects of insurrection. Their plans were betrayed. They were left to the justice of the laws they had vitiated. . . . Every day produced some fresh instance of servile submission.[23]

This was the pattern of alternating turbulence and submission, anarchy and despotism, that was observable during most of the seventeenth century in England and in Europe following the French Revolution.

Macaulay also discerned this pattern of historical change when he wrote the *History*. Prior to William's appearance in England there had been a century of revolutions and counterrevolutions,[24] and each successive regime had vindictively punished its opponents:

> From the commencement of the civil troubles of the seventeenth century down to the Revolution, every victory gained by either party had been followed by a sanguinary proscription. When the Roundheads triumphed over the Cavaliers, when the Cavaliers triumphed over the Roundheads, when the fable of the Popish plot gave the ascendancy to the Whigs, when the detection of the Rye House Plot transferred the ascendancy to the Tories, blood, and more blood, and still more blood, had flowed. Every great explosion and every great recoil of public feeling had been accompanied by severities which, at the time, the predominant faction loudly applauded, but which, on a calm review, history and posterity have condemned. No wise and humane man, whatever may be his political opinions, now mentions without reprehension the death either of Laud or of Vane, either of Stafford or of Russell.

The last butchery was associated with James and Jeffreys. "But it assuredly would not have been the last, perhaps it might not have been the worst, if William had not had the virtue and the firmness resolutely to withstand the importunity of his most zealous adherents." These men had vivid memories of Sidney on the scaffold, Elizabeth Gaunt at the stake, the Bloody Assizes, the prison ships to Jamaica, of languishing in Newgate, of cold garrets in Amsterdam, and they "were bent on exacting a terrible retribution for all they had undergone during seven disastrous years. . . . Nothing stood between them and their victims, but William's immutable resolution that the glory of the great deliverance which he had wrought should not be sullied by cruelty."[25]

William put an end to all this. "Till his accession the British Constitution was in its Chaos." He interrupted the cyclical pattern in which alternating regimes, each representing opposite principles, experienced persecution in defeat, vengeance when in power. Before 1688 there had always been the risk and sometimes the actuality of either tyranny or anarchy; after the Revolution, these dangers were greatly reduced.[26] Politicians and parties were tamed; they ceased to advocate extreme remedies. It was no longer a matter of the greatest importance that one set of politicians be in power and that the other be excluded. The nation was placed on a safe and steady course, and dangerous oscillations no longer threatened. Politics, in a sense, suddenly ceased to be a dangerous enterprise. This was William's achievement. Of course there was a multitude of circumstances that facilitated it—fear of civil war, a promise of prosperity, unity in the face of French power, perhaps a weariness with religious conflict. These circumstances were recognized by William, who is portrayed as one who discerned in them an opportunity to impose his own benevolent design.

What is more, William's achievement was enduring. Since the seventeenth century "no statesman, while engaged in constitutional opposition to a government, has had the axe before his eyes." Political disputes no longer carried a high degree of risk of civil war, nor did attempts at reform lead to revolution. "The highest eulogy which can be pronounced on the revolution of 1688 is this, that it was our last revolution. Several generations have now passed away since any wise and patriotic Englisheman has meditated resistance to the established government." The contrast in

1848 between London and the Continental capitals, where passion, the thirst for gain and vengeance, and class conflict and civil war prevailed, seemed to support this analysis (which was written in November 1848). Yet, if there had been no more revolution, there had still been opportunities for reform. "In all honest and reflecting minds there is a conviction, daily strengthened by experience, that the means of effecting every improvement which the constitution requires may be found within the constitution itself." For all this—for freedom and authority, for security and peace—"our gratitude is due, under Him who raises up and pulls down nations at his pleasure, to the Long Parliament, to the Convention, and to William of Orange."[27]

William's achievement was not accomplished in a brief historical moment. It was the product of many specific acts and policies during the decade before his death in 1702. William is portrayed by Macaulay as being a trimmer (in the favorable sense of the word) throughout this period, even though Macaulay had not seen the documents in which it was recorded that William, in conversations with Halifax, had adopted this label. Macaulay describes William as adopting the principles of no one party. None of the sects or parties could look upon him as their agent or spokesman. Although this made him unpopular, it was for this reason, according to Macaulay, that he was effective.[28] With this approach he succeeded in blunting destructive conflict and in gaining consent for the new regime.

Facing the angry, ambitious, embittered, vindictive men whose memories were scarred by the suppressions and persecutions and defeats of the revolutions and counterrevolutions of the preceding decades, William's difficulties were great. "A single false step might be fatal; and it was impossible to take any step without offending prejudices and rousing angry passions." No matter which course he chose, it carried the risk that it would alienate some body of opinion. "It was impossible to make an arrangement [filling the major offices of state] that would please everybody, and difficult to make an arrangement that would please anybody; but an arrangement must be made." The problem of gaining and keeping a modicum of support without driving some of the parliamentary politicians into opposition, and even to treasonable opposition, was a continuing problem. What barely saved the situation was, in Macaulay's view, the fact that England had "a prince who belonged to neither of her factions, who loved neither, who hated neither, and who, for the accomplishment of a great design wished to make use of both, was the moderator between them."[29]

Even when not successful, William's conduct was interpreted as at least a search for reconciliation and, as a step toward it, for moderation of passions and compromise of differences. With regard to religious sects, "personal ambition, as well as higher motives, prompted him to act as mediator." He established permission for dissenting Protestants to practice their religion without interference. He also tried to remove obstacles to their holding civil offices, but in this he failed. He was also unsuccessful in changing Anglican ritual and polity in a manner that, "without offending those to whom that ritual and that polity were dear, might conciliate the moderate nonconformists."[30]

William had a similar object in Scotland, where the question of church government was in dispute. He impartially listened to "eager advocates" — Episcopalians, Latitudinarians, and Presbyterians — as he sought to serve as "umpire in that great contention." He balanced conflicting considerations to avoid "leaning unduly to either side." Macaulay, in analyzing William's outlook, pointed to the restraint and comprehensiveness that qualified him to seek conciliation or, at least, to reduce irreconcilable conflict:

> His conscience was perfectly neutral. For it was his deliberate opinion that no form of ecclesiastical polity was of divine institution. He dissented equally . . . from the men who held that there could not be a Christian Church without Bishops, and from the men who held that there could not be a Christian Church without synods. Which form of Government should be adopted was in his judgment a question of mere expediency . . . ; he was far too wise a man to think of settling such a matter according to his personal tastes.

William determined that "if there was on both sides a disposition to compromise, he would act as mediator." But he would not force either Scotland or England into conformity with the other, nor would he allow persecution or encroachments on the jurisdiction of the civil magistrate.[31]

Macaulay describes William's character as having many qualifications that allowed him to play the role of mediator, conciliator, trimmer. For one thing, he felt a sense of distance, even disdain, for many of the politicians with whom he was to cooperate. Yet this made it possible for the new king to be manipulative in his dealings with them:

> He knew that he must work with such tools as he had. If he was to govern England he must employ the public men of England; and, in his age, the public men of England, with much of a peculiar kind of ability, were, as a class, lowminded and immoral. There were doubtless exceptions. . . . But the majority, both of the Tory and of the Whig ministers of William . . . had been formed in two evil schools, in the most unprincipled of . . . oppositions. . . . But though they could not be trusted, they might be used; and they might be useful. No reliance could be placed on their principles: but much reliance might be placed on their hopes and on their fears.[32]

Another of William's qualities was his willingness to subordinate his own preferences to what was feasible, given the range of policies for which consent could be achieved. On many of the questions that agitated his subjects he had preferred remedies. Although bred a Presbyterian, "he was, from rational conviction, a Latitudinarian." As to the relation of the monarchy to Parliament, "he was, by nature, at least as covetous of power and as impatient of restraint as any of the Stuarts."[33] Yet he was able to form his judgments without allowing these views a determining influence.

William had still another quality that made him effective. He practiced restraint in his own conduct and in the expression of his feelings. When faced with a report of Jacobite plotting, he recognized that

> it contained little more than what he had long known, and had long, with politic and generous dissimulation, affected not to know. If he spared, employed, and promoted men who had been false to him, it was not because he was their dupe. . . . It has seemed strange to many that a prince of high spirit and acrimonious temper should have treated servants, who had so deeply wronged him, with a kindness hardly to be expected from the meekest of human beings. But William was emphatically a statesman. Ill humour, the natural and pardonable effect of much bodily and much mental suffering, might sometimes impel him to give a tart answer. But never did he on any important occasion indulge his angry passions at the expense of the great interests of which he was the guardian. For the sake of those interests, proud and imperious as he was by nature, he

submitted patiently to galling restraints, bore cruel indignities and disappointments with the outward show of serenity, and not only forgave, but often pretended not to see, offences which might well have moved him to bitter resentment.

If he was not uniformly successful, he yet conducted himself on the whole "with that air of stoical apathy under which he had, from a boy, been in the habit of concealing his strongest emotions."[34]

William was also skillful at discerning the circumstances in which preferred outcomes would result from the unfolding of circumstances, whereas, were he to try to force the event, the results would be contrary to his wishes. This required patience as well as perceptiveness. "No part of statesmanship is more important than the art of taking the tide of public opinion at the turn. On more than one occasion William showed himself a master of that art." This talent helped him gain the crown. Since he could not prudently admit to the desire, "he uttered not a word indicating any design on the English Crown.... His only chance of obtaining the splendid prize was not to seize it rudely, but to wait till, without any appearance of exertion or stratagem on his part, his secret wish should be accomplished by the force of circumstances, by the blunders of his opponents, and by the free choice of the Estates of the Realm."[35]

Standing aside from all parties and sects, yet manipulating and using them, William is portrayed as a supremely successful politician:

> In the highest parts of statesmanship, he had no equal among his contemporaries. He had formed plans not inferior in grandeur and boldness to those of Richelieu, and had carried them into effect with a tact and wariness worthy of Mazarin. Two countries, the seats of civil liberties and of the Reformed Faith, had been preserved by his wisdom and courage from extreme perils. Holland he had delivered from foreign and England from domestic foes.

Macaulay seems to have admired William's artfulness and his skill as much as his success:

> Obstacles apparently insurmountable had been interposed between him and the ends on which he was intent; and those obstacles his genius had turned into stepping stones. Under his dexterous management the hereditary enemies of his house had

helped him to mount a throne; and the persecutors of his
religion had helped him to rescue his religion from persecution.

In both the alliance against France and in post-Revolutionary
England he had the satisfaction of finding that "factions and sects,
divided by mortal antipathies, had recognized him as their
common head."[36]

William's trimming policy could not be described adequately by
any of the conventional labels. He was "a Sovereign, yet the
champion of liberty, — a revolutionary leader, yet the supporter of
social order." He also combined old and new: "this great prince,
in attacking a system of oppression, summoned to his aid the
venerable principles and deeply seated feelings to which it was
indebted for protection": by making important changes without
destroying old institutions, he successfully "transferred to a hap-
pier order of things the associations which had attached the
people to their former government."[37]

William's achievement was shared by Halifax — "the Trimmer
of Trimmers."[38] "Our Revolution," Macaulay asserts, "as far as it
can be said to bear the character of any single mind, assuredly
bears the character of the large yet cautious mind of Halifax."
William and Halifax shared Macaulay's highest esteem. The
former had been a heroic figure for Macaulay from early manhood on; his judgment of the latter was formed more slowly.[39]
Halifax's career was more varied and more complex than
William's; for Halifax had attempted to preserve the Stuart
monarchy, and, after that failed, he had contributed to the
shaping of the Revolutionary settlement. Whereas William gained
consent for the post-Revolutionary regime, Halifax not only
shared this achievement but also attempted to alter the pre-Revo-
lutionary regime so as to make it palatable to all factions and
opinions, yet within a context of liberty, religious toleration, and
the rule of law. This exemplified Macaulay's conception of the
politician's first task, especially when undertaken in times of deep
distrust and intense conflict. For this reason, Halifax, perhaps
even more than William, served as a model. Furthermore, unlike
William, Halifax left writings on politics that Macaulay recognized as being highly relevant to the politics of divided regimes
requiring reform in order to promote stability yet without sacrifice
of constitutionality.

George Savile, Marquis of Halifax, is best remembered for these writings, particularly "The Character of a Trimmer," in which he seeks to provide an honorable defense for the epithet that had been used to signify inconsistency and therefore unprincipled conduct, as well as inconstancy and therefore betrayal of one's associates. Halifax could not deny having changed sides. He opposed the Exclusion Bill and served James, yet he also led the legal opposition to James and opposed James's use of the dispensing power. He refused to take part in the conspiracy against James, yet he played so important a part in gaining consent for William's accession that he was chosen as the one to present the crown to William and Mary.[40] Halifax defended such shifts in the name of stability. "This innocent word *Trimmer* signifieth no more than this, That if Men are together in a boat, and one part of the company would weigh it down on one side, another would make it lean as much to the contrary; it happeneth there is a third Opinion of those, who conceive it would do as well, if the Boat went even, without endangering the passengers."[41]

The defense—indeed, the proud assertion—of trimming was temperamentally congenial to Halifax, but it also had an intellectual origin. If "Halifax was a Trimmer on principle," Macaulay observed that "he was also a Trimmer by the constitution both of his head and of his heart." Halifax felt great distaste for zealous, sectarian outlooks in both religion and politics, regardless of the substance of the views. He was "singularly unsusceptible of enthusiasm, and singularly averse to extremes." In religion, Macaulay said, "he was so far from being a zealot that he was called by the uncharitable an atheist," though Halifax, of course, denied this. He was so detached that Macaulay wrote, with awe: "He was treating of the most exciting subjects in the most agitated times—he was himself placed in the very thick of the civil conflict:—yet there is no acrimony, nothing inflammatory, nothing personal. He preserves an air of cold superiority,—a certain philosophical serenity, which is perfectly marvellous." Such a man was "by no means prone either to malevolence or to enthusiastic admiration," and consequently he found it easy to stand apart. Not sharing the passions of others, whether they expressed antagonism or promoted solidarity, he "could not long be constant to any band of political allies."[42]

Macaulay, recognizing that there was a principled foundation for Halifax's trimming, found it in Halifax's belief in the impor-

tance of stability for a political system that also provided rule of
law, limited monarchy, and the maximization of liberty and
religious toleration. This required the consent of the populace;
but the preponderance of any sect or faction would alienate and
perhaps provoke rebellion in its rival. The extremes of prelacy and
Puritanism were incompatible, as were the extremes of absolute
monarchy and Whiggism as represented by Sidney. Thus, like one
who shifts his position on a boat in order to correct its list,
regardless of the side to which it leans, so Halifax advocated
shifting one's political position in order to keep the polity from
moving too far in any one direction. "His place was on the
debatable ground between the hostile divisions of the community,
and he never wandered far beyond the frontier of either. The
party to which he at any moment belonged was the party which, at
that moment, he liked least." Thus "he passed from faction to
faction," always seeking to reduce the differences between them.
Therefore, "instead of adopting and inflaming the passions of
those whom he joined, he tried to diffuse among them something
of the spirit of those whom he had just left." And this purpose led
him to be "severe upon his violent associates, and . . . in friendly
relations with his moderate opponents." Consequently, he was "an
uncertain friend, [and] . . . a placable enemy." The wish to
reconcile opponents also made him magnanimous and forgiving
to the vanquished.[43]

It is thus not surprising that Halifax sought to play "the part of
mediator between the throne and the nation," a role for which, as
Macaulay said, he was best qualified and most ambitious. To
James, Halifax recommended concessions that might make his
regime palatable to the populace and to the politicians (the
dismissal of Roman Catholics from office, a foreign policy independent from France, and an amnesty to those already in
rebellion against him). James refused, of course. This did not
prevent Halifax from attempting, even as the Dutch were march-
ing toward London, to effect a reconciliation, for "the eloquent
and ingenious Trimmer might flatter himself that he should be
able to mediate between infuriated factions, to dictate a compromise between extreme opinions, to secure the liberties and religion
of his country, without exposing her to the risks inseparable from
a change of dynasty and a disputed succession."[44]

Macaulay did not blame Halifax for the failure of the scheme, for "the failure is to be ascribed to causes against which no human skill could contend." Although unwilling to take part in the conspiracy against James, Halifax helped place William on the throne once James had gone to France. "From the moment of that shameful flight, the sagacious Trimmer, convinced that compromise was thenceforth impossible, had taken a decided part." His support was of course thrown to one on whom he could rely to seek reconciliation.[45]

Macaulay's admiration for Halifax was almost without qualification, and this is extraordinary in view of his mixed judgments of most other men of great achievement. His writings, Macaulay said, had "amplitude and acuteness of intellect, that vivacity of fancy, that terse and energetic style, that placid dignity, half courtly half philosophical, which the utmost excitement of conflict could not for a moment derange." Furthermore, "in wit and eloquence, in amplitude of comprehension and subtlety of disquisition, he had no equal among the statesmen of his time."[46]

Apart from the immediate appeal of the style and wit of Halifax's writings, what explains Macaulay's great praise? For one thing, Halifax's judgments were based on that combination of general understanding with awareness of particular circumstances that Macaulay thought essential. Untouched by fashionable prejudice and not sharing prevailing passions, he discerned the essential circumstances. "He always saw passing events, not in the point of view in which they commonly appear to one who bears a part in them, but in the point of view in which, after the lapse of many years, they appear to the philosophic historian." His judgments were those of neither "the mere man of theory" nor "the mere man of business." It was for this reason that "the memory of Halifax is entitled in an especial manner to the protection of history. For what distinguishes him from all other English statesmen is this, that, through a long public life, and through frequent and violent revolutions of public feeling, he almost invariably took that view of the great questions of his time which history has finally adopted."[47]

Macaulay obviously thought of himself as the voice of posterity, as the philosophical historian who properly understood Halifax. Macaulay's appreciation of Halifax was enhanced by affinities with him. Like Halifax, Macaulay also was a trimmer from principle (though not by temperament). Halifax, like Macaulay, was nervous that public discontents would lead to violence, and he feared the possibility of civil war and revolution. For both men, the zealot, the doctrinaire extremist, in religion as in politics, was a bugbear. The main purpose for each was the cooling of passions and the relief of grievances in order to reduce the risks of violent conflict. Halifax, "from temper averse to violent changes," was, Macaulay said, what "in our time, is called a Conservative"; yet, at the same time, he noted that in speculation Halifax was attracted to doctrines—notably, republicanism—that outraged most of his contemporaries. Macaulay similarly combined conservative inclinations with many advanced if not outrageous beliefs, and both, despite their conservatism, were, in a sense, reluctant revolutionaries—Halifax in practice, Macaulay in judgment. But their greatest affinity was in their shared way of understanding politics. Macaulay understood Halifax's politics precisely as he did his own. Halifax "trimmed," he said, "as the temperate zone trims between intolerable heat and intolerable cold—as a good government trims between despotism and anarchy—as a pure church trims between the errors of the Papist and those of the Anabaptist"—or, we might add, as Macaulay thought Whigs ought to trim between ultra-Tories, with their threat of despotism, and Radicals, with their threat of anarchy.[48]

It is instructive to compare Macaulay's unqualified esteem for Halifax with Mackintosh's view that Halifax was an important but not extraordinary political figure. Mackintosh—who lacked Macaulay's hypersensitivity to the existence of dangerous cleavages that call for the comprehensive vision of crisis-oriented, trimming politicians—did not see Halifax as an extraordinary statesman. He recognized his "brilliant genius" and that he played a "great part" during the reign of Charles II and during the period following 1688, but he also found much to dislike. "His political speculations being soon found incapable of being reduced to practice, melted away in the sunshine of royal favour; the disappointment of visionary hopes led him to despair of great improvements, to despise the moderate services which an individual may render to the community, and to turn with disgust from public principles to the indulgence of his own vanity and ambition." Instead of recognizing and praising the conduct of a trimmer, Mackintosh describes it without sympathy:

> He was too acute in discovering difficulties, too ingenious in
> devising objections. He had too keen a perception of human
> weakness and folly not to find many pretexts and temptations
> for changing his measures and deserting his connections. The
> subtlety of his genius tempted him to projects too refined to be
> understood or supported by numerous bodies of men. His
> appetite for praise, when sated by the admiration of his friends,
> was too apt to seek a new and more stimulating gratification in
> the applause of opponents. His weaknesses and even his talents
> contributed to betray him into inconstancy; which, if not the
> worst quality of a statesman, is the most fatal to his permanent
> importance.[49]

When Mackintosh does discern Halifax's trimming policy, he
judges it to be ineffective and self-defeating. He sees that during
the last years of Charles's reign Halifax practiced "his refined
policy . . . of balancing factions, of occasionally leaning to the
vanquished, and always tempering the triumph of the victorious
party." He served Charles during the period of the Rye House Plot
but tried to save Russell from the gallows. "Perhaps he satisfied
himself with the reflection, that his compliance with all the evil
which was then done was necessary to enable him to save his country from the arbitrary and bigotted faction which was eager to rule
it," but he was unsuccessful. Mackintosh even suggested that he
unintentionally contributed to Sidney's execution as a consequence of his manipulations, which were intended to balance the
duke of York's influence on the king by enhancing the status of
Monmouth. In the end, these manipulations, these "refinements,"
backfired:

> The compliances and refinements of that period pursued him
> with, perhaps, too just a retribution during the remainder of his
> life. James was anxious to be rid of him who had checked his
> influence during the last years of his brother, and the friends of
> liberty could never place any lasting trust in the man who
> remained a member of the government which put to death
> Russell and Sidney.[50]

Mackintosh's estimate was the conventional one; it was similar to
Hallam's and to Hume's. Macaulay's appreciative judgment,
then, was quite novel.[51]

There is still another difference between the two historians that reflects the distinctive character of Macaulay's political outlook as it is revealed in his *History*. Much more than Mackintosh, Macaulay elevated some politicians to heroic status. But heroes require heroic situations. Since it was the function of his hero to interrupt the pattern of destructive conflict and to help the nation give shape to new institutions, he needed to understand social and political processes in a way that made it possible for him to play his heroic role. Macaulay assumed that there were critical situations in which there is a last opportunity to salvage what had not been provided for through foresight and prudence. These crises developed because grievances had not been dealt with, because the tactics of conciliatory politics and timely concession had not been adopted. That this happens Macaulay knew from the examples of Hampden, of Halifax before the Revolution, and of Turgot. Thus no matter how perceptive, far-seeing, and wise a politician, if suspicions and mutual hostilities prevail among a divided people, he may not gain support sufficient to implement a policy of concession and conciliation. Consequently, crises may be unavoidable. Yet, even then, not all need be lost. If there is some latent basis of reconciliation, recognized by a politician who has the skill to help men discover it, the outcome may yet be favorable. Macaulay called these crises "conjunctures." His best examples of conjunctures were the Restoration, the period immediately following James's departure, and the Reform Bill period of 1831–32.

In using the term "conjuncture," Macaulay seems to have meant something more than the conventional dictionary definition, for he often used the term to refer to a crisis that could be resolved in an unexpected and highly favorable way.[52] The possibility of a favorable outcome arose from the fact that during many conjunctures old antipathies were submerged and new alliances between usually hostile parties were formed, perhaps only temporarily, but for a sufficient time that some significant development, possibly of an apocalyptic character, could take place. The alliance among usually antipathetic parties made it possible to establish consent for a policy that otherwise would be an occasion for dispute between those parties. Thus a conjuncture had the effect of temporarily, perhaps only momentarily, reconciling parties that were usually in conflict and of making palatable what was usually rejected.[53] Such a conjuncture occurred, for example, in 1660, when, with the army disunited, there was an opportunity to restore civil rule:

On the use which might be made of one auspicious moment
depended the future destiny of the nation. Our ancestors used
that moment well. They forgot old injuries, waved [*sic*] petty
scruples, adjourned to a more convenient season all disputes
about the reforms which our institutions needed, and stood
together, Cavaliers and Roundheads, Episcopalians and
Presbyterians, in firm union, for the old laws of the land against
military despotism. . . . The old civil polity was, therefore, by
the general consent of both the great parties, reestablished.

Much hung in the balance; for Macaulay thought that, had this
not occurred, England would have fallen "under the tyranny of a
succession of small men raised up and pulled down by military
caprice." A conjuncture presents great opportunity, yet it is
dangerous. Thus, of 1660 he said, "It was a stirring time, a time of
anxiety, yet of hope."[54]

Of course the events of 1688–89 best exemplify what he meant
by a conjuncture. James's tyranny provoked opposition in the
entire nation, which became "one huge compact mass. All ranks,
all parties, all Protestant sects, made up that vast phalanx." As a
result, old enmities were temporarily forgotten, and men could
act in a new way. "All party prejudices, all recollections of former
hostility, all apprehensions of danger, were forgotten in the sense of
intolerable oppression. Mutual antipathies gave way to common
perils. Whigs and Tories, prelates and field preachers, were
combined by the dread of tyranny and persecution." In these
circumstances there was a novel willingness to modify old loyalties
and to befriend new institutions and new practices.[55]

Macaulay had in mind something like a revolutionary situation
—one in which historical memories were altered, factions and
parties were suddenly realigned, and, despite usually fundamental
differences in interest, or class, or religious outlook, men were
united by a shared fear and a common hostility. Yet it was not the
conventional revolutionary situation. For the changes that were
made, though they might be large, did not involve a break with
the past; instead, there was a continuity with it, and the views of
those who would impose novel institutions and practices, whether
religious or constitutional, were rejected. Thus in 1660 the
Protectorate was terminated; in 1688 a Catholic king was
removed. Although these situations were filled with danger, by
skillful management they were turned into consolidating, concil-

iatory experiences. It was, in a sense, a revolutionary situation that had a revolutionary yet conservative outcome.

It was in this way that Macaulay saw the Revolution of 1688. In a well-known passage he gave an account of the peculiar character of that event. He pointed to the absence of violence and the continuity with the past, and to the prescription and legitimacy that accompanied it. Those who made and those who supported the Revolution shared a belief in a fundamental law in support of individual rights and against arbitrary government, and this belief was supported by statute and common sentiment, as it had been during the previous four centuries. "As our Revolution was a vindication of ancient rights, so it was conducted with strict attention to ancient formalities. In almost every word and act may be discerned a profound reverence for the past." All was done according to the old rules, in accordance with accustomed forms, and with the antique ceremonial.

> The speeches present an almost ludicrous contrast to the revolutionary oratory of every other country. . . . To us, who have lived in the year 1848, it may seem almost an abuse of terms to call a proceeding, conducted with so much deliberation, with so much sobriety, and with such minute attention to prescriptive etiquette, by the terrible name of Revolution.

Its distinguishing characteristic was that it maintained continuity with the past, in contrast to revolutions in other countries, where a "gulf . . . completely separates the new from the old system." For these reasons he called it a "defensive" and "preserving" revolution.[56]

To turn a conjuncture to good account, political leadership of a special order was necessary. It required, among other things, a sensitivity to the way feelings about the past can be made to support innovations, for such support gave to revolutions their conservative, defensive character. And this sensitivity William had to a preeminent degree:

> He outraged no national prejudice. He abolished no ancient form. He altered no venerable name. He saw that the existing institutions possessed the greatest capabilities of excellence, and that stronger sanctions and clearer definitions were alone required to make the practice as admirable as the theory. Thus

he imparted to innovation the dignity and stability of
antiquity. [57]

Only one who could dispassionately analyze the past, without
feeling that it was in some sense sacred and without feeling that it
was abhorrent, could play this role. In other words, he would have
to be without the typical attitude toward the past of either the
Tory or the Radical.

The leader who successfully managed a conjuncture also needed
a quality of perception that made it possible to recognize, beneath
the appearance of dispute and fragmentation, the potential for
agreement. Of course it was necessary that there be some common
ground that would allow him to alter political alignments. Thus,
after the Civil War and the Protectorate, it was possible to seek
reconciliation because such common ground existed:

> A few enthusiasts on one side were ready to lay all our laws
> and franchises at the feet of our Kings. A few enthusiasts on
> the other side were bent on pursuing, through endless civil
> troubles, their darling phantom of a republic. But the great
> majority of those who fought for the crown were averse to
> despotism; and the great majority of the champions of
> popular rights were averse to anarchy. [58]

A similar situation existed after James's flight. A small faction
wanted to recall the old king; another small faction wanted to set
up a commonwealth. "But these extreme opinions were generally
held in abhorrence. Nineteen twentieths of the nation consisted of
persons in whom love of hereditary monarchy and love of
constitutional freedom were combined, though in different proportions, and who were equally opposed to the total abolition of
the kingly office and to the unconditional restoration of the
King." [59] Reflecting these shades of difference, as well as the
potential for agreement, the majority consisted of two classes:

> One class consisted of eager and vehement Whigs, who, if they
> had been able to take their own course, would have given to the
> proceedings of the Convention a decidedly revolutionary char-
> acter. The other class admitted that a revolution was necessary,
> but regarded it as a necessary evil, and wished to disguise it, as
> much as possible, under the show of legitimacy. The former
> class demanded a distinct recognition of the rights of subjects
> to dethrone bad princes. The latter class desired to rid the
> country of one bad prince, without promulgating any doctrine
> which might be abused for the purpose of weakening the just

and salutary authority of future monarchs. The former class dwelt chiefly on the King's misgovernment; the latter on his flight. The former class considered him as having forfeited his crown; the latter as having resigned it.[60]

The political problem was to draw up a resolution that would gain the consent of this varied majority. It was the achievement of the leading politicians of 1689 that in face of the cleavages and disputes of their time they fashioned consent for what came to be known as the Revolution settlement. Preeminent among them were Halifax and William. Somers and Maynard also earned Macaulay's esteem for their contributions to it.

Macaulay was aware that, if an underlying basis of agreement did not exist, even the finest political leadership would be helpless. Thus even Cromwell—"the most profound politician of that age"—was unsuccessful in his attempt to heal the wounds left by the Civil War. And by 1689, even if William had been inclined to establish a just government in Ireland, he would have failed, for "the opportunity had passed away: compromise had become impossible: the two infuriated castes were alike convinced that it was necessary to oppress or to be oppressed, and that there could be no safety but in victory, vengeance, and dominion."[61]

The revolutionary leader who managed to turn dangerous conjunctures into unifying events with great significance in the nation's history might be compared with other types of leadership. Macaulay's hero is not a prophet of a future order, nor is he the spokesman for a class or an ideological view. His distinguishing characteristic is his lack of ideological commitment to any position that would have a divisive effect. In some respects he resembles Rousseau's Legislator. Of course, he lacks the mystery of the Legislator. Not only is he not godlike, but he avoids any appearance of that character. But, like the Legislator, his function is to reform or renovate a political order that is corrupt, that is, unable to function properly. He does this by seeking to gain consent for new political arrangements among men who, were they to conduct themselves in their routine manner, would withhold consent. Thus he makes them behave in a new way—in a sense, as Rousseau would have said, to change their natures. His achievement rests upon his ability to discern and elicit the sentiments that, despite enmities and suspicions, are capable of binding men together.

Although Macaulay and Mackintosh were both in some sense

Whig historians, they were yet markedly different in important ways. Whereas Mackintosh was the more conventional historian, Macaulay used history to justify his own understanding of political practice. He wrote his *History* as if he were helping his contemporaries to follow his advice not to do what their ancestors had done but rather what their ancestors would do, were they facing contemporary circumstances. This meant that he assumed a similarity in the kinds of considerations that would be relevant to political practice at all times. As in the nineteenth century, the seventeenth-century politician had had to deal with extremists. The Puritans, the early Whigs, and James were all — whether from temper or principle — unable to practice the art of timely concession and conciliatory politics. Thus there would always be conjunctures — situations in which skillful politicians could discern the bonds that might unify men whose passions and shortsightedness made them dangerously contentious. And there would be the need for statesmen who could elicit the sentiments that would make those bonds politically effective, thus assuring continuity with the past in the midst of far-reaching change. Macaulay, in other words, not only generalized, but he sought politically relevant generalizations. Mackintosh, in contrast, conducted historical inquiry in order to elucidate "general causes"; history was part of the attempt to "philosophise on the nature of man and of society." Using it as a source of political maxims was secondary, even unimportant.[62] Consequently, Mackintosh's history of the events leading up to the Revolution is filled with acute observations and sustained analyses of complex events (for example, on the sudden shift from toleration to persecution in France in the 1680s and on the growth of disaffection and the sudden development of a revolutionary situation under James).[63] But these parts are not bound together to support a general interpretation that is relevant to comparable situations at other times. Perhaps this is why Macaulay said of Mackintosh's book, "too many plums, and no suet."[64]

One more difference between the two historians should be mentioned. Macaulay deals extensively with the arguments and doctrines that actually affected the main actors: the Anglicans and their view of resistance, the exclusionist Whigs, the Jesuits, the nonjurors. He analyzes these as ingredients of the historical situation as it unfolded. He does not present the conventional

Whig justification of the Revolution which in large part could be understood in Lockean terms and which became historically important during the eighteenth century. Indeed, he barely mentions Locke; and, when he does, it is mainly in connection with Locke's (and Newton's) part in promoting the recoinage in 1695.[65]

This does not mean that Macaulay did not appreciate the Revolution or that he failed to emphasize its importance as the source of much that was still valuable; but he did not portray the Revolution as the responsibility of men who were implementing Lockean ideas about trusteeship and resistance. Mackintosh, on the other hand, incorporates into his history an essay on political obligations and resistance in which he outlines the grounds of the just rebellion. Although there are references to seventeenth-century beliefs, it is not a historical essay but rather a discourse in legal and political philosophy. Without mentioning Locke, it is Lockean; that is, it defines the grounds of resistance, and it circumscribes them much more than Locke did. Notable in itself, it also identifies Mackintosh as one whose Whiggism is derived from the Revolution of 1688. In Macaulay's *History*, where such considerations are not to be found, the emphasis is given to an approach to politics that was meant to be as relevant to the nineteenth century as to the seventeenth — or to any period. For Macaulay made a trimmer's assumption about politics and aspired to adopt a trimmer's remedies. Significantly, the political thinker most celebrated by Macaulay is not Locke but Halifax.[66]

The novelty of Macaulay's views among Whig historians does not depend on the comparison with Mackintosh alone. Henry Hallam (1777–1859) was the other notable Whig historian (among other things) of the seventeenth century who was contemporary with Macaulay, and a comparison of his work with Macaulay's confirms the finding that the political teaching included in Macaulay's historical writing distinguishes him from other Whig historians.

Hallam demonstrated no interest in the trimming theme, which was the distinguishing feature of Macaulay's *History*, nor did he display any sensitivity to it. He appreciated Halifax's skills and his "sound principles," such as his opposition to unlimited monarchy. But to Hallam, Halifax was not significantly different from other politicians. He noted that Halifax was "not uniform in conduct"; but whereas Macaulay recognized the trimmer beneath such apparent inconsistency, Hallam interpreted it as the result of a defective character. Thus Halifax was unwilling to sign the invitation to the Prince of Orange because his "conscience or [his] courage [was] unequal to the crisis."[67]

The trimming outlook is most congenial to those who assume that movement to the extremes is likely and that there can well be destructive conflict between extremist groups. But Hallam made no such assumption. On the contrary, he wrote of "that centripetal force, that moral attraction towards uniformity and obedience to custom, which Providence has rendered one of the great preservatives of political society."[68] His belief that the political center can be easily maintained was also reflected in his characterizations of political parties in the seventeenth century. The Whigs, he said, wanted to protect the privileges of the subject, while the Tories cared most about the crown's prerogative, and thus the principle of the Whigs was amelioration, of the Tories, conservation. But despite these differences, they "both ... admitted a common principle, the maintenance of the constitution." Although there was a risk that in some circumstances the Tory might aid in establishing despotism and the Whig in subverting monarchy, generally they shared a belief in the constitution, that is, in a government in which sovereignty was shared between monarch and Parliament. The Tories did not believe in unlimited monarchy, and the Whigs were not republicans.[69] With this view of parties, there was not much need for trimming.

Another difference between the two historians concerns the Revolution of 1688. Macaulay thought the main features of the constitution were established with the Revolution settlement, but in Hallam's judgment "the long parliament formed our constitution such nearly as it now exists." He was thinking of provisions for the return of Parliaments at fixed intervals and the abolition of the Star Chamber. "Laws of great importance were doubtless enacted in subsequent times, particularly at the Revolution [of 1688]; but none of them, perhaps, were strictly necessary for the preservation of our civil and political privileges; and it is rather from 1641 than any other epoch, that we may date their full legal establishment."[70]

Since Hallam somewhat diminished the constitutional significance of the Revolution of 1688, he was not inconsistent in his view that James II was not very oppressive. James was not a Caligula or a Commodus or a Galeazzo Sforza. His encroachments were "rather felt in prospect than [in] much actual injury."[71]

> Though the reigns of the two latter Stuarts, accordingly, are justly obnoxious, and were marked by several illegal measures, yet, whether we consider the number and magnitude of their transgressions of law, or the practical oppression of their government, these princes fell very short of the despotism that had been exercised, either under the Tudors or the first two of their own family.[72]

With this characterization of James II as comparatively moderate, it would have been difficult to interpret the change in the succession as Macaulay did—as a defensive revolution.

Macaulay understood the political situation in 1688 as a conjuncture: usually antagonistic parties agreed to a course of action that resolved a crisis and removed a threat of civil war. The policy to which they agreed was not imposed by one party and accepted by the other. But as Hallam interpreted the Revolution, it was the victory of one party—the Whigs. It was the triumph of liberal principles, which were Whig principles. "The king had been raised to the throne by the vigour and zeal of the Whigs." Hallam acknowledged Tory cooperation in the successful conspiracy; but that party, he held, was insincere, since it looked forward to a compromise that would leave to James his throne and his constitutional prerogatives. "The revolution, to which at the outset a coalition of whigs and tories had conspired, became, in the final result, in the settlement of the crown upon William and Mary, almost entirely the work of the former party." Consequently, William was a Whig king—"he was the legitimate and natural ally of the whig party."[73] Whereas Macaulay avoided this attribution of party affiliation, since he placed William above party politics and made him a sympathetic ally of Halifax's, in contrast, Hallam announced that "a high regard for the memory of William III may justly be reckoned one of the tests by which genuine whiggism, as opposed both to tory and republican principles, has always been recognized."[74]

In addition to being a Whig achievement that placed a Whig king on the throne, the Revolution of 1688 was understood by

Hallam in Lockean terms. In this respect, too, the contrast with Macaulay could hardly be greater. Locke's spirit, Hallam said, characterized the age of William III. The Revolution had been undertaken for the sake of fundamental rights and liberties. The great advantage of the Revolution was that it broke the line of succession, and this was justified on theoretical grounds: "The right of excluding an unworthy heir from the succession" was supported not only by constitutional principles but also "by the plain and fundamental principles of civil society." The outcome was a "chosen sovereign" on his "elective throne."[75] This Lockean-Whig rhetoric, which Hallam found congenial, persuaded him that "the whigs appear to have taken a far more comprehensive view of the nature and ends of civil society"; and to the extent that they were guided by their principles, they were "far more friendly to the great interests of the commonwealth than their adversaries."[76] Thus Hallam subscribed to the theoretical ideas of one of the contestants, but Macaulay, in contrast, thought that the Lockean rhetoric was an obstacle to the mediation and trimming that the situation required. For the same reason Macaulay was severely critical of the Whigs' vindictiveness; Hallam, however, as a defender of the Whigs, justified it.[77]

Although these historians are usually considered intellectually and politically similar, the differences between them were considerable. Already in 1828 Macaulay, although approving some aspects of Hallam's *Constitutional History,* differed on many important points.[78] But it is the differences that appear from a comparison of Macaulay's *History* with Hallam's work that confirm what was found by the comparison with Mackintosh—that interwoven in Macaulay's historical writing was a strong emphasis on the role and usefulness of trimming, and that this distinguished Macaulay from other Whig historians.

History for Macaulay was political, for its function was "to supply statesmen with examples and warnings."[79] Macaulay called upon politicians to consult history when he advised them to respect their ancestors, "not by superstitiously adhering to what they, in other circumstances, did, but by doing what they, in our circumstances, would have done."[80] This required understanding not only what ancestors had done but why they had done it, which, in the case of the fortunate examples found in the past, revealed what Macaulay meant by civil prudence or civil wisdom.

Thus history provided the politician with examples of the circumstances when conciliatory politics and trimming were necessary in order to avoid the extremes that brought either anarchy or despotism or both; and it identified examples of the kind of politician and political thinking that were obstacles to the practice of conciliatory politics. To do this properly was to be a "philosophical historian," and there was no greater achievement for the statesman than to look "on the events which were passing before him with the eye of a philosophical historian."[81] Historical inquiry, then, linked past and present and future, for it not only directed the politician's vision as he looked to the past for models, but, by perpetuating a tradition in which these models were given an honored place, it extended its influence into the future, thereby giving historians an indirect but pervasive influence on future politicians.

With historical inquiry serving politics, Macaulay's *History* could not meet the standards of professional historians, and it is not surprising that he has been severely criticized by them. For his understanding of the purpose of history led to what the professionals have considered his most serious faults. This does not include inaccuracies as to facts; there are some, but they are not the usual target of criticism.[82] But he has been accused of exaggerating the importance of some events and neglecting others. For example, he is thought to have made the Glorious Revolution too significant, and, in explaining it, he is said to have overemphasized domestic developments and neglected the context of foreign affairs within which domestic developments can best be understood. Such distortions may be avoided by the professional historian who is careful to see things from all angles; for whom the context is as important as the event; who prefers to discern continuities within which even significant events have diminished importance. But history written in this way does not allow the historian to direct the thoughts of the statesman, for that requires focusing on one event and neglecting the background. The statesman's responsibility is to shape and direct, not primarily to understand all aspects of the situation. His purpose is different from the professional historian's, and a historian who writes history to serve statesmanship will necessarily not satisfy his professional colleagues.[83]

We can see the difference between the two approaches to historical inquiry by considering the charge that Macaulay oversimplified individual character. Not only is he said to have lacked sympathetic understanding for those he disapproved of; he is also charged with failure to appreciate the complexity of his favorite historical figures. For example, it can be shown that he under-estimated James II, making him into a mere "stage-tyrant."[84] He also ignored the complexity of Archbishop Laud in casting him as a diehard opponent of all change. It is also argued that Macaulay could not empathize with those who had intense religious feeling; these he characterized as fanatics. If the purpose of historical inquiry is to achieve full comprehension of all aspects of situations and individual character, many of Macaulay's judgments are overly simple and unfair.

However, from Macaulay's point of view it was not the purpose of history to appreciate the intentions or to understand the complexity of diehards and fanatics. On the contrary, it was the purpose of history to demonstrate the dangers of such persons, even if this meant ignoring complexity and making imbalanced judgments. Only in this way could history educate politicians by demonstrating how diehards and fanatics provoked each other, bringing about, alternately, despotism and anarchy; and only in this way could history remind statesmen of their responsibility to protect the state from such extremes. In addition to the warnings, historians should also provide examples of the great men who, recognizing fanaticism as the most important problem, success-fully dealt with it. Perhaps this purpose led to exaggeration of their achievements, but this was the way models for politicians were established. Given this political and didactic role of the historian, it became thematically necessary for Macaulay in his *History* to cast historical figures as fanatics, demagogues, despots, and (in rare cases) conciliators and trimmers. Only in this way could they be portrayed as playing a part in the historical drama which, as he described it, could provide the basis for the understanding of politics that he wanted to define and perpetuate among future politicians.[85]

While Macaulay intended his *History* to contain a political teaching, it was not narrow party history that he wrote. Yet he is most often accused of this—of producing biased, Whig interpreta-tions.[86] In view of his celebration of trimming, which distin-guishes his *History* and creates a sharp contrast with Hallam and

Mackintosh (the two most prominent Whig historians before Macaulay published his *History*), it would be surprising to find that he shared the typical views of Whig history. For example, a Whig historian is supposed to consider the constitution as it emerged after 1688 as a Whig achievement and to glorify the Whig politicians of the late seventeenth century.

What were Macaulay's views on these questions? There is one sense in which Macaulay was not a typical Whig historian: his *History* did not give a favorable interpretation of the seventeenth-century Whigs. They were portrayed as impassioned, fanatical, uncompromising — the very opposite of the qualities Macaulay most admired. Rejecting the "absurd panegyrics which have been lavished on the Whigs of the reign of Charles the Second," he was already critical of the Whigs in his Cambridge prize essay in 1822, where he noted their part in the Popish Plot and in the Rye House Conspiracy. To oppose James II was commendable,

> But nothing can justify the conduct of the whigs, which was generally insincere, and often sanguinary. And the results of that conduct form a great and important lesson for posterity. Woe to those mistaken friends of Liberty who separate her from humanity and justice! Woe to the statesman who with intentions however upright, and for ends however noble, employs popular delusion and violence as his instrument. He evokes a daemon of whom he may for a short time be the master, but must ultimately become the slave and the victim.[87]

The Whig's violent factionalism is seen as a major cause of the political deterioration that followed. Having projected insurrection, only to be betrayed, the Whig leaders were left, not only to the mercy of the angered king, but "to the justice of the laws which they had vitiated":

> By popular clamour, by infamous testimony, by sophisticated law, they had poured forth innocent and honourable blood like water. By the same arts they were now destined to perish. When their victims were in their power, they had interfered to prevent their Sovereign from remitting the last brutal mutilations prescribed by a barbarous Code. They were now compelled to implore the exercise of a prerogative which they had endeavoured to curtail.[88]

Macaulay can be found in an election speech in 1839 to be glo-
rifying all Whigs at all times, including the seventeenth century,
in contradiction to what he said in less politically motivated
writings; but in the *History* (1849) he was still sufficiently critical
for his observations there to provoke criticism on this point from
Lord John Russell, to whom he wrote: "I am not surprised that
you think me too much of a Trimmer." It was natural, he
acknowledged, that a Russell should be partial to the Exclusionists.
Macaulay agreed that the Exclusion Bill ought to have passed.
"But the question is whether, when it was clear that the exclusion
bill would not pass, it was wise to reject all compromise, and,
instead of framing laws which might have secured the liberties and
religion of the nation, to proceed to excesses which produced a
violent reaction in the public mind."[89]

The victorious Whigs of 1688–89 fared no better in Macaulay's
judgment. For one thing, they experienced, in the moment of
triumph, "a revenge too delicious to be relinquished."[90] This was
perhaps understandable in view of their defeats and sufferings,
but it hardly contributed to the conciliatory policies that the
divided country so much needed:

> Vindictive as had been the mood in which the Whigs had left
> Westminster, the mood in which they returned was more
> vindictive still. Smarting from old sufferings, drunk with recent
> prosperity, burning with implacable resentment, confident of
> irresistible strength, they were not less rash and headstrong than
> in the days of the Exclusion Bill. Sixteen hundred and eighty
> was come again. Again all compromise was rejected. Again the
> voices of the wisest and most upright friends of liberty were
> drowned by the clamour of hotheaded and designing agitators.
> Again moderation was despised as cowardice, or execrated as
> treachery.[91]

What is more, they failed to learn from history:

> All the lessons taught by a cruel experience were forgotten. The
> very same men who had expiated, by years of humiliation, of
> imprisonment, of penury, of exile, the folly with which they had
> misused the advantage given them by the Popish plot, now
> misused with equal folly the advantage given them by the Rev-
> olution. The second madness would, in all probability, like the
> first, have ended in their proscription, dispersion, decimation,
> but for the magnanimity and wisdom of that great prince,
> who . . . saved them.[92]

Furthermore, in this mood the Whigs were unable to appreciate the wisdom of William's policies. The new king appointed a few Tories and trimmers to high office, and he tried to obtain a general amnesty. But the "intemperate friends of liberty . . . were clamouring for a new proscription." However, the king "had no sympathy with the just resentments of the Whigs"; indeed, "he was in truth not a man to be popular with the vindictive zealots of any faction." His efforts to establish an amnesty attracted "the savage invectives of those whose malevolent passions he refused to satisfy."[93]

Macaulay's difficulty in sympathizing with the Whigs of the Revolution is also revealed in his characterization of their doctrine. Their beliefs supported those who would have given the Convention "a decidedly revolutionary character" — hardly what Macaulay was likely to welcome. They "demanded a distinct recognition of the rights of subjects to dethrone bad princes."[94] This position represented one of the extremes between which Macaulay's trimming heroes had to work in order to gain consent for a constitutionally agreeable and politically effective compromise. This lack of sympathy for Whig doctrine is perhaps one of the reasons Macaulay barely mentions Locke.

Macaulay also condemns the early Whigs for their Irish policy. They were utterly indifferent to the fate of the Irish, and they were hypocritical as well.

> While ostentatiously professing the political doctrines of Locke and Sidney, [they] held that a people who spoke the Celtic tongue and heard mass could have no concern in those doctrines. . . . Indeed, during the century which followed the Revolution, the inclination of an English Protestant to trample on the Irishry was generally proportioned to the zeal which he professed for political liberty in the abstract.

It would not always be like this. After the rebellion of 1798, "the vanquished people found protection in a quarter from which they would once have had to expect nothing but implacable severity. By this time the philosophy of the eighteenth century had purified English Whiggism from that deep taint of intolerance which had been contracted during a long and close alliance with the Puritanism of the seventeenth century."[95]

Some historical legends give the Whigs credit for the Revolution of 1688, but Macaulay did not share this view. As early as 1822 he rejected the suggestion that the Whigs of Charles II's reign contributed to the Revolution. And in the *History*, far from ignoring the role of the Tories, he emphasizes that it could not have taken place without the cooperation of all parties and groups. James was hated, Macaulay said, by Tories even more than by Whigs, for to them he was not an enemy but a faithless friend.[96] In the face of James's depredations,

> the ablest and most enlightened Tories began to admit that they had overstrained the doctrine of passive obedience. The difference between these men and the Whigs as to the reciprocal obligations of kings and subjects was now no longer a difference of principle. There still remained, it is true, many historical controversies between the party which had always maintained the lawfulness of resistance and the new converts. The memory of the blessed Martyr was still as much revered as ever by those old Cavaliers who were ready to take arms against his degenerate son. They still spoke with abhorrence of the Long Parliament, of the Rye House plot, and of the Western insurrection. But whatever they might think about the past, the view which they took of the present was altogether Whiggish; for they now held that extreme oppression might justify resistance, and they held that the oppression which the nation suffered was extreme.[97]

The coalition that emerged was temporary, formed to deal with the common danger. "The oppressor learned that an armed deliverer was at hand and would be eagerly welcomed by Whigs and Tories, Dissenters and Churchmen." The Revolution was accomplished by a coalition: "those politicians who were peculiarly zealous for monarchy assisted to vindicate liberty."[98]

Although not a defender of the seventeenth-century Whigs or a supporter of the Whig legend that the Revolution of 1688 was solely a Whig achievement, there is one sense in which Macaulay was something of a Whig historian. His wish to have history teach led him to assume that the problems of different historical periods were fundamentally similar and that the task of statesmanship in each era was therefore the same. This made it possible to learn from the mistakes and the achievements of earlier periods. These assumptions gave him some affinity with the Whig interpretation of history as Butterfield has described it. According to this view, the Whig historian studies the past with reference to the present, using categories that have relevance at the present time to analyze the past and using present-day values in judging the past. Many consequences follow from this, according to Butterfield. It is assumed that there are basic similarities between past and present; consequently the past is not interpreted in terms appropriate to it. A misunderstanding of the past is the result. Another consequence is the tendency to judge developments in the past by considering whether they may be seen as congenial to institutions and beliefs that are valued today. In this way certain men, movements, and decisions are seen as contributing to the emergence of beliefs and institutions that prevail at the present time, whereas others are judged harshly for having been obstacles to the developments that led to present-day arrangements. For example, the seventeenth-century parliamentarians are praised for anticipating the later development of parliamentary democracy; or sixteenth-century religious reformers are praised for anticipating the later development of religious freedom. The result is a bias in favor of Protestants, progressives, and Whigs and a serious misunderstanding of the purposes and expectations of historical actors of all sides.[99] Butterfield did not suggest that it was merely a matter of party bias. "The Protestant and whig interpretation of history is the result of something much more subtle than actual Protestant or party bias.... [It] is not merely the property of Whigs and it is much more subtle than mental bias; it lies in a trick of organization, an unexamined habit of mind that any historian may fall into."[100]

Macaulay, with many others, investigated the past in this way. Of course he was sympathetic to the parliamentary cause and critical of the Stuarts. He did look on the technological achievements of the seventeenth century as a foundation for the economic progress that he observed in his own time. He did have a vague conception of a fundamental law and an ancient constitution that was recognizable and which was seen as being violated by the Stuarts. And he did judge the conduct of seventeenth-century politicians by the standards of rectitude that were established only in his time.

Yet, tarnished though it is, Macaulay's record in this respect is mixed, for in many ways he avoided the Whig interpretation as Butterfield has described it. Although he was critical of the Stuarts, he saw the Restoration as an opportunity for the development of the constitution in a way that would allow for a reasonable balance

between king and Parliament. Although he did occasionally refer
to the ancient constitution and identify violations of it by James II,
he can also be found to acknowledge that "all along the line which
separates the functions of the prince from those of the legislator
there was long a disputed territory."[101] Although he did appreciate
the Puritans' contribution to the later development of liberty, this
did not exonerate them in Macaulay's judgment, for he condemned
their fanaticism for its contribution to intolerance and civil war.
And while he did judge much conduct of the past by standards of
his own time, there were exceptions, for example, in his understanding of the obstacles to full toleration, for Catholics as well as
for all Protestant sects in the 1690s.[102] Furthermore, in his analysis
of the Toleration Act, the growth of ministerial government, the
development of liberty of the press, the decisions of the Convention,
and of noiseless revolutions generally, Macaulay explained historical developments as the undesigned results of the clash of opposing
opinions in which all sides contributed to the outcome. He thus
complies with Butterfield's recommendation that the historian
explain developments as "the result of the continual interplay and
perpetual collision" of both sides in a conflict.[103]

Finally, there is Macaulay's complaint (already quoted) that,
among the errors committed by those who study the past, one is
especially pernicious in a historian—"the error of judging the past
by the present." He had observed contemporaries who produced
distorted histories to serve their partisan purposes as they debated
the question whether Roman Catholics should be allowed to sit in
Parliament; as Macaulay remarked, "It may be doubted whether
any dispute has produced stranger perversions of history. The
whole past was falsified for the sake of the present. All the great
events of three centuries long appeared to us distorted and
discoloured by a mist sprung from our own theories and our own
passions." These statements (and others) indicate that Macaulay
would at least have recognized the merit of Butterfield's argument
even if he did not always comply with the precepts that may be
derived from it.[104]

There were some affinities between Macaulay and the Whig
interpretation, and there were interpretations of events and
developments in which he carefully avoided the Whig fallacy,
especially with regard to the distinguishing characteristic of
Butterfield's Whig historian, namely, the tendency to interpret

and judge the past with categories and values derived from present-day experience. Although Macaulay in one sense did do this, it is also possible to understand his categories of analysis as being not solely derived from nineteenth-century experience. On the contrary, his understanding of seventeenth-century problems in an important way informed his analysis of nineteenth-century politics. The religious conflict of the seventeenth century became the prototype for all other kinds of conflict; it provided the example of the dogmatist who inflexibly defends the existing order regardless of consequence and the example of the visionary who sweeps away that order to make possible the actualization of his utopian dream. Thus he saw the extreme Radicals of his own time as being like the revolutionary Puritans, and he saw Eldonine Tories as being modeled on Laud. He showed coercion in the nineteenth century to be imprudent by pointing out that it failed when Charles tried it against Hampden and when James tried it against the bishops. In the same vein, he described Lord John Russell in 1840, when pressed by both Tories and Radicals, as being "exposed to the fury of a Laud on one side, and to the fanaticism of a Praise-God-Barebones." This represents more than convenient reference to familiar historical examples. The problems of the seventeenth century were, to Macaulay, real and enduring, and they became the model with which he interpreted the events of his own time.[105] This is not to say that his historical judgments were unaffected by nineteenth-century experience. There was an interplay between the two, because he assumed that there were similarities between the two periods. This assumption was, for Macaulay, part of his trimmer's outlook, which also included the assumptions that in all societies there are potentialities for destructive conflict and that one can discover its character and the remedies for it by looking to examples of such conflict in the past.

The seventeenth-century model was, however, somewhat dysfunctional in that it led him to expect severe conflict, with class replacing religion as the occasion for it. Macaulay often seemed to be expecting destructive conflict. Each symptom was looked upon as significant, and the specter of civil war was almost never far beyond his range of vision. After 1850 he was less alarmed, but he was never complacent. It might be argued that his concern was misplaced in view of the rapidly diminishing risk of revolution as the Victorian decades passed. Yet it remained a fundamental maxim for Macaulay that the risks of civil war, anarchy, and despotism were never entirely eliminated. "Till Sovereigns and nations learn to act with perpetual attention to this great principle, mankind can hope for little through the future, as they have experienced little through the past, except an alternation of miseries and errors."[106]

Macaulay made a trimmer's assumptions about his own time. He assumed that there was instability; that the social foundations might contain rot and decay; and therefore that there were real risks of social disorder. He was aware of poverty, and he suspected that it might not be eliminated easily. Religious feeling still ran strong and intensified many political conflicts; and although religious issues were not as divisive as they had been in the past, there were many signs that class might be replacing religion as the source of unmanageable conflicts. All this might be understood in relation to the cyclical pattern that Macaulay discerned in modern history. The eighteenth century had been a period of tranquillity; as in the seventeenth century, now perhaps it was time to experience turbulence. The riots, which were not uncommon in his time, did nothing to reduce these feelings of uneasiness. Consequently, during the late 1820s he found it easy to believe that there was a real possibility of civil war. His expectation of dangerous conflict was so great that when, on his return from India in 1838, he found the country enjoying social peace, he recorded genuine surprise.[1] His fears, which were shared by many, made him something of an alarmist at the moments of Chartist agitation in 1842 and 1848.[2] The Newport rising (in 1839) also stimulated his fantasy of civil war:

> This attack was intended to lead to a great rising of the
> Chartists in the middle and northern counties of England....
> When we imagine the effect of a great civil war between classes
> in England—and that is what these persons projected—that is
> what they desired—that is what they intended—it would be

worse than any war we ever read of. Remember the wealth—
remember the civilization—remember the power of all those
classes. They were possessed of advantages, to retain which they
would have made every possible effort. A civil war commenced
under these circumstances, and with such objects in view, would
be a visitation more horrible than can possibly be conceived. . . .
It would be more dreadful than the wars of the cavaliers and the
roundheads in the seventeenth century. . . . The land may
recover after such battles even as those of Towton or of
Bosworth; but do you imagine that such would be the case
after a great war of classes in this country? All the power of
imagination fails to paint the horrors of such a contest.

Macaulay was unwilling to recommend mercy for the convicted
leaders of the uprising: "Is it not possible that these men may not
find imitators, if it shall go forth to the world that persons guilty of
high treason—men who have shed blood, who have meditated a
great civil war, a civil war of the worst of all kinds, a war of class
against class—are to escape with a less amount of punishment
than the shop boy who filches five shillings from the till?"[3] With
these fears, it is not surprising that he was fond of quoting Bacon
on the importance of noticing apparently insignificant symptoms
—that even the direction of a straw shows where a storm is coming
from. He was hypersensitive to small signs because of his basic
assumption that a storm was very likely to come.[4]

In a society characterized by discontents and conflicts, the way
politicians conducted themselves was especially important. Conflicts could be either reconciled or exacerbated. Discontents might
be relieved or they might be stimulated. Macaulay saw an
unfortunate tendency among politicians and political journalists
to stimulate political passions and to give expression to popular
hostilities—a tendency not confined to agitators on the periphery
of the major parties. Macaulay often saw the Radicals and
particularly the Tories as extremists whose success carried with it a
risk of civil war. He had no difficulty in seeing most extraparliamentary Radicals in this way; whether Henry Hunt, William
Cobbett, the early socialists who wrote for the inexpensive,
unstamped newspapers, or the Chartists, they all seemed to him to
be encouraging the workingman to assume that there were easy
political remedies for intractable economic problems. Moreover,
during the 1830s many of the parliamentary (so-called Philosophic) Radicals made it their greatest priority to realign parties

so that party conflict would reflect what they assumed to be the fundamental conflicts of class interest in society. Macaulay saw the Tories, on the other hand, as a party of squires and parsons who were firmly committed to unrealistic creeds of protectionism and Protestant exclusiveness. Although Peel was flexible, he could not control, or lead, his bigoted back-benchers. At the extremes one found enthusiasts on one side, bigots on the other. Both were unrealistic, and both made conflict more likely. One represented anarchy, the other an unrealistic, ineffective response to it. Together they gave plausibility to Macaulay's nightmare of a society that alternated between anarchy and despotism.

With centrifugal forces operating to give prominence and appeal to the extreme positions, Macaulay, in the tradition of trimming, sought to preserve the center against the extremes. Protecting the center was not a matter of hedging or of compromising differences. The purpose was to preserve consent for the constitutional system against one extreme (the Radicals), which encouraged anarchy, and the other (the Tory extreme), which would provoke rebelliousness and so create a justification for repression. When successful, this policy would leave society in "that happy central point in which alone it can repose."[5] This was the goal Macaulay defended as early as 1822, although he did not then identify it with the Whigs; and it was the policy he outlined in 1827, when he defended the Canningite coalition against Radicals, Eldonine Tories, and those Whigs reluctant to support it. By the time of the Reform Bill crisis, he saw this policy as the rationale for the Whig party.

Macaulay held that the merit of being at the center was not that such a position was more liberal than the Right or less hasty than the Left. Despite his reputed belief in progress, he did not think of politics developing historically toward some ideal end. Indeed, Macaulay expected that whatever improvement was to take place would occur outside the realm of politics—the product of beneficent, noiseless revolutions taking place in the sciences, the practical arts, and the economy. Government might facilitate improvements, but its main task was to avoid that easy descent into anarchy or despotism that characterized the politics of most nations through most of their histories.

An explicit statement of the importance of the center as a bulwark against the danger from the extremes was novel in the 1820s. Macaulay was not unique in making it, however, for

Francis Jeffrey, who was editor of the *Edinburgh Review* when
Macaulay first contributed to it, argued, in passages suggesting
that Halifax's *Character of a Trimmer* was his model, that the
Whigs would have no excuse for existing if the nation were not
plagued by extremist parties:

> [There are] dangers to which the conflict of opposite extremes
> must always expose the peace and the liberty of a country like
> England. . . . We acknowledge that we are fairly chargeable
> with a fear of opposite excesses — a desire to compromise and
> reconcile the claims of all the great parties in the State — an
> anxiety to temper and qualify whatever may be said in favour
> of one, with a steady reservation of whatever may be due to the
> rest . . .; the real reason of the animosity with which we are
> honoured by the more eager of the two extreme parties, is, that
> we afford a covering and a shelter to each — impede the assault
> they are impatient mutually to make on each other, and take
> away from them the means of that direct onset, by which the
> sanguine in both hosts imagine they might at once achieve a
> decisive victory. If there were indeed no belligerents, it is plain
> enough that there could be no neutrals and no mediators. If
> there was no natural war between Democracy and Monarchy,
> no true ground of discord between Tories and Radical Reform-
> ers — we admit there would be no vocation for Whigs. . . . If
> there were no such middle body [as the Whigs], who saw faults
> and merits in both [Tories and Radicals], and could not consent
> to the unqualified triumph or unqualified extirpation of either
> — if the whole population of the country was composed of intol-
> erant Tories and fiery reformers . . . does any man imagine
> that its peace or its constitution could be maintained for a
> single year?[6]

Like Jeffrey, Macaulay also placed a reforming, conciliatory
policy in a context of social conflict. As his defense of the
Canningite coalition shows, he too justified a defense of the center
against extremes by the need to reduce the risk of ideologically
nourished class warfare that carried the threat of open combat.
However, it should be noted that Jeffrey saw the Whig party as
responsible for defending the center, whereas Macaulay initially
formulated the problem without attributing to the Whigs any
responsibilities of this kind. But by the time of the Reform Bill,
following Jeffrey's example, he thought that without the Whigs,
"the country [would be] divided between the Radicals and the
Ultra-Tories." And later he was to make a major contribution

toward establishing the association between the trimmer's rationale and Whiggism.[7]

Macaulay believed that the extremes could be defeated, but it
depended on skillful leadership of the center, for he also discerned
potentially great strength at the extremes. He witnessed the
predominance of ultra-Tory resistance to change during the late
1820s and again during the Reform Bill debates. He thought it
quite conceivable that Radical middle-class leadership might
forge an alliance with working-class radicalism and that such an
alliance would be most ominous for civil peace. Later, during the
forties, he feared the influence of Chartism, especially as it
combined with Toryism to oppose free trade.[8] So there was no lack
of threats from the extremes. The task was to confine extremist
groups to the periphery.

Macaulay's concern with the center was made evident in many
ways. He identified it on one of the few occasions on which he used
the language of Left and Right:[9]

> The strongest party, beyond all comparison, in the empire,
> is what I call the *centre gauche,* the party which goes further
> than the majority of the present [1834] ministry, and yet stops
> short of the lengths to which Hume and Warburton go. That
> party is a match for all the other parties in the state together.
> It contains, I imagine, three fourths of the constituent body.
> But it has no head.... Stick to the *Centre Gauche.* Gain
> their confidence. And you may do what you please. This is the
> game I would have tried to play, if I had remained in England.[10]

This advice, written from India, where Macaulay had gone in
1834 to serve on the Governor-General's Council, indicates that he
did not identify himself solely with the Whigs. The party he had in
mind excluded the doctrinaire Radicals in Parliament, that is, the
self-styled Philosophic Radicals, as the reference to Hume and
Warburton indicates. He would also have shunned a coalition
between the Whigs and the Tories, as the label *centre gauche*
shows. (Such a coalition had been rumored during the mid-
1830s.)[11] The party he visualized would have included the large
body of Members of Parliament who were liberal in opinion but
not doctrinaire Radicals. These were men who would have
favored more reform, especially the secret ballot. Indeed, they
were sometimes referred to as the "200-ballot men." They sometimes thought of themselves as Radical; but, unlike the doctrinaire Radicals, their radicalism did not go so far as to make them

indifferent as to whether the Tories replaced the Whigs. For this party of Whigs and moderate Radicals, Macaulay would have accepted conventional Whig leadership, had it been available. But he was not without personal ambition. His great success during the Reform Bill debates must have given plausibility to such aspirations. The game he would have played had at one point been more than a daydream, for he confessed that he had once had longings to play the part of a political leader.[12]

The *centre gauche* appeared to be flourishing during the year or so after the passage of the Reform Act. It had carried that Act, and the elections of 1832 gave it a predominant position in the House of Commons. Macaulay's confidence in it reflects this strength. However, during the decade that followed, it dwindled in size; and, as it did, Macaulay was among those who sought to sustain it by making concessions to the moderate Radicals. In advocating flexibility he was trying to adjust the boundaries of the center in order to preserve it as a politically effective body.

One way of enlarging the center was to extend the boundary on its left. Macaulay proposed to do this by making the issue of the secret ballot an open question, that is, by allowing members of the cabinet to openly disagree about it. To demand the secret ballot had been one of the identifying marks of Radicalism (along with universal suffrage and short parliaments). But it was not only the doctrinaire Radicals who attached great importance to it. The large group of moderate Radicals (or liberal Whigs) on whom the Whig governments of the 1830s depended for their majorities also attached great importance to it. The Whig governments tried to keep their votes, yet without allowing any member of the government to advocate the ballot. It was against this position that Macaulay urged that the ballot be made an open question. This would allow spokesmen for the ballot to enter the government, giving it a more liberal posture. And this, in turn, would allow the moderate Radicals in the House of Commons to support the government, thereby undermining the extreme, doctrinaire, anti-Whig Radicals and preserving the *centre gauche*. Leaving the question of the ballot open, Macaulay argued, would "do more than anything else to cement the league between Whigs and Radicals, — a league on the continuance of which the welfare of the state seems to me to depend." Probably for the same reason, he thought many other matters of public policy ought to be open questions as well.[13]

Macaulay's advocacy of the ballot separated him from the conventional Whig position. His views on the place of the House of Lords in the constitution separated him still further. Here, too, his purpose was to preserve and strengthen the center. Macaulay made the assumption that popular agitation for reform, which had become so intense during the Reform Bill period, would continue. Writing from India, where in his isolation he could not test his assumption, he expressed this view:

> The probability is that popular opinions will gather strength every year. At the next general election the reformers will probably have a far greater majority in the House of Commons than at the present. . . . The minds of men are fast becoming familiarized to the contemplation of changes which, even when I left England, would have been regarded with dismay by a great majority of the middle classes. The institution of a hereditary aristocracy is one which it is not easy to defend in theory. But it had, till lately, a very strong hold on the feelings and imagination of the people. It is losing that hold. Opinions on this subject which, a few years ago, few people entertained and scarcely any ventured openly to express, are now constantly repeated in the most respectable newspapers, and have been very plainly hinted in parliament without calling forth any strong disapprobation. These opinions, I firmly believe, will spread and strengthen.

The difficulty arose from the Lords' resistance to the tide of public opinion. They resisted the Reform Bill until intimidated by the threat of the creation of a large number of new peers. But their resistance was only temporarily extinguished. "The Lords are out of their senses. What they want—unless they want revolution—I am at a loss to comprehend." After reading accounts of their response to the Municipal Corporations Bill, he observed that "the Lords are becoming fiercer and more obstinate day by day. The young aristocrats who are destined to fill the seats of the present peers are even more bigotted than their fathers."[14]

The outcome would be conflict between the two Houses, reflecting conflict between the aristocracy and the populace. The crisis was not to be expected immediately, but it would have to be faced during the years immediately ahead, Against the great and increasing popular pressure, the upper House had little chance: "unless I am quite mistaken, the days of the House of Lords are numbered." Their imprudence was only "hastening the day of reckoning." Macaulay, observing this conflict between the Lords and the populace, and assuming that it was going to intensify as popular pressures increased, condemned the Lords' resistance, for it prevented the government, with its majority in the House of Commons, from implementing the conciliatory policies that would hold together the center and so undermine the immoderate Radicals. To allow Tory resistance in the House of Lords "would make the present generation the mere slaves of the past, and be utterly inconsistent with the first principles of politics." To avoid this, he was quite willing to allow the House of Lords to "go after Old Sarum and Gatton," those other relics of the past which had been abandoned in 1832. He even proposed a scheme for reconstructing the upper House on an elective basis.[15]

The wish to preserve the center against the extremes was also revealed in Macaulay's readiness to support coalitions. In 1827 he defended Canning's administration, which included Whigs, as the best defense against both the anti-Catholic, backward-looking ultra-Tories and the Radicals; and after Canning's death, he wanted the coalition to continue. Again, in late 1838, when the Whig majority was reduced and Whig leaders were reluctant to make concessions to the Radicals, Macaulay, observing division among the Tories, expected coalition. "The Duke and Peel will drop the Orangemen and the opponents of the new poor law . . .; the ministers will drop the Radicals . . .; as to most English questions there is, I imagine, little difference of opinion, and none which might not be easily accommodated." This was more than a forecast; he would not have considered such a coalition outrageous. "Should such a ministry be formed I should, if I were in public life, be disposed to give it a fair trial and [page torn] to go into regular opposition." Again in 1852 he was strongly in favor of the coalition of Whigs and Peelites led by Aberdeen.[16]

Although often favorably disposed toward coalitions, Macaulay did not always look to the *centre gauche* as the basis of them. The turning point in this respect came about 1838–39, after his return from India. Having observed the growth of popular interest in reform during the 1820s and the Reform Bill period, Macaulay

assumed that it would continue; but in 1838, on his return, he
found that it had diminished and, with it, parliamentary Radicalism. It was at this time that he uttered the famous witticism that
"the Radicals were clearly extinct, being reduced, as far as he
could learn, 'to Grote and his wife.'"[17] Not only had the funda-
mentalist, extreme Radical group been depleted, but moderate
Radical support for the Whig governments during the late 1830s
was also reduced in both numbers and determination. Moreover,
the antagonist against which the *centre gauche* was to have been
organized was also changing. During Macaulay's youth and early
manhood the deeply divided Tory leadership often appeared to be
dominated by the ultras, but by the early forties this ceased to be
the case. With Wellington withdrawn and Peel's move away from
protectionism, it was possible to see the antiprotectionist Tories as
allies. A moderate now dominated the Tory party. These shifts
within the Tory camp were taking place against the background
of another development. With the decline of parliamentary
Radicalism, the Chartist movement was gaining ground among
the unenfranchised. There were disturbances at Newport and
Birmingham in 1839, the Plug Plot riots in 1842, economic
heresies in the Chartist press, and, of course, the demonstration
and threat of worse in April 1848. All this appeared to be a new
threat against which politicians at the center ought to unite.
These developments might be seen as the dwindling of the
moderate left, while the more extreme left came into greater
prominence; and, on the other side, the extreme right had
retreated, while the moderate right became much stronger. The
distribution of opinion at the center was changing, and, at the
same time, the most serious threat to the center no longer came
from the ultra-Tories but from the Chartists. In these circumstances Macaulay turned away from the *centre gauche* and
became increasingly willing to include conservative politicians
among those he would look to for support of the center.

Macaulay's purpose was unchanged; he still sought a strong
center against the extremes, but, to achieve this, it was necessary,
given the new circumstances, to bolster a different part of the
political spectrum. Accordingly, some of his opinions were
altered. Whereas earlier he was certain that the House of Lords
would require reform, in 1838 he "did not think it worth while to
give such projects a thought." Whereas he had been for the secret

ballot, by the late forties he had changed his mind. His evaluation of the French Revolution also changed; having found it on the whole beneficial to mankind during the earlier period, he now became more severe in his judgment. And with some other Whig politicians he found it easy to support Peel on the reduction of the duties on corn and on the Maynooth grant. Whereas in 1836 he did not approve of coalition with the Tories and held that "the league between the Whigs and Radicals [was one] . . . on the continuance of which the welfare of the state seems to me to depend," by 1852 he supported Whig coalition with the Peelites.[18]

Following on these developments, there was also a revision in his view of political parties. Earlier, when the ultras appeared to dominate the Tory party, he regarded them as a threat to the state. At that time he viewed the Tory party, like the extreme Radicals, as threatening constitutional stability. But from the early 1840s he willingly acknowledged that the Tory party had something to contribute and that the two major parties complemented each other. Now (1844), he said,

> we look at the essential characteristics of the Whig and the
> Tory, we may consider each of them as the representative of
> a great principle, essential to the welfare of nations. One is,
> in an especial manner, the guardian of liberty, and the other,
> of order. One is the moving power, and the other the steadying
> power of the state. One is the sail, without which society would
> make no progress, the other the ballast, without which there
> would be small safety in a tempest.[19]

Neither party went to extremes; in the sentiments of both parties—one favoring innovation, the other seeing the risks that attend it—"there is something to approve." Indeed, "of both the best specimens will be found not far from the common frontier." Leaving aside the few enthusiasts in each party—on one side leaning to anarchy, on the other to despotism—"the difference . . . has always been a difference rather of degree than of principle." Each contributed to the quality of political life, so that there was a fortunate combination of antiquity and progress, authority and liberty. The nation "could have spared neither."[20] In this situation there could be an alternation of parties in office, for both could be counted on to defend the center. He no longer saw the Whigs as the only center party on which the state depended for its safety.

As a trimmer, in these new circumstances, Macaulay shifted his political focus as he looked for support at the center. Therefore, he looked favorably on alliances that in earlier decades he had viewed as abhorrent and even dangerous. He recognized that new labels might now be applicable. He had called himself progressive when he began his parliamentary career, but in 1839 he said, in a half-flippant observation, that if the Corn Laws were abolished and the Irish Church reformed, he would "begin to think of being a Conservative." By 1852 he acknowledged that "he had grown more conservative on some points."[21] And in 1853 he identified himself as "at once a Liberal and a Conservative politician."[22]

Macaulay's attempt to redraw the boundaries around the center in face of the decline of ultra-Tory leadership and the rise of Chartism was also reflected in his changing estimate of democracy. During the 1820s and well into the thirties he thought the main danger of revolution would come from the unyielding ultra-Tories, who would provoke the middle ranks into a revolutionary posture. Wishing then to enlarge the center as a way of countering the powerful ultra-Tories, he was favorable to an extension of the suffrage and not dogmatically opposed to democracy. However, by about 1840 he could locate the threat to the constitutional system among the Chartists, where violence in rhetoric, and at times in practice, was to be found. Such violence in itself would make him hesitant about democracy, for the Chartists were the most prominent advocates of universal suffrage. In addition, by 1840, with moderates in command of the Tory party and with the decline of middle-class support for the program of political Radicalism, he was willing to see the center enlarged on its conservative side. This also made it unlikely that he would be favorable to democracy. But, above all, the Chartist movement affected Macaulay's judgment of democracy by providing the evidence he used when he visualized how the working classes would take part in politics if democratic conditions were to prevail.

From the beginning Macaulay formulated his view of the suffrage issue in a way that facilitated a shift in judgment.[23] For while many of his contemporaries took doctrinaire positions on both sides of the issue, his response was anything but rigidly fixed. Macaulay acknowledged that in some circumstances democracy might be desirable. He emphasized not any particular form of government but the need to have a form of government suited to all the circumstances of the people who were to live with it. "I distrust all general theories of government. I will not positively say, that there is any form of polity which may not, in some conceivable circumstances, be the best possible. I believe that there are societies in which every man may safely be admitted to vote." However, even if democracy were the best form of government, this would not justify advocacy of it. "The fact is, that a good government, like a good coat, is that which fits the body for which it is designed. A man who, upon abstract principles, pronounces a constitution to be good, without an exact knowledge of the people who are to be governed by it, judges as absurdly as a tailor who should measure the Belvidere [*sic*] Apollo for the clothes of all his customers."[24]

In his earliest statements about democracy he was already trimming between the antidemocrat Mitford and the prodemocrat James Mill. In his review of Mitford's *History of Greece* (1824) he emphasized the arguments for democracy, and in his review of Mill's "Essay on Government" (1829) he emphasized its dangers. But the prevailing tone of his statements, compared with what was to come, was not unfavorable. Even in one of his articles against the Utilitarians he pointed out that he was not rejecting democracy: "Our object was to prove, not that monarchy and aristocracy are good, but that Mr. Mill had not proved them to be bad; not that democracy is bad, but that Mr. Mill had not proved it to be good."[25] Indeed, in his most favorable statement there is Benthamite influence in his formulation of the problem. There were, he said, two ingredients for the best government: the desire to make the people happy and the knowledge as to how this can be done. Neither alone is sufficient, but it is difficult to find the two together. One of these two requirements was met by democracy (and conceivably both might be). Only pure democracy assured that the government would wish to make the people happy: "That the government may be solicitous only for the interests of the governed, it is necessary that the interests of the governors and the governed should be the same. . . . But the interests of the subjects and the rulers never absolutely coincide till the subjects themselves become the rulers, that is, till the government be either immediately or mediately democratical." Having concluded that democracy assures that the government will seek to gratify the people's wishes, Macaulay turned to the other ingredient. Here he raised the question whether the people, when they became rulers, would be sufficiently educated to understand their own wishes. Would they know how to make themselves happy? If this requirement could be met—and it was a matter of education—then democratic government would be justified. "Hence it may be concluded that the happiest state of society is that in which supreme power resides in the whole body of a well-informed people." This, he added, may appear to be an imaginary goal, "yet, in some measure, we may approximate to it; and he alone deserves the name of a great statesman, whose principle it is to extend the power of the people in proportion to the extent of their knowledge, and to give them every facility for obtaining such a degree of knowledge as may render it safe to trust them with absolute power."[26]

Favorable as he was to the idea of democracy, Macaulay always saw the circumstances of the working classes as an obstacle to universal suffrage. Distress and ignorance disposed the working-man to endorse policies that would only worsen his economic situation; and there was the threat of class hostility arising from resentment and political opportunity. However, during the early period (the 1820s and 1830s) Macaulay did not emphasize these considerations. At this time the United States was still an example of how abundance might make democracy safe for property and liberty. He saw it as a new country "where the necessaries of life are cheap and the wages of labour high, where a man who has no capital but his legs and arms may expect to become rich by industry and frugality."[27] In such a place there would be so little class conflict that universal suffrage might not be dangerous.

Macaulay's optimistic expectations about the possibility of democracy were also sustained by his Baconian vision, for it allowed him to believe that the historian's observation of social, economic, and educational improvements would continue. Were this to happen—were "progress" to occur—the ignorance and poverty that prevented the workingman from playing a full citizen's role would be eliminated. Just as the decline of religious passion had reduced the danger of destructive conflict along religious lines, so in the long run a gradual improvement in living conditions could reduce the danger of class conflict. Macaulay observed that improvement was occurring, and there is no doubt that he welcomed it and expected it to continue. "The history of England is emphatically the history of progress. It is the history of a constant movement of the public mind which produced a constant change in the institutions of a great society." Such progress might not be evident in the short run; but if centuries are compared, if we compare 1794 with, say, 1685, then "we cannot doubt in which direction society is proceeding."[28] In the eighteenth century one needed

> only to open his eyes, and to see improvement all around him, cities increasing, cultivation extending, marts too small for the crowd of buyers and sellers, harbours insufficient to contain the shipping, artificial rivers joining the chief inland seats of industry to the chief seaports, streets better lighted, houses better furnished, richer wares exposed to sale in statelier shops, swifter carriages rolling along smoother roads.

This had been going on since the twelfth century. Furthermore, "this progress, having continued during many ages, became at length, about the middle of the eighteenth century, portentously rapid, and has proceeded, during the nineteenth, with accelerated velocity."[29]

Nor had improvement been confined to production and consumption. With advancement from poverty, there was advancement in knowledge. It was evident in the arts and sciences—in medicine, surgery, chemistry, engineering, and navigation. It was evident in the success of the struggles against caste distinctions and tyrannical regimes. It was evident in the "changes of manners and morals . . . from ferocity to humanity." And it was evident in the spread of knowledge. "Time advances, facts accumulate, doubts arise. Faint glimpses of truth begin to appear. . . . The sound opinion, held for a time by one bold speculator, becomes the opinion of a small minority, of a strong minority, of a majority— of mankind. Thus, the great progress goes on." This was the beneficial result of the so-called scientific revolution, which Macaulay celebrated in his essay on Bacon. Some nations, pre-eminently his own, were the first to reap the fruits of this development. But it could be observed in others as well, and he thought that none would be untouched by these blessings.[30]

Macaulay insisted that even the humblest shared in these improvements. Despite the considerable increase in population since the sixteenth century, it appeared certain "that a greater share falls to almost every individual than fell to the share of any of the corresponding class in the sixteenth century." The court and the establishments of the nobility are more splendid than before; merchants and shopkeepers are richer; and the servants, artisans, and agricultural workers "have a more copious and palatable supply of food, better clothing, and better furniture." Macaulay quickly added that "this is no reason for tolerating abuses, or for neglecting any means of ameliorating the condition of our poorer countrymen." Nor was it a reason for "telling them . . . that they are the most wretched people who ever existed on the face of the earth."[31]

Having observed improvement in the past, Macaulay expected it to continue:

> We rely on the natural tendency of the human intellect to truth, and on the natural tendency of society to improvement. We know no well authenticated instance of a people which has decidedly retrograded in civilization and prosperity, except from the influence of violent and terrible calamities. . . . We know of no country which, at the end of fifty years of peace and tolerably good government, has been less prosperous than at the beginning of that period. . . . History is full of the signs of this natural progress of society.

He also revealed his vision of what life would be like a century hence. There would be a population of fifty million (in 1830 it was about fifteen million), "better fed, clad, and lodged than the English of our time . . .; machines, constructed on principles yet undiscovered, will be in every house . . .; there will be no highways but rail-roads, no travelling but by steam."[32]

Not only did Macaulay reveal his great satisfaction with the fact of long-run improvement in the conditions of living; he also rarely neglected an opportunity to emphasize it. When he described the scene for a seventeenth-century event, he alluded to the favorable contrast that could be made by considering the same place in his own time. Whether he was describing Exeter or Torbay, the Trossachs or Cork, or the countryside and towns mentioned in his account of England in 1685, he never tired of pointing to the contrast between conditions in the past and what he could observe in his own time: the flourishing agriculture, the signs of commerce and prosperity, the size and number of dwellings, and the state of the roads.

Macaulay's evident satisfaction in reporting improvements and his forecasts of more have elicited a good deal of criticism. He has been accused of insensitivity to the poverty and misery that clearly existed.[33] He is not invulnerable on this count. He knew about great distress but evidently assumed that it was not novel; and he firmly held that the real income of the working classes had increased.[34] The ample sympathies of a Carlyle or a Sadler he tended to discount as romantic distortion, lacking historical foundation. On the other hand, he was not the stereotypical doctrinaire advocate of laissez-faire, complacent and indifferent to suffering. He provided some compelling accounts of the suffering of the poor, in which he recorded "the most appalling misery, and heart-breaking famine and wretchedness." He did come to support factory regulation. And his sympathetic concern for the people of Ireland was genuine.[35]

Macaulay's expectation of continued improvement in living conditions and the favor with which he looked on this prospect have also elicited charges of materialism and vulgarity. If this means that he was unbothered by a prospect of general opulence, this may be true. Far from denying the accusation, Macaulay would have acknowledged it. His celebration of the Baconian philosophy shows how little he would have regarded this charge:

> The end is the well-being of the people. The means are the imparting of moral and religious education; the providing of every thing necessary for defense against foreign enemies; the maintaining of internal order; the establishing of a judicial, financial, and commercial system, under which wealth may be rapidly accumulated and securely enjoyed . . . ; the aim of the Baconian philosophy was to supply our vulgar wants. . . .
> Some people may think the object of the Baconian philosophy a low object, but they cannot deny that, high or low, it has been attained. . . . They cannot deny that mankind have made, and are making, great and constant progress in the road which [Bacon] pointed out to them.

Had he been asked about moral, intellectual, and cultural values, he would have shown that he was not indifferent to them, but he would also have called them utopian, unattainable for the mass of men; indeed, he would have argued that too eager a pursuit of them is an obstacle to reaching the modest goal set by Bacon. This was the trouble with the Platonic philosophy. Although more noble, it encouraged men to reach for goals beyond their capacity, whereas the Baconian philosophy aimed less high but at attainable goals.[36]

Macaulay lived at a time when one could have a prospect of greater affluence, and this to him was a welcome development, for it held out promise that the passions of class conflict might be attenuated. His hope for this was the background to his defense of the manufacturing system, private property, and a government that provided a legal framework conducive to the pursuit of improvement and enrichment. By providing amplitude and domestic peace, the satisfaction of private goals would be sufficient for most men, and the threat of class conflict would be reduced. In these circumstances, the workingman might not be disqualified from political participation. Macaulay suggested as much: "If employment were always plentiful, wages always high, food always cheap, if a large family were considered not as an encumbrance but as a blessing, the principal objections to Universal Suffrage would, I think, be removed" (1831). Even in his most outspoken statement against democracy—in the speech on the Chartists' demands—he indicated that it was conceivable that universal suffrage could be safely introduced if there were universal education.[37]

Macaulay continued to entertain the prospect of future improvement in social and economic conditions for the workingman. However, with the rise of Chartism, and his changing view of the way in which the center ought to be supported against the extremes, his expectation of future improvement ceased to sustain his belief that the educational and economic disqualifications of the workingman would be removed, at least in the foreseeable future. Instead, his observation of improvement was turned against the Radicals and Chartists, who assumed that economic conditions had deteriorated in modern times. Seeing this as needless stimulation of discontent, as a politician he used his historian's understanding in order to dispel romantic myths that depreciated the present time. "Those who compare the age on which their lot has fallen with a golden age in their imagination may talk of degeneracy and decay: but no man who is correctly informed as to the past will be disposed to take a morose or desponding view of the present." He had in mind those who pointed to the conditions of life for the workers, including women and children, in the manufacturing industries. But he denied their claims and attributed this to a tendency in all ages to depreciate the present and long for the past. "Ever since I began to make observations on the state of my country, I have been seeing nothing but growth, and hearing of nothing but decay."[38]

Having leaned during the earlier period to the optimistic side in his evaluation of the possibility of democracy, about 1840, as his political outlook shifted, Macaulay came to emphasize the risks in allowing the workingman to vote, and even a note of hysteria entered his reflections when he emphasized that democratic government was objectionable because the working classes were too prone to follow demagogic leadership. This propensity was due not only to their inadequate education but to the resentments that naturally accompanied their situation:

> Nothing is more natural than that the labouring people should be deceived by the arts of such men as the author of this absurd and wicked composition [the Chartists' petition of 1842]. We ourselves, with all our advantages of education, are often very credulous, very impatient, very shortsighted, when we are tried by pecuniary distress or bodily pain. We often resort to means of immediate relief which, as Reason tells us, if we would listen to her, are certain to aggravate our sufferings. Men of great abilities and knowledge have ruined their estates and their constitutions in this way. How then can we wonder that men less instructed than ourselves, and tried by privations such as we have never known, should be easily misled by mountebanks who promise impossibilities? Imagine a well meaning laborious mechanic fondly attached to his wife and children. Bad times come. He sees the wife whom he loves grow thinner and paler every day. His little ones cry for bread; and he has none to give them. Then come the professional agitators, the tempters, and tell him that there is enough and more than enough for everybody, and that he has too little only because landed gentlemen, fundholders, bankers, manufacturers, railway proprietors, shopkeepers, have too much. Is it strange that the poor man should be deluded, and should eagerly sign such a petition as this?[39]

Universal suffrage, according to Macaulay, would lead to violations of property rights and a general reduction of economic activity, which would affect all classes. Already in his critique of James Mill he had forecast that the people, "if they have the power, ... will commit waste of every sort on the estate of mankind, and transmit it to posterity impoverished and desolated"—a statement he repeated in 1842, when Chartism was under discussion. In view of the importance of property, "it would be madness to give supreme power in a state to a class which would not be likely to respect that institution." The result would be plunder of the well-off by the poor.[40]

Macaulay was not so much concerned with actual pillage as with the adoption of an economic policy that would disrupt the economy and reduce the standard of life for all classes. He had in mind the simplistic slogans of the cheap economic tracts of his time. They assumed that scarcity was not a problem and that redistribution of wealth and income could be achieved by a democratically elected government without producing undesirable economic consequences. He visualized well-meaning but unsophisticated workingmen, in times of distress, bewildered and credulous before agitators who, at best, were themselves deluded by unsound economic doctrines. Such doctrines, if implemented, would lead to economic chaos, with "many millions of human beings, crowded in a narrow space, deprived of all those resources which alone had made it possible for them to exist in so narrow a space; trade gone; manufactures gone; credit gone."[41]

Despite his reputation as a believer in progress and his genuine expectation that, in the long run, improvement in living conditions would be increasingly shared by all, Macaulay was quite gloomy about the immediate future. He accepted the Malthusian doctrine and the assumptions of the political economists about scarcity. He was aware of the existence of a lumpenproletariat, and his historical knowledge allowed him to visualize its political role in severe crises. He was intimately familiar (as has been mentioned) with the many disturbances of the early nineteenth century that were part of the "tradition of riot" which prevailed at that time. He could not but be aware of poverty, for he was an indefatigible London walker. Indeed, the scenes described by Mayhew must have been familiar to Macaulay, who regularly, over many decades, walked from Albany (and later from Campden Hill) to the House of Commons, to the British Museum, to the City, to Clapham, and to the bookstalls in Holborn.[42] These experiences were interwoven in his outlook with his understanding, derived from seventeenth-century history, of the way anger, fear, and moral indignation can sustain social and political upheavals. All this facilitated his probably unrealistic belief that the working classes, if given the vote, would act in accordance with the hostile, class-conscious rhetoric of the vaguely socialist pamphleteers who wrote for the unstamped press.[43]

There was also a political dimension to his fear of the consequences of universal suffrage. Economic chaos would lead to a Hobbesian struggle for necessities, and "out of the confusion a strong military despotism may arise." He had this vision before the coup of Napoleon III, but after 1851 it became much more real for him. "Either the poor would plunder the rich, and civilization would perish, or order and property would be saved by a strong military government, and liberty would perish." Given his expectation that universal suffrage would bring class conflict, he could conclude that "institutions purely democratic must, sooner of later, destroy liberty, or civilization, or both." This harsh judgment is consistent with (and may have been partly derived from) his early view of history as alternating between anarchy and despotism. The ignorant, resentful working class, given political power, would bring chaos; those resisting would sacrifice liberty in order to preserve order. If he were obliged to choose, he would accept — of course without enthusiasm — the latter alternative. As he put it, "What must the state of things be, if an Englishman and a Whig calls such an event the very best?"[44]

This dilemma was faced by the French, whose situation served to persuade Macaulay that his way of seeing the problem was not unrealistic. Seeing mid-century events in France in these terms, Macaulay, though liking neither of the alternatives, decided that it was better to preserve order. Thus he did not object to the reign of Louis Napoleon. "I am for the President against the mountain and for freedom and order against the President, if there be any possibility of having freedom and order in France." But he assumed that there was no such alternative. "What is there steady or well-organized or deserving of trust but the army? Whatever is not army is chaos. The soldier in France now is what the priest was in Europe six centuries ago — he must govern, and ought to govern." Furthermore, to pull down the emperor would only renew the cycle:

> I do not like the Emperor or his system. But I cannot find that his enemies are able to hold out any reasonable hope that if he is pulled down, a better govt will be set up. His govt is better

than the Red Republic — better probably than that of the military Chief who may take his place — better than civil war.

Fortunately, this dilemma was not Britain's. She was saved from it by the statesmen who managed conjunctures and practiced the arts of conciliatory politics. Unlike the French, Macaulay said, "We should have reformed the gov[ernmen]t of the H[ouse] of Orleans without subverting it. We should not have borne the yoke of celui-ci for one day."[45]

Macaulay's changing estimate of the possibility of democracy in a well-ordered constitutional state was reflected in the way he thought about the United States. In his earlier view it was the place where democracy was compatible with liberty and property because it was a new country; toward the end of his life he came to fear that new nations would become old and unfit for the democracy they had previously enjoyed. Economic development would bring increased population, scarcity, lower wages, and class conflict:

> As long as you have a boundless extent of fertile soil and unoc-
> cupied land [he wrote to an American], your labouring popu-
> lation will be far more at ease than the labouring population
> of the old world; and, while this is the case, the Jeffersonian
> polity may continue to exist without causing any fatal calamity.
> But the time will come when New England will be as thickly
> peopled as old England. Wages will be as low, and will fluc-
> tuate as much with you as with us. You will have your Man-
> chesters and Birminghams, and in those Manchesters and
> Birminghams, hundreds of thousands of artisans will assuredly
> be sometimes out of work. Then your institutions will be fairly
> brought to the test.

When in this mood, Macaulay thought democratic institutions would fail. The American Constitution was "all sail and no anchor." If in bad times the sufferers are also the rulers, class conflict will lead to civil war, anarchy, and perhaps, in the end, despotism. "You may think [again to his American correspondent] that your country enjoys an exemption from these evils. I will frankly own to you that I am of a very different opinion. Your fate I believe to be certain, though it is deferred by a physical cause."[46] Somewhat more poignantly, he argued that it "would not be wise to reason . . . from the behaviour of a dog pampered with the best morsels of a plentiful kitchen, which is the case of the people of America, to the behaviour of a wolf."[47]

Although his judgment of democracy changed with his changing estimate of circumstances, Macaulay never adopted a doctrinaire position, and regardless of his evaluation of democracy in
the abstract, he was willing to enlarge the electorate. At some
times he was more yielding than others. During the 1820s and
1830s, when he wanted to strengthen the center against the
Tories, he was willing to make large concessions. As he put it, "he
was as great a Radical as anybody, that is, that if ever the voice of
the nation should be as clearly and universally pronounced for
reform of the H[ouse] of Lords, or any other great change, as it
had been for the Reform Bill, he should be for it too."[48] After
1839, however, when Radicalism appeared to be a smaller but
more virulent movement, and when he wanted to strengthen the
center in order to resist the threat from Chartism, he was more
reluctant to make large concessions. Yet, even at this time he was
somewhat yielding. He had never held the view that the Reform
Act should be final. It is true that he wanted it to be a settlement
of the question, that is, to put an end to agitation and popular
discussion of first principles; but he realistically recognized that at
best it could last only a decade or perhaps a generation. It would
be "final in the only sense in which a wise man ever uses that
word ...; it will last during the time for which alone we ought at
present to think of legislating. Another generation may find in the
new representative system defects.... Wealth will increase.
Industry and trade will find out new seats."[49] He had opposed the
Chartists' demand for universal suffrage (he was more agreeable
to the other points of the charter),[50] yet in 1852, when the
question of electoral reform was broached again, he agreed that it
would be necessary to amend the Act of 1832, "temperately and
cautiously, but in a larger and liberal spirit." Macaulay's views on
this question can be misrepresented by the notoriety of his
arguments against universal suffrage. Most of his contemporaries
among the political and intellectual classes were antidemocratic;
indeed, they were more emphatically opposed to universal suffrage than he was.[51]

Trimming is a consistent theme in all that Macaulay did. It was the great trimmers of the late seventeenth century that he honored in his *History,* where he presented them as models for future politicians; and in his own time it was as a trimmer that he justified his political postures—when supportive of democratization and when opposed to it, when in favor of the secret ballot and when opposing it, when predominantly anti-Tory and when predominantly anti-Radical, when affiliated to the *centre gauche* and when identified with conservative centrists, when identified with public opinion and when resisting it. Like a true trimmer, he sometimes found himself comfortably identified with his party's leadership and on some occasions quite separate from it.

Trimmer though he was, Macaulay's name is not easily separated from Whiggism. Of course there is a connection between trimming and Whiggism, but it is not a necessary connection, nor did it always exist. Macaulay in his historical writing makes it clear that they were separate, indeed, often opposed. The close association between them developed during the early nineteenth century, and Macaulay, for whom they were analytically separate, perhaps did more than anyone to bring about the association that has become so close that the idea of nineteenth-century Whiggism now suggests trimming. Butterfield's view is in this respect typical, although it is more explicit than most. Whiggism is a method of conducting politics that seeks to reconcile opponents and avoid extremes. It makes adjustments to new circumstances, yet it emphasizes the importance of continuity amid change. This is the Whiggism familiar to historians—"the whiggism that chooses only a moderate pace of reform, a cautious progress to whatever end may be desired; the whiggism which, abhorring revolutionary methods, seems now mildly left-wing, now almost indistinguishable from conservatism itself." It is opposed to abstractions and doctrinairism, and it is based on reflection on past mistakes, that is, on historical inquiry.[1]

The development of this outlook is a matter of interest in view of its having become, in the view of Butterfield and many others, the national attitude. Butterfield has argued that "the Whig method ... became the English tradition" and that "the virtues of the whigs have been distributed through all the great parties of this country; ... they have liberalized English politics generally, and given a colour to all our progress; standing in protest equally against die-hard-ism [i.e., ultra-Toryism] on the one hand and mere lust for overthrow [i.e., extreme radicalism] on the other."[2] Thus he says that "in every Englishman there is hidden something of a whig that seems to tug at the heart-strings."[3] Bagehot also saw this moderateness, along with a tendency to compromise and an opposition to doctrinairism and dogmatism, as national characteristics; and he saw Whiggism as the exemplification of this character. It was a practicality of outlook that would be undisturbed by enthusiasm of temperament or attachment to grand theories.[4]

The association between trimming and the Whig party had not always existed. Although there were anticipations, it was essentially a nineteenth-century development. During much of the eighteenth century, particularly before the accession of George III, there was little occasion for trimming, which is called for in times of sharp conflict and instability. Yet the period of the first two Georges was not a time of deep divisions and destructive conflict. On this most contemporary historians agree with Macaulay.

Butterfield, however, has suggested that the Whigs had already become trimmers in the early eighteenth century. His contention that the Whigs had already then adopted a policy of moderation and trimming, whereas the extremists dominated the Tory party, is based on an essay by the Huguenot historian Rapin de Thoyras. Using the testimony of Rapin's *Dissertation sur les Whigs et les Torys* (London, 1717), Butterfield argues that by 1717 "it would appear that the cautions of the 'trimmers' have been adopted by the Whigs and have come to be associated with the policy of their party."[5] However, Rapin's remarkable pamphlet does not fully support Butterfield, for Rapin emphasized that both parties were divided between extremists and moderates and that, although extremism may have been a greater problem among the Tories, neither party had a monopoly of either moderation or extremism. Each party was divided into Political and Ecclesiastical sections, and each of these had a moderate and an extremist side. Consequently, there were four extremist and four moderate groups. Among the Political Tories there were High Flyers (or Arbitrary Tories) and Moderates; among the Ecclesiastical Tories there were Rigids and Mitigates. Among the Political Whigs there were Republicans and Moderates; among the Ecclesiastical Whigs there were Rigid Presbyterians and Mitigate Presbyterians, as well as Church of England spokesmen.[6] Rapin called the moderates in each party "true *Englishmen*," for they wanted to preserve the constitution against the immoderates of both parties. The moderates in both parties shared outlooks and opinions, and Rapin emphasized that the moderates would realign themselves if circumstances required. The moderate Whigs would join the Tories if the Republicans on their side grew too powerful. And the moderate Tories would act in the same way: "They have often saved the State, and will save it again, whenever they see it in Danger, either from the *arbitrary Tories,* or the *republican Whigs,* by making a noble stand against all such as would break in upon the Constitution. It would be Injustice to these, to confound them with the former [Arbitrary Tories], under the same name of *Tories.*"[7] Clearly there were trimmers among Tories as well as Whigs, according to Rapin, and his essay does not provide support for the proposition that trimming was a Whig monopoly. Furthermore, and more important, it is doubtful that, even without a monopoly, the Whigs were trimmers during this early period. Butterfield himself did not quite defend his argument, for he became somewhat equivocal, stating that "Rapin's account was almost prophetic; for it was written before the age of Sir Robert Walpole had really opened. It was to be truer for the Whigs of the future than for those of the present or the past."[8] This qualification was appropriate; indeed, it has been suggested that it was even insufficient, for the work of historians since Butterfield presented this argument has cast doubt on Rapin's account of the early-eighteenth-century Whigs.[9]

It might be said that the Whigs during the last decades of the eighteenth century sought to play a mediatorial role. But their mediatorial role, at that time, served a purpose different from Macaulay's. These Whigs saw themselves—and the Parliament in which they served—as intermediaries between crown and people; and this way of visualizing the political spectrum was made possible by their traditional suspicion of the power of the crown and their legendary assumption that, as natural leaders of the people, it was their duty to control the executive and restore balance to the mixed constitution. This mediatorial role was derived from two circumstances: from the rise of the Radicalism associated with Wilkes and later with Paine and the French Revolution, and from the belief that took shape among the Whigs during the reign of George III—and given impetus by Burke's *Thoughts on the Present Discontents*—that there was a plan to discredit the Whigs and to restore both the crown and the Tory party to new strength. Thus there was the threat of the crown on one side and the people on the other. In this situation, according to such Whigs as Fox and Grey and Mackintosh, it was necessary to reform Parliament. Such reform would blunt the power of the crown and reduce pressure from the people. In between would be the Whigs in a reformed Parliament.[10]

This mediatorial role was much more modest than the one visualized by Macaulay, for whom the forces that produced extremism and undermined the center were much more varied and threatening. For Macaulay there was an intermingling of political, social, and economic considerations in the creation of the threat of both anarchy and despotism. Whereas the eighteenth-century concern centered on the distribution of power within the constitutional system, Macaulay's nightmare was a civil war, perhaps a class war, that would lead to the overturning of the constitution and the social order. For Macaulay the trimming role was more central in his understanding of politics. In contrast, the mediatorial theme had a minor place in eighteenth-century Whiggism, in which the preponderant motif was glorification of the Revolution settlement and the principles that justified it. However little continuity is granted to the Whig party in eighteenth-century politics, it would appear that belief in the principles of the Revolution settlement was shared by all varieties of Whigs. The Protestant succession, the mixed constitution, the absence of censorship, trial by jury, an independent judiciary, broad limits of toleration — these were the principles of Whiggism. They were often associated with statements of abstract Lockean principles concerned with power being held in trust for the people, the illegitimacy of arbitrarily exercised power, the importance of free speculation, and the right to withhold obedience from those who abuse power.[11]

This version of Whig doctrine, which was closely connected with the Revolution and with Locke as he was understood during the eighteenth century, ceased to be a distinguishing outlook once Jacobitism had visibly and finally become a lost cause. During the reign of George II "Whiggism had become the creed of the age."[12] The issues that divided the nation when this version of Whig doctrine first developed were no longer salient questions. Acceptance of the Revolution settlement and its justifying principles was transformed into belief. Locke's *Second Treatise* was frequently reprinted throughout the century. The system was codified and celebrated in Blackstone's *Commentaries*.[13] The kind of Whiggism that was derived from the events and debates of the Revolution was not uncongenial to early-nineteenth-century Tories, who revered the "Protestant Constitution." Indeed, they thought of themselves as its best defenders and the Whigs as deserters of their own cause.[14]

Nineteenth-century Whig politicians retained this eighteenth-century outlook, but it came to be alloyed with other themes. Most of the leading Whig politicians had connections, some of them personal, with Fox and the Society of Friends of the People, and their rhetoric was given a liberal stamp by this heritage.[15] Their version of the constitution emphasized liberties of the subject, including the rights to hold public meetings and to use the press with minimum risk of prosecution for seditious libel; that is, it interpreted the constitution in a way that allowed for the legitimacy of free and ample expression of grievances. In subscribing to the mixed constitution, consisting of king, Lords, and Commons, they used the term "Commons" loosely to include "the people" — at least some parts of the populace who were not yet qualified to vote. This heritage also made them uneasy with exclusions on religious grounds. Consequently, many early-nineteenth-century Whigs were opposed to the exclusion of Catholics and to the legal disabilities of Protestant Dissenters; they proposed various schemes of parliamentary reform; and they opposed some of the proposals to suppress political dissent during the panic-ridden years of 1816–22.

These liberal convictions, derived from traditional Whig principles and emphasized by the Foxite influence, were the source of a reformist impulse that made some Whig politicians willing to make concessions to radical movements. But this willingness to make concessions was reinforced by motivations of a fundamentally different kind: by fear of the consequences of withholding them. The two motivations — liberal conviction and prudent consideration of consequences — were often interwoven. With the passage of time, after the tumultuous agitation of the post-Waterloo period and its renewal in 1830, considerations of prudence, fear, and necessity became increasingly important.

The chief source of such motivations lay in the trauma caused by the French Revolution, even among Foxites, who shared the nervousness of the years leading up to Peterloo.[16] The example of France and an awareness of the reality of "two nations" made fear of instability almost endemic. Many expressed it in near-hysterical references to the revolutionary significance of any symptom of disorder. An extreme yet symbolic example of this is provided by Lord John Russell, who had lived through these years; lying on his deathbed (in 1869), he "heard a loud noise in the street and thought it was the revolution breaking out."[17] These fears were not confined to Whigs, nor were concessions made only by Whigs; but Whigs were more forthright in acknowledging their motives and in justifying their policies. Their deliberations on the Reform Bill demonstrate this, as do Sydney Smith's claim that they practiced "prudence of the highest order," which he defined as "the deliberate reflection of a wise man, who does not like what he is going to do, but likes still less the consequences of not doing it, and who of two evils chooses the least."[18]

These two themes — the liberal conviction and the prudential consideration — gave nineteenth-century Whiggism a double pedigree.[19] The liberal conviction could be traced back to Fox and, further, to the traditional Whig doctrine associated with the "old cause," of which Foxite doctrine was an extension. The prudential theme might have been traced back to Halifax, but most Whigs did not make this connection (this was left for Macaulay to do). Indeed, the Whigs typically judged Halifax with severity, for he had opposed the Whig exclusionists and was said to have shared responsibility for Algernon Sydney's death on the scaffold. The prudential consideration need not have had an intellectual pedigree; but it can also be traced back to Burke, whose writings provided both a rationale for prudence and conciliation and a wealth of maxims on these matters.

Because of this double pedigree there was a mixture of themes when Whigs explained their positions. The liberal conviction that exclusions and privileges were incompatible with constitutional principles coexisted with the prudential objection to exclusions because they were a source of grievance and discontent. The liberal conviction that freedom of assembly and discussion and liberty of the press were rights provided by the constitution coexisted with the prudential consideration that to deny their exercise might be "dangerous to the tranquillity of the country, and ultimately subversive to the authority of the state."[20] The proportions varied, but the mixture is to be found in the pronouncements of most of the leading Whig politicians of the early nineteenth century. (Melbourne is perhaps an exception, for prudential considerations predominated with him; and he did not begin his career as a Whig.)

The trimming component in Whig doctrine only gradually came to have a foundation in principle. The leading Whig magnates adopted trimming tactics as a matter of necessity, and what they considered necessary was shaped by their fears. "To avoid crisis was their desire, their instinct, their interest, their technique." To use Macaulay's categories (which he had used in analyzing Halifax), they were trimmers by temperament but not yet from principle. (The very opposite characterized Macaulay, and this gave him a critically important influence on the development of Whiggism.) There was a "tendency apparent in the Whig party ... to move with public opinion and introduce reform measures"; and "under Melbourne the tendency became a policy." It was this tendency that contributed to the Whigs' reputation for playing a mediatorial role.[21] At some times among some of the Whigs their liberal convictions nourished their reformist impulse; but the main source of that impulse was a concern to ward off danger.

The trimming component in Whiggism was systematized by Macaulay, for, unlike most of the leading Whig politicians, he was a trimmer from principle. For him it was not a matter of adopting

Whig ideas as an amalgam of Lockean ideas, Foxite principles, and the precepts of trimmers.[22] Although he recognized the inclination to trim in the Whig politicians, he also saw that trimming was historically and logically separate from Whiggism, as he makes clear in his treatment of the seventeenth- and eighteenth-century Whigs. Acton described the Whigs as unphilosophic and unsystematic, as men who were compromising, expediential, as patching-up and making-do — as politicians with a very short-term point of view. And he used this image to distinguish the Whig from the Liberal: "One is practical, gradual, ready for compromise. The other [the Liberal] works out a principle philosophically. One is a policy aiming at a philosophy. The other is a philosophy seeking a policy."[23] This distinction allows us to identify the important role Macaulay played as a Whig intellectual (although Acton would not have approved the result). The party Macaulay adopted had inclinations, tendencies, sometimes a policy; but it had need of a philosophy. And it was a philosophy (in the sense of a systematic, reasoned outlook) that Macaulay sought to provide. Of course he had recent predecessors in this role, most notably Francis Jeffrey and Burke (at least in some of his teachings). Macaulay's contribution was to apply systematically the trimmer's outlook to nineteenth-century problems and to explain it persuasively, notably during the Reform Bill debates and in his *History,* thereby significantly contributing to the shaping of national consciousness about the role of trimming in the political tradition and in the distinctively British approach to politics.

To attribute this role to Macaulay is to suggest that he was a trimmer before he became a Whig and that he could become a Whig because he recognized in the leading politicians of that party an inclination to promote the trimmer's purpose.

Macaulay's early political beliefs are difficult to determine, for the evidence is sparse and contemporary descriptions of them use ambiguous language. For example, it is difficult to interpret descriptions of his early political opinions by those who knew him at Cambridge but who recollect those years after observing his later career as a prominent spokesman for the Whigs, for such testimony tends to describe his earlier views in language appropriate only to the later period. Furthermore, his opinions fluctuated,

as he himself claimed. He had gone to Cambridge bearing the
influence of his father's Evangelical views and Toryism,[24] but
during his undergraduate years (1818–22) this outlook was undermined. His correspondence with his father at this time reveals parental concern and filial defensiveness about the new opinions. In
one of his letters to his family young Macaulay acknowledged
having written "a few democratical sentences," and there is an implication of liberal and perhaps even Radical sympathies in his
indignation against those responsible for the events at Peterloo, in
his disapproval of the government's conduct in the trial concerning the queen in 1820, and in his insistence that his opinions "were
learnt not from [the Radicals] Hunt and Waithman, but from
Cicero, from Tacitus, and from Milton." He also found it
necessary to assure his father that he had not joined any "democratical societies" and that he was not — what his mother thought
possible — "one of the 'sons of anarchy and confusion.'"[25] He was
also influenced by Charles Austin, younger brother of the now
more famous legal philosopher, John Austin, and already a
proselytizer on behalf of Benthamism and Radicalism. Macaulay's
family were said to have been startled by accounts of Austin's
opinions and influence. His nephew and biographer has said of
Austin that he "certainly was the only man who ever succeeded in
dominating Macaulay" and that he "cured the young undergraduate of his Tory opinions, which were never more than skin deep,
and brought him nearer to Radicalism than he ever was before or
since."[26]

One thing is clear: many attitudes and judgments that Zachary
upheld at home and in the *Christian Observer* were undermined
at Cambridge. But it is uncertain how far in the direction of
Radicalism Macaulay went. The suggestion that he had become a
Radical should be taken seriously; however, it should be recognized that the term "Radical" comprehends a wide range of
beliefs, and, furthermore, the available evidence does little to
dispel our uncertainty. Although it is clear that Austin had a
powerful influence on him, Macaulay was not a docile learner. It
is reported that he disputed with Austin over the comparative
merits of induction and the a priori method in politics — an issue
which lay at the heart of their respective political outlooks.[27] And
regardless of how influential Austin was, a doubt is cast upon his
reputation as a Radical by his claim "that, in his most Radical

days, he had never desired universal suffrage."[28] Austin contributed to Macaulay's disenchantment with Toryism, and he must
have facilitated Macaulay's growing independence of mind and
even his adoption of a rationalistic approach to religion and
politics. Macaulay appears to have experienced a disturbance of
belief in home orthodoxies and to have considered the merits of
popular, liberal opinions.

His own accounts, written during his first years at Cambridge,
give the impression that he had no settled views, to say nothing of
firm convictions defined in doctrinal terms, at that time. He said
that he knew "no people who make politics a common or frequent
topic of conversation, except one man who is a determined Tory";
that he himself "made it a rule never to talk on politics except in
the most general manner"; and that his "most intimate associates
have no idea of my opinions on the general questions of party."
The popular, liberal, mildly Radical sentiments found in some of
his letters to his father were tentative and fluctuating, and in any
case, he explained, they were not to be taken too seriously. His
father was not to think him "a precipitate, silly, shallow, sciolist in
politics," nor was Zachary to suppose "that every frivolous word
that falls from my pen is a dogma which I mean to advance as
indisputable."

> If I say, as I know I do, a thousand wild and inaccurate things,
> and employ exaggerated expressions about persons or events in
> writing to you or to my mother, it is not, I believe, that I want
> power to systematize my ideas or to measure my expressions, but
> because I have no objection to letting you see my mind in
> dishabille.[29]

Possibly he was saying these things to mollify his hypercritical
father. But if we were to take Macaulay at his word, his version
would be confirmed by the recollection of his Trinity contemporary and Clapham family acquaintance Henry Sykes Thornton,
who said that at Cambridge Macaulay "was thought to have no
political opinions, so often did he evince contrary views."[30]

This understanding of Macaulay's political outlook during his
undergraduate years (1818–21) provides a plausible transition to
the nonparty and between-party posture that is so evident in his
notable prize essay of 1822. In this essay Macaulay clearly had
adopted the posture of a trimmer (though not yet acknowledging
his intellectual lineage back to Halifax). Anti-Whig, antiextrem-

ist, in the essay he tries to formulate a position that might be called one of principled moderation. Centrist politics are defended on the ground that they are the basis of constitutionalism. Stability is made to be important because in its absence a polity is led, alternately, to anarchy and to despotism. From this point of view, any party is suspect if it moves to an extreme; such an understanding of politics is an obstacle to any firm party commitment. In light of this it is understandable that Macaulay, still at Cambridge but now (1823) tutoring and trying to qualify for a fellowship, said that he would listen with "composure and impartiality . . . on most of the subjects which interest politicians. We are neutrals"; and he added, "We espouse no party. . . . [But] if we ever descend into the field of battle, it . . . will be our object, not to fight under the banners of either army, but to render the offices of humanity and courtesy to both."[31]

This aspiration to be independent of party did not prevent Macaulay from having opinions that leaned sometimes to the liberal side and at other times in the opposite direction. However much he looked with sympathy on the victims of Peterloo, and whatever rumors reached his family regarding his undergraduate views, there is evidence that he held moderately conservative opinions, while at Cambridge, through 1822. This is evident in his speeches at the Union Society, in which he actively took part for a year or so, in 1822 and also in early 1823. For example, in 1822 he defended the political character of George III; he denied that Hampden's political conduct deserved approval; he defended the British constitution rather than the American; and he defended the proposal that Burke's political conduct deserved the approbation of posterity.[32]

There was a shift, however, and it came in early 1823. Contemporaries recalled that he had altered his opinions, and they associated it with the Union.[33] Moreover, the record of Union debates shows that, whereas he was consistently somewhat conservative in the 1822 debates, in early 1823 he became rather liberal. For example, he defended Mirabeau and Charles James Fox, condemned foreign interference in French affairs in 1792, and defended the idea of parliamentary reform. These opinions reflect a liberal outlook that predominated during the mid-1820s.[34]

While still taking part in the Cambridge debates, Macaulay wrote the review of Mitford's *History of Greece* in which he complained, "Democracy he hates with a perfect hatred," and "he never fails to inveigh with hearty bitterness against democracy as the source of every species of crime."[35] In this review Macaulay, without endorsing democracy, came closer than he ever would again to a sympathetic defense of it. "The interests of the subjects and the rulers never absolutely coincide till the subjects themselves become the rulers, that is, till the government be either immediately or mediately democratical."[36] Such formulations betray the influence of either Bentham or James Mill. It could have been these sentiments that led Macaulay to assert, "I have been a Tory; I am a Radical; *but I never will be a Whig.*"[37]

During these few years when Macaulay affirmed popular convictions, his historical view of seventeenth-century constitutional struggles reflected his political beliefs, for he described the rebellion against Charles I with language that identified him with political figures in his own time who were popular, liberal, perhaps Radical. The 1630s and 1640s witnessed a conflict between "liberty and despotism, reason and prejudice. That great battle was fought for no single generation, for no single land." As a result, mighty principles were proclaimed that since then "have kindled an unquenchable fire in the hearts of the oppressed, and loosed the knees of the oppressors with a strange and unwonted fear." Charles he labeled a tyrant; and although Macaulay did not approve of regicide, he did approve Milton's justification of it. Indeed, though he acknowledged that many evils were produced by the Civil War, "they were the price of our liberty."[38]

If one considers the shift in Macaulay's opinions in Union Society debates, his observations about democracy in 1824, and the language with which he described the Civil War period, it is not surprising that he actively supported a liberal Whig candidate at Leicester in 1826, or that Henry Crabb Robinson at this time described him as "Liberal in opinion, but no Radical," or that in his brief association with the London Debating Society (in 1825-26), which John Stuart Mill did much to organize, he was known as one of the liberals.[39] All this represents a liberal mood that contrasts somewhat with his views both before and after. His views after 1826 continued to be liberal, but his rationale for them emphasized prudential considerations, whereas during the years 1823-26 there was something resembling liberal conviction in his outlook. From 1827 onward, and emphatically during the debates on the Reform Bill, liberal reform would be justified by Macaulay as a means of protecting the established order against the threat of immediate disturbance and, in the long run, revolution.

Yet the liberal language of even these years is restrained and intermingled with the language of trimming. In his review of Mitford, where Macaulay was more favorable to democracy than he ever would be again, he argued, not as a spokesman for democracy against Mitford, but rather as a mediator between the opposing sides. "The errors of both parties arise from an ignorance or a neglect of the fundamental principles of political science. The writers on one side imagine popular government to be always a blessing; Mr. Mitford omits no opportunity of assuring us that it is always a curse."[40]

The outlook of the trimmer is also evident in what Macaulay wrote about Milton and the Civil War period. Although he praised Milton and Cromwell, he did not write about this period as a spokesman for the Puritans or for the ideas of the Commonwealthman. He did not feel identified with the Commonwealthman tradition, as has been claimed. Had he been, he would have subscribed to the ideas of natural rights, republicanism, and liberty associated with Price and Priestley and Godwin and the seventeenth-century authors to whom their ideas can be traced.[41] But in the essay on Milton (1825) he defended the rebellion because it defeated the tyranny of Charles I and not because it led to the establishment of the Commonwealth. Indeed, in another essay on Milton, although he praised the Long Parliament as "the best and most useful" assembly that ever existed, he located its merits in the period before "it became subject to the soldiers," i.e., before Pride's Purge in 1649 and before the execution of the king and the establishment of the Commonwealth.[42] Nor did Macaulay endorse all the rhetoric about liberty. Milton was to be praised for fighting "for that species of freedom which is the most valuable, and which was then the least understood, the freedom of the human mind"; in contrast, the Puritans, who were often intolerant, "espoused the cause of civil liberty mainly because it was the cause of religion."[43] Finally, Macaulay implicitly but clearly criticizes the Commonwealth by criticizing extreme reform: reverence for ancient usage is foolish but cannot be wholly removed, and "therefore those who would amend evil laws should consider rather how much it may be safe to spare, than how much it may be possible to change."[44]

Furthermore, Macaulay, in interpreting mid-seventeenth-century developments, used the categories of trimming he had already used in the 1822 essay, and this way of thinking prevented him from unequivocally endorsing either the Puritans or the Commonwealth cause. Milton was identified with the center and against the extremists on his own political side. There were "blameable excesses" and much "that was ridiculous and hateful." But Milton was not responsible. The regicides were blameable, but not Milton. Macaulay also attributed to Milton his own thoughts about the need to protect the center against the extremes of both anarchy and despotism and on the need, not only to provide for liberty, but to avoid rebellion.[45]

He described Cromwell in similar terms. Cromwell was not the despot of royalist legend nor the republican of the Commonwealth tradition. In Macaulay's eyes he was a moderate driven by extraordinary circumstances to an extremism he did not approve. "The ambition of Oliver was of no vulgar kind. He never seems to have coveted despotic power." Cromwell's goal was to reconcile, for he tried to give the nation "a constitution far more perfect than any which had at that time been known in the world." But the intensity of religious and political conflict prevented this. So Cromwell was a failure; but he was not to be blamed, for the failure was due to circumstances he could not control. "We believe that he was driven from the noble course which he had marked out for himself by the almost irresistible force of circumstances." What these circumstances were is indicated by what happened when he died. "His death dissolved the whole frame of society." That is, there was anarchy, which Cromwell had resisted. Thus Cromwell is placed in the position of the trimmer, between the despotism of Charles and the anarchy threatened by fanatics, such as the Fifth Monarchy men. Between these extremes Cromwell is portrayed as a moderate in immoderate times. He might have been a William III; as it was, "he will not lose by comparison with Washington or Bolivar. Had his moderation been met by corresponding moderation, there is no reason to think that he would have overstepped the line which he had traced for himself."[46]

Although Macaulay became associated with the liberal cause during these few years (c. 1823–26), he did not abandon the outlook of trimming. The praise of moderation and condemnation of extremes in his descriptions of men and events regarded by most historians of his time as occupying the extremes of the political spectrum indicates that Macaulay, even when located to the left of the political center, retained the understanding and the values that are so evident in his 1822 essay on William III. This is also revealed in his association with the London Debating Society, where he was known as a liberal. According to the surviving records of the society, he never spoke, even though the topics of debate would have been of great interest to him and would have allowed him to assert liberal or antiestablishment views. (For example, on 9 December 1825 the topic was "That the Influence of the Aristocracy in the Government of this Country is beneficial"; and on 5 and 19 May 1826, "That the practical Constitution of Great Britain is adequate to all the Purposes of good Government.")[47] What evidently happened was that the society, as John Mill proudly revealed, was a place where ideologically extreme sides confronted each other; and this was a kind of political discourse that a trimmer would instinctively shun.[48]

During the years that immediately followed (from 1827) Macaulay spoke like one who was more a trimmer than a Whig. The trimming theme is especially evident in his important essay of 1827 defending the Canningite coalition. Macaulay's strong support is notable in view of Canning's history and political views. Although he had a reputation for being somewhat liberal at the end of his life, a reputation based on his views of foreign affairs, the Catholic question, and economic policy, Canning also had a record that Macaulay could have found abhorrent. He had justified Peterloo; he defended the government's policy of political repression in 1816-22; and he was opposed to parliamentary reform. Thus there was no easy ideological affinity between them. With this record in mind, those who have defended Canning as a liberal claim that he would have adjusted his opinion as circumstances changed; nevertheless, his ultra-Tory colleagues during the early 1820s considered him orthodox on the question of parliamentary reform.[49] The Whigs disagreed about the propriety of joining Canning's government. Some did take part, notably Lansdowne and Holland, though with a disappointingly meager share of offices, and Brougham enthusiastically supported it. But Grey and Althorp withheld support. Grey feared that Canning's success would cause the dissolution of the Whigs as a party; and, even more, he objected as one who had been a follower of Fox and who therefore distrusted the leading author of the *Anti-Jacobin* and heir to Pitt.[50] Macaulay, however, felt so strongly about Canning's government that, even though unwell with a cough and a cold, he went off to Cambridge to vote for Sir Nicolas Tindal, the solicitor-general in Canning's government. "We were all unwilling to have him leave home," his sister Selina recorded, "but he says that in the present state of things every victory gained by the Government interest is of the greatest consequence, and that were he certain of being ill for a month by going it would not have prevented him."[51]

What made Canning's government so attractive to Macaulay? The new prime minister's opposition to slavery and to Catholic exclusion was part of it. There was also his record of having shifted his views with changing circumstances (on the French Revolution, foreign policy, party alignments). But Macaulay's support was not based on Canning's political record or even on hope of what the coalition government would achieve. Whereas the Whigs justified their taking part by the hope that some of their favored policies might be promoted, particularly in regard to the Catholic question and Ireland, Macaulay's rationale was different. For him the coalition had the negative attraction of avoiding the disastrous situation that would prevail if Canning were to fail. In this event, with Whig strength so insignificant, the ultra-Tories would dominate the government and the Radical movement would become more visible.[52] He urged support for the coalition because it avoided Radicalism and its revolutionary implications and, alternatively, the repressiveness of an ultra-Tory government. On the one side there was a threat of anarchy; on the other, of despotism. The analysis is in terms also to be found in the 1822 essay.

Similar themes appear in Macaulay's review of Hallam's *Constitutional History* (1828). Here again Macaulay applies the trimmer's approach to contemporary problems, for he alludes several times to the development of intense conflicts, difficult to reconcile; and he also presents a rationale for concession and reconciliation that anticipates the formulation he later presented during the Reform Bill debates. Yet in this essay he disputed many of Hallam's historical judgments (and Hallam was a Whig historian in opposition to Hume). Hallam is honored by Macaulay, but for his way of dealing with historical problems rather than for his

particular historical judgments. We can see another projection of
Macaulay's image of himself in his description of Hallam as one
who, "steadily attached to principles, is indifferent about names
and badges, — and who judges of characters with equable severity,
not altogether untinctured with cynicism, but free from the
slightest touch of passion, party spirit, or caprice."[53]

Macaulay's severe criticisms (1829–30) of James Mill's "Essay on
Government" are to be seen in the same light. They should be
considered in combination with his review of Mitford (1824).
Whereas Macaulay criticizes Mitford for being too harsh on
democracy, in the later essays he is critical of Mill for being too
generous in his evaluation of democracy. Whereas Mitford "hates
democracy with a perfect hatred," Mill's view of democracy is
utopian.[54] We are reminded of Macaulay's opposition to the
ultra-Tories, on one side, and to Radicalism, on the other.

These essays on democracy also reveal that during this early
period Macaulay's trimming is expressed in the language of
science. The sensible, statesmanlike position is associated with
common sense and "political science." The language of Baconian
induction and political science, which was a prominent theme in
his writings from the mid-1820s until the early 1840s, was used to
express the trimmer's judgment. With it he searched for neutrality
and a nonparty position, and it only later receded, to be gradually
replaced by an explicit admiration for Halifax, in whom he found
a formulation of an intellectual heritage with which he could
identify. He criticized both Mitford and James Mill, not on party
grounds, but because their reasoning was not in keeping with
Baconian induction. It is significant that, as late as 1829, he
criticized James Mill, not from the point of view of a Whig,
although Mill was notoriously and explicitly anti-Whig, but
because Mill's argument was contrary to what Macaulay called
political science. As yet Macaulay had not unequivocally identified
himself with the Whig party.

During this early period there was a coincidence of judgment
(though not necessarily of reasons) between Macaulay and the
liberal Whigs. Macaulay during these early years was a thoughtful
and concerned person whose political thinking cannot be encap-
sulated in the party slogans of the time. That he leaned to the
Whigs is indicated by his connection with the *Edinburgh Review*.
But his *Edinburgh Review* essays, in which he provided a trimmer's

rationale for policies that were supported by Whigs, but for different reasons, were congenial to Francis Jeffrey on other than narrow party grounds, for Jeffrey was also sensitive to the need for trimming.[55] The most important thing about Macaulay during the 1820s was that his thinking ranged far beyond the particular programs and interests of parties. The emphasis was on the survival of the political system in the face of threats of rebellion and oppression. Having disassociated himself from Toryism, he was, during this period, unaffiliated. If he leaned to the Whigs, it was perhaps because, given his outlook, the other alternatives were even less attractive. It is important, however, since later he became a prominent and intense Whig, to avoid assuming that after he rejected Toryism (while at Cambridge) he immediately became a Whig.[56] Unless his having contributed since 1825 to the *Edinburgh Review* in itself made him a Whig, it was not until 1830 that he formally adopted the Whig label, when he accepted the nomination to represent Lord Lansdowne's pocket borough at Calne.[57] In either case, assuming that trimming is distinguishable from Whiggism — and Macaulay clearly thought it was — it is fairly certain that he became affiliated with the Whigs after he set forth his initial defense of trimming.[58]

Since Macaulay adopted the trimmer's outlook before he became a Whig, one may speculate about why he chose to be a Whig (which is not to suggest that this took place at a decisive moment). It was not because he accepted, as relevant to the nineteenth century, that conception of Whiggism that was defined in Lockean terms or that was associated with the so-called Commonwealthman tradition as it affected Whig thought. Indeed, according to Robbins, the Commonwealth tradition did not survive as a living tradition far into the nineteenth century; at most there were mere echoes of it.[59] And by 1828, when Macaulay encountered such an echo, his response was to ridicule it as an example of the mythology of politics. This was a recurring theme in most of his comments on Commonwealthmen.[60] Nor did he identify himself with the Foxites, even though the memory of Fox and what he stood for was perhaps the most prominent theme in the thinking of the early-nineteenth-century Whig leadership. Indeed, as G. M. Trevelyan has said, "Whereas the Whigs who followed Burke were merged among the other supporters of the Tory Ministry, the Whigs who followed Fox remained the nucleus of the party, and the keepers of its traditions.... Where [Fox] was, there would the Whig party be." Yet Macaulay's observations on Fox were respectful but vague, whereas Fox's great antagonist Burke is elevated to heroic status.[61] Even Pitt, who still more than Burke was the occasion for Fox's continuing parliamentary antagonism and who came to be idolized by the Tories, was given much, though qualified, admiration by Macaulay.[62] In this, and even more in the very high praise given to Burke, Macaulay by implication was derogating Fox and what the Foxites stood for.

It may well be that he was drawn to the Whig party because he recognized in its leading politicians an inclination to promote the trimmer's purposes. The combination of flexible tactics and conservative interests made them the most appropriate party to implement a trimmer's policy. The other parties were doctrinaire, according to Macaulay. This was not an inaccurate characterization of many Radicals at that time. Macaulay saw the Tories in the same way. In their hearts they were ultras, that is, doctrinaires, still wishing to use Pittite methods to resist changes in the church, the economy, and in public opinion:

> We look at the two extreme parties in this country; a narrow oligarchy above; an infuriated multitude below; on the one side the vices engendered by power; on the other side the vices engendered by distress; one party blindly averse to improvement; the other party blindly clamouring for destruction; one party ascribing to political abuses the sanctity of property; the other party crying out against property as a political abuse. Both these parties are alike ignorant of their true interest. God forbid that the State should ever be at the mercy of either, or should ever experience the calamities which must result from a collision between them! I anticipate no such horrible event. For between those two parties stands a third party.[63]

Were the Whigs to fail, they would be "scattered and dispersed, so that there [would be] scarcely a trace left of it [the Whig party], and the country [would be] divided between the Radicals and the Ultra-Tories."[64] Combining the Tory's concern for order (while avoiding his inflexibility), with the Radical's capacity for change (while avoiding his misguided ideas), the Whigs could play the role of a center party whose most important function would be to prevent either extreme from gaining power. After the Canning coalition proved unsuccessful in this, Macaulay looked to the Whigs.[65]

Macaulay became one of the most prominent spokesmen for the Whig party during the Reform Bill debates, just a year after he had entered Parliament. His impact on the House of Commons and on the political world could hardly have been greater. Gladstone said his speeches on the Reform Bill "achieved for him, years before he had reached the middle point of life, what may justly be termed an immense distinction." His political prominence enlarged the fame he had already achieved as the author of such *Edinburgh Review* articles as those on James Mill, Milton, and Hallam. "For a century and more," Gladstone added, "perhaps no man in this country, with the exceptions of Mr. Pitt and of Lord Byron, had attained at thirty-two the fame of Macaulay. His parliamentary success, and his literary eminence, were each of them enough, as they stood at this date, to intoxicate any brain and heart of a meaner order."[66] Another contemporary has described him as one who in a brief but brilliant career (before going to India in 1834) "at once raised himself to the first rank in the Senate." His speeches (and at this period this meant, in the main, his Reform Bill speeches) were such that "in every sentence you saw the man of genius—the profound scholar—the deep thinker—the close and powerful reasoner. You scarcely knew which most to admire—the beauty of his ideas, or of the language in which they were clothed. . . . Time after time has the House listened to him as if entranced."[67]

He quickly became known as having a gift for oratory and invective. His support of the Reform Bill and his display of intense party feeling have lent support to the belief that he was preeminently the spokesman for the Whig cause. It was perhaps the animosity he directed at some members of the Tory party that gives plausibility to this notion. Croker and Peel were the targets of his outspoken, severe criticism, leading Peel to complain of his "sweltered venom." Nor was his criticism confined to the House of Commons. In the *Edinburgh Review* he displayed literary animosities that often were directed at men who were also his political opponents. Thus Macaulay acquired a reputation. Sir John Graham in 1845 complained of "the bitter party and personal invective . . . [with which Macaulay], as usual, has accompanied his arguments."[68]

There is no doubt that Macaulay took part in political controversy with intense and sometimes bitter feeling. It is reported that
his college friends thought vindictiveness and generosity his
leading qualities.[69] His journals are filled with scurrilous, contemptuous observations on opponents, literary as well as political.[70] Once again Macaulay's description of a historical figure, on
this occasion Francis Atterbury, applies to himself: "it was his
nature to be vehement and pugnacious in the cause of every
fraternity of which he was a member."[71] This was a characteristic
that seriously hampered him in playing the trimmer's role, which
required detachment and the capacity, which Halifax possessed to
so eminent a degree, to befriend former opponents and to treat
with enemies in a way that would permit alliance with them on
future occasions. Macaulay understood the importance of this but
was temperamentally unsuited to play this role. Thus whereas he
idealized trimming as a matter of principle, in the realm of
practice, however much he thought like a trimmer, his conduct
sometimes revealed the loyalties of an intense partisan. However,
it should be noted that in this Macaulay was not unique. He
entered politics at a time when "hatreds, suspicion, and habitual
depreciation of each other's character and motives ... affected
even the best men on both sides." As Melbourne observed in 1835,
"the great fault of the present time is that men hate each other so
damnably."[72]

Macaulay's intense partisanship and his loyalty to his party have
obscured the extent of his belief in trimming. However, he was a
less-orthodox Whig than his political animosities indicated. At
least his opinions did not coincide with those of the party
leadership. During the Reform Bill debates, while providing
intellectual weapons to the Whig ministry, he was continually
critical of it. He thought it weak, infirm, and without courage
and determination. He (with many others) wanted a large creation of peers to resolve the Reform Bill crisis, whereas most of the
Whig leaders were reluctant to adopt such tactics. He thought
they lacked aggressiveness and that this deficiency placed the
nation, as well as its government, in peril. He therefore tried to
organize back-bench pressure to make them assume a more
assertive role. On many other issues he went far beyond the Whig
leadership. On changes in the constitution of the House of Lords,
on the "finality" question, and on the ballot he was anything but
typical of the Whig leadership.[73]

Macaulay was an atypical Whig in still another way. Socially he was marginal. The Whigs "always bore the stamp of aristocracy...; Whigs in every age were magnates, relatives, privileged associates or clients of magnates."[74] If Macaulay fitted any part of this description, it would be the last. But neither his own character nor Lord Lansdowne's requirements made him a client. Furthermore, his fame quickly allowed him to be rid of his dependence on Lansdowne, for he was nominated at Leeds in 1832, just two years after entering as a Member for Calne, where he had been elected by about twenty voters and without opposition.[75] Soon afterward, late in 1833, he decided to accept the appointment to the Governor-General's Council in India, partly to accumulate sufficient capital so that, if he chose to stay in politics, he could do so with complete independence.[76] Yet during his first session as an MP he was anything but an integral part of Whig society. Lionized though he was, this made him feel only more of an outsider:

> I have learned [he wrote to a sister in 1833] where most people
> unlearn all their philosophy, in crowded senates and fine
> drawing rooms. I will say for myself that I am the only *parvenu*
> I ever heard of, who, after being courted into splendid circles,
> and after having succeeded beyond expectation in political life,
> acquired in a few months a profound contempt for rank,
> fashion, power, and popularity, and money, — for all pleasures
> in short but those which arise from the exercise of the intellect
> and of the affections.[77]

This feeling of distance from those with whom he worked and lived never quite left him; after he was given a peerage in 1857, two years before his death, he again described himself—in the privacy of his journal and with a certain pride—as a *parvenu*.[78]

Macaulay was too suspicious of creeds and slogans to feel a sense of identity with any party, even the Whigs. He frequently criticized the images, emblems, myths, and creeds to which ordinary men were unthinkingly devoted. Such blind attachments were obstacles to realistic understanding. "The multitude is more easily interested for the most unmeaning badge, or the most insignificant name, than for the most important principle." Parties had dogmas, creeds, mythologies. The Tories celebrated theirs in the Pitt clubs, and on the other side Hampden and Sydney were treated hagiographically. "In religion, so in politics, few even of those who are enlightened enough to comprehend the meaning latent under the emblems of their faith can resist the contagion of the popular superstition."[79] Macaulay held out as a model the statesman who was unaffected by such superstition. Such a statesman would use the myths and the creeds to organize support and to challenge opponents, but he would not lose sight of the realities. Macaulay's analysis of political problems was remarkably free of the mythological beliefs that prevailed in his time. His wish to identify the realities of grievances that arose from frustrated aspiration and from distress was evident in his Reform Bill speeches. Significantly, the most notable occasion on which he subscribed to Whig myths regarding the "old cause" was on an occasion (in 1839) when he was electioneering and not playing the role of legislator.[80]

For Macaulay when he entered politics, what were the realities? A divided nation, growing discontents, the potentiality for growth of radicalism, a backward-looking party, resistant to change, that had enjoyed power without interruption for a generation, and a discontented middle class that could be radicalized if it were not conciliated. The targets of Macaulay's bitterest attacks were those who did not share this understanding of the political situation, indeed, who were spokesmen for the extreme parties that were leading the nation to destructive conflict. Croker and Peel were men who in Macaulay's view were insensitive to the need for concession, reform, and conciliation as a way of preserving the constitution. The same can be said of his literary targets. Southey, for example, he castigated for holding a romantic view of society that was an obstacle to realistic political judgment. Nor were his targets selected only from the Tory camp. The three essays of 1829–30 criticizing James Mill and the Utilitarians (and the criticism of the same men included in the 1827 essay on the coalition government) were aimed in the opposite direction but from the same point of view, and in these he was no less severe than he was with Southey or Sadler or Croker. Between these two extremes Macaulay found himself with the Whig party, but he did not associate himself with it because its traditional creed was congenial. During this period he not only ridiculed the worship of Hampden and Sydney, but he also said that the Revolution of 1688, although useful, "was not, what it has often been called, a glorious revolution."[81] He opposed the parties that occupied the extreme positions, and this put him in company with Whigs who also occupied middle ground. That they also were willing to trim (although this was more "instinctual" than principled) made them more acceptable to him.

Even though not a typical Whig, either socially or in his opinions, Macaulay had a very considerable influence on the party and on the development of the doctrines associated with it. Entering the House of Commons just as the critical debates on parliamentary reform were about to get under way, he was qualified to play an important role by his already established concern for a stable constitutional order and for the necessity of concessions in order to undermine the extremes and strengthen the center. Having systematically thought about the problem, he was in a position to formulate a rationale for reform much more fully and persuasively than the Whig leaders, and this greatly enhanced his influence on the development of Whiggism. He was able to cast his rationale in terms of an understanding of how revolutions could be avoided, and he did this in a way that was congenial to Whig legends about 1688 while it appeased Whig fears about 1789.

Macaulay spoke at every crisis during the fifteen months of debate on the Reform Bills, and according to Francis Jeffrey he defined the terms of debate: "the views of Macaulay, advanced perhaps at the fifth or sixth day's debate, formed the topic of discussion for the remainder of the time that the subject was under consideration."[82] His speeches provided a rationale for reform that was related to a general understanding of the process of change and an analysis of the interests and passions that both urged and resisted it. Since he went beyond the other supporters of the government, including the ministers themselves, in this respect, his aid was welcomed by the Whig leaders, who were, if not desperate for help, divided and uncertain about their policy. The eager and enthusiastic cheers from those who welcomed his support suggest that, in providing an authoritative rationale for reform, Macaulay was performing an important service. This is confirmed by accounts of his speeches. One (on 5 July 1831) was judged as having "had more of argument and profound philosophy, given in the most appropriate language ... than I ever before witnessed." Althorp thought most of his speeches "distinguished as beautiful philosophical essays, and for their splendid generalizations." Such comments suggest that the Whigs had a policy but needed a philosophy and that they looked to Macaulay as one who could effectively defend their position by the use of political maxims and historical examples. It is not surprising to find that when, in 1833, Macaulay decided to go to India, Lord Lansdowne worried that no adequate successor would be found.[83]

The association between Macaulay and these events was so close that it became a kind of legend that Macaulay was shaped by this first exciting experience of politics. Bagehot in 1856 saw him as "still the man of '32."[84] But it would be more accurate to see him, not as the loyal Whig who eloquently defended his party's cause, but as a thoughtful and independent politician who helped shape his party's cause by reviving the idea of trimming and emphasizing its relevance for the nineteenth century. In this sense (which allows us to recall the essay on William III, where he first revealed his adoption of the trimmer's outlook) he should be seen not as the man of '32 but as the man of '22. And as such a man he not only helped shape his party's cause at a climactic moment in its history, but he also contributed greatly to the reputation for trimming that has since been associated with Whigs and Whiggism.

Macaulay's contribution to the giving of this imprint to Whiggism was not confined to his significant role at the time of the Reform Bill crises. His writings also contributed, above all the *History,* and this was an effect which, as has been argued, he intended it to have. Near the beginning of the *History* he noted that, unlike the Continent, in England statesmen were especially under the influence of the past and consequently the work of the historian had great significance for the practice of politics.[85] The writing of history, then, did not represent an abandonment of politics but the pursuit of political goals through literary means.

In 1835, while in India, Macaulay developed the intention "to undertake some great historical work," and by 1838 his initial plan was formed. However, he was slow to implement it, for he found it difficult to tear himself away from active politics. Genuinely repelled by the drudgery of parliamentary life and worried that he would repeat Mackintosh's mistake of falling between two stools, with meager achievement in both politics and history, he nevertheless resumed his parliamentary career soon after returning from India in 1838.[86] He was elected Member from Edinburgh in 1839 and continued until he was defeated in 1847, and he served in the cabinet during some of this period.

Throughout these decades he often struggled with the choice, as he put it, between politics and literature.

Why did he continue in politics despite his feeling that "litera- ture is my vocation, and not politics"? Ambition, perhaps; the excitement of political life; the gratification of being in the councils of his party.[87] But it also must have been a sense of responsibility about the social and economic crises that were evident in the violent rhetoric of class conflict, the demonstra- tions, and the occasional rioting that accompanied Chartism and the anti-Corn Law movement. Despite the conciliatory effects that had been anticipated from parliamentary reform, and despite the decline of parliamentary Radicalism during the late 1830s, ner- vousness about the economic and social health of the nation persisted. Although one great crisis was resolved in 1832, a sense of crisis continued, and this contributed to Macaulay's remaining in active politics.[88]

During these years, especially while in opposition (1841–46), he worked at the *History,* and gradually he was being weaned away from politics. Finally, his defeat in 1847 emancipated him (he did return to the House in 1852, but not as an active Member). After the failure of the Chartist demonstration in 1848, he felt much less nervous about the state of the nation; indeed, his earlier nervous- ness soon turned, if not to complacency, to something close to confidence. He now turned full time to his pen and his books and completed the first two (of five) volumes of the *History.* Whereas his way of living changed drastically, his choice of the radically different alternative of literature over politics did not disturb the continuity in his way of thinking. For his political concerns remained the same. Whereas contemporary politics, especially in 1831–32 but also during the 1840s, provided him with an opportunity to deal with the problem of conflict and stability and legitimacy, when he turned to his *History,* it was to deal with the same kind of problem — but in its seventeenth-century setting. As he said when he foresaw electoral defeat in 1847, "I do not altogether despair of being able to show, that even in retirement, something may be done for the greatest and most lasting interests of society."[89]

The popularity of his writings, which was almost unprece- dented, made the political lessons that Macaulay wished to teach available to a vast audience. During the twenty-seven years following its first publication, more than 140,000 copies of the *History* were sold. In 1855 he received the famous royalty check from Longmans for £20,000. The essays were frequently reprinted in cheap editions. The *History* was found to be a "seducing" book that could hardly be put down until finished; even hostile critics confessed feeling "breathless interest" in the narrative.[90] Many have testified to the very great "appeal" he had for his Victorian audience. This suggests that he merely put into attractive words the values and prejudices his readers already possessed. On some subjects this may have been so; for example, Restoration morality, national pride, and satisfaction with technological and economic progress. But there was more to the *History* than this; above all, there was Macaulay's attempt to identify an approach to politics and an appreciation of the attitudes and institutions that allowed that approach to be successful. This became part of a tradition of thinking about politics, and he contributed to it by virtue of having established, as Gladstone put it, a "monarchy over the world of readers."[91]

In fact, Macaulay became a legend in his own time. Anecdotes were repeated about his extraordinary memory and his brilliant monologues, his vast range of knowledge and his varied talents as administrator, politician, and author. The legend gave added authority to his ideas, so that, along with Francis Jeffrey, Sydney Smith, and a few others, he became something of an oracle whose words were repeated and remembered. This position is revealed in a description of the way a well-known churchman (Dean Milman) thought and spoke:

> His whole conversation was about the men who formed its [the Whig party's] leaders. It was Sydney Smith and Macaulay, Lord Holland and Lord Lansdowne, Tommy Moore and Rogers, at every word. You would have supposed from his discourse not only that the Whig leaders had been and were the greatest men of the age, but that they were the *only ones* who were worth thinking of or speaking about. This is a singular circumstance, which I have also observed in the old Whig set in London.[92]

It was this position that allowed James Fitzjames Stephen to say that Macaulay "was the greatest, and indeed almost the only great, advocate and expounder of Whig principles since the time of Burke."[93] And it led Henry Reeve to conclude that Macaulay gave to Whig principles "a broader and more universal character. . . . [In both his essays and the *History*] . . . these truths will be remembered in the language he gave them."[94]

Macaulay was bound to be influential, particularly as he had an opportunity to fill what was then a large gap in historical knowledge of the seventeenth century at a time when legends about it still survived to affect nineteenth-century conduct.[95] But influential in what way? Many have testified to Macaulay's role in reinforcing belief in liberal values. He had great "success in making the achievement of the constitutional struggles of the past once more a living possession of every educated Englishman."[96] But he aimed at much more than this, as Francis Jeffrey recognized when he claimed to find in the *History* "original and profound reflective suggestion . . . on innumerable questions of great difficulty and general interest; though these precious contributions," he said, "are not ostentatiously ticketted and labelled, as separate gifts to mankind, but woven, with far better grace and effect, into the net tissue of the story."[97]

What were these suggestions that were woven into the narrative? Macaulay sought to have his contemporaries and his posterity enjoy as a living possession an understanding of the way in which the constitutional struggles had been fought and won. The outcomes of old struggles would become obsolete. It was the way in which they were successfully conducted that was to be perpetuated, for this knowledge was permanently useful. The important thing was to have trained perceptions that allowed one to recognize the ways in which cleavage, disruption, and conflict might undermine the social order in new ways. It was equally necessary to be able to recognize the ways in which men might be reconciled, for, without this, consent and legitimacy were impossible; and this required an understanding of the way institutions might be artfully altered so as to allow them to perform their old functions in new ways and so enjoy support and loyalty instead of being subjected to the withdrawal of consent and to hostility. Since there were parallels between past, present, and future examples of this kind of problem, one might learn from history, both from its favorable and its unfortunate episodes. This was the purpose of the *History*, particularly as it focused on an example of civil prudence that had reduced religious and political passions, attenuated conflict, reconciled classes, conducted a revolution with scarcely any violence, and, finally, had established a new regime without sacrificing old values. Macaulay played the role of philosophical historian whose duty it was to recognize great historical acts of civil prudence and so to identify models for statesmen in his own time and in the future.

Macaulay was preeminently political. The political dimension of any situation was uppermost in his perceptions and his thoughts. Much of his poetry dealt with political themes, and even his literary judgments were influenced by political considerations. "Literature," he said, "is, and always must be, inseparably blended with politics and theology."[1] Gladstone observed with regret that he "carried the passions of politics into the Elysian fields of literature."[2] The *History* was informed by the same purposes, and its judgments by the same criteria, that characterized Macaulay as an essayist and a politician.[3] It was not simply a matter of narrow partisan judgments, though he was guilty of these, as often charged. He thought of politics as supremely important because of the dangers created by the many centrifugal forces operating in society, not least by men's passions, stimulated as these were by religious fanatics, ideologies, and distress.

Macaulay's breadth of interest and versatility amazed his contemporaries. As a poet, critic, and historian he wrote about antiquity, the Renaissance, and modern times. He dealt with French as well as British affairs, with philosophy and literature as well as politics. Yet there is hardly a field in which he is not vulnerable to criticism. Although extravagantly (but not unanimously) praised in his own time, he has been severely criticized since then. His poetry is no longer appreciated, and many particular historical judgments, now even more than in his own time, have been disputed. His style, though still widely admired, has been blamed for contributing to historical misrepresentations.[4] His understanding of antiquity is said to be shallow, and his interpretation of Bacon can be faulted. The criticisms, many of them substantiated, of his understanding of specific historical situations and personages are seemingly endless.[5] It was only in politics that he overcame all but partisan criticism. As a parliamentary orator he attracted the appreciation of his party leaders and the admiration of veterans, regardless of party. In ministerial office he was successful. As an Indian politician and administrator his achievements were considerable and his influence enduring.[6] And it was his political sense, cultivated during a varied and successful career in Parliament, that added to his achievement as a historian. Indeed, it is this political sense, according to Trevor-Roper, that "makes his *History,* in spite of all its blemishes, so difficult to fault."[7]

Yet it was perhaps his tendency to see all things with practical political considerations in mind that has reduced his intellectual stature, giving him a reputation for shallowness and narrowness, for being a philistine who appealed to the educated (and inevitably "middle") classes but not to those for whom intellectualism was the highest calling.

One manifestation of this was his unwillingness to take political philosophers seriously. He read them, as did many educated men of his time. But it was not their philosophy that interested him; they were important only as they influenced opinion. Thus, in the *History,* the writings of Filmer and Lilburne are considered only for their effect, respectively, on the beliefs and conduct of the nonjurors and the independents in the parliamentary army.[8]

Philosophy was potentially dangerous to the political order because, if allowed to influence politicians, it would prevent them from performing their most important function as custodians of the fragile sense of legitimacy. Philosophy, as Macaulay thought of it, was abstract, logical, and therefore rigid and remote from the experience of most men, including politicians, who thought in terms of myths and "emblems." For one thing, philosophy, with its emphasis on logical consistency, was an obstacle to the practice of conciliatory politics. "Logic admits of no compromise. The essence of politics is compromise."[9] Furthermore, philosophy rationalistically emphasized the statement of reasons for policy and the articulation of the relationship between principles and policy. In Macaulay's view, this had the awkward effect of stimulating prejudice and provoking opposition among ideologically oriented persons, who oppose a principle more than the policy justified by it.

This attitude is exemplified by Macaulay's understanding of the virtues of the Toleration Act passed in 1689. On the surface the Act appears to endorse intolerance. It did not repeal any of the penal statutes passed since the time of Elizabeth, which required all persons to attend the services of the Church of England and forbade their attendance at conventicles. Instead of proclaiming "the sound principle . . . that mere theological error ought not to be punished by the civil magistrate," the Toleration Act "not only does not recognize, but positively disclaims" this principle. "Not a single one of the cruel laws enacted against nonconformists by the Tudors or the Stuarts is repealed. Persecution continues to be the general rule. Toleration is the exception." Yet this was the law that for the first time permitted Protestant Dissenters to worship according to their consciences (Catholics continued to be excluded). Indeed, the Act for a long time was considered "the Great Charter of religious liberty."[10]

Toleration was effectively promoted, according to Macaulay, because it was not proclaimed and because, on the surface, the Act appeared to continue the policy of penalties for nonconformity. Thus to a logically inclined jurist, "not intimately acquainted with the temper of the sects and parties into which the nation was divided at the time of the Revolution, that Act would seem to be a mere chaos of absurdities and contradictions." But the fact is that "the English, in 1689, were by no means disposed to admit the doctrine that religious error ought to be left unpunished." Indeed, if a bill had been drawn up granting liberty of conscience to all Protestants, it would have failed, according to Macaulay. Nottingham would not have introduced it; all the bishops, including Burnet, would have voted against it; it would have been denounced from most pulpits "as an insult to God and to all Christian men, and as a license to the worst heretics and blasphemers; . . . it would have been burned by the mob in half the market-places of England; . . . it would never have become the law of the land, and . . . it would have made the very name of toleration odious during many years to the majority of the people." On the other hand, the Act that was passed, though offensive to logic and philosophy, and though it "recognized persecution as the rule, and granted liberty of conscience only as the exception," effectively produced toleration, for the rule was enforceable against only a few hundreds of Protestant Dissenters, while the exceptions included hundreds of thousands. [11]

Macaulay saw this as something that could not have been achieved by men for whom it was important to proclaim general principles. Preoccupied with theory, such men would not "take into consideration the passions and prejudices of those for whom the Toleration Act was framed." He acknowledged that the Act was "abounding with contradictions which every smatterer in political philosophy can detect ... [and] that the provisions ... are cumbrous, puerile, inconsistent with each other, inconsistent with the true theory of religious liberty." However, the men who framed the Act "did what a law framed by the utmost skill of the greatest masters of political philosophy might have failed to do ...; they removed a vast mass of evil without shocking a vast mass of prejudice."

> They put an end, at once and for ever, without one division in either House of Parliament, without one riot in the streets, with scarcely one audible murmur even from the classes most deeply tainted with bigotry, to a persecution which had raged during four generations, which had broken innumerable hearts, which had made innumerable firesides desolate, which had filled the prisons with men of whom the world was not worthy, which had driven thousands of those honest, dilligent, and godfearing yeomen and artisans, who are the true strength of a nation, to seek a refuge beyond the ocean.

"Such a defense, however weak it may appear to some shallow speculators, will probably be thought complete by statesmen." [12]

Macaulay often expressed his disapproval of philosophy and his fear that it might mislead legislators; and he attributed his own distaste for philosophy to the nation as a whole:

> In English legislation the practical element has always predominated, and not seldom unduly predominated, over the speculative. To think nothing of symmetry and much of convenience; never to remove an anomaly merely because it is an anomaly; never to innovate except when some grievance is felt; never to innovate except so far as to get rid of the grievance; never to lay down any proposition of wider extent than the particular case for which it is necessary to provide; these are the rules which have, from the age of John to the age of Victoria, generally guided the deliberations of our two hundred and fifty Parliaments.

He acknowledged that the national distaste for the abstract was a fault, but suggested it was "a fault on the right side," and he pointed to the "scores of abortive constitutions," produced in the world since the end of the eighteenth century, "which have lived just long enough to make a miserable noise, and have then gone off in convulsions." They were the work "of lawgivers in whom the speculative element has prevailed to the exclusion of the practical."[13]

Macaulay's belief that philosophy held out dangers for politics and his interpretation of philosophy as abstract and rigid were in part derived from the prevailing image of the role philosophers had played in bringing about the French Revolution. While this view may have been novel in Burke's time, by mid-century it had become conventional. In this image philosophers were speculative and utopian. They thought in universal categories, were indifferent to the past, and lacked the practical experience that might have made them sensitive to the value of tradition.[14] Such philosophers had no part in the English Revolution, as Macaulay interpreted it. In 1688 historical continuity was not disturbed. The practical statesmen who played the major role in that Revolution were without the aspirations or the illusions that are sustained by abstract, utopian philosophy. Instead, they were guided by precedent and prescription. Halifax, William, Danby, Maynard, and Somers were distinguished by their realism and the immediacy of their concerns. They justified their proposals and their conduct by appeals to law and custom. They firmly rejected persecution and tyranny, yet did so without reference to the state of nature, the law of nature, or the social contract.[15] It was perhaps because Macaulay understood the Revolution to be the work of such men that he hardly mentioned Locke as one of its architects in the *History*. This has subjected Macaulay to indignant criticism. Yet it is consistent with his interpretation that he should play down the role of a philosopher who was famous for a treatise that was as yet unpublished when the Revolution occurred and who was isolated from events by extreme secretiveness and exile. Locke's theories concerning government are historically important; but, as Firth, who criticized Macaulay's neglect of Locke, acknowledged, they are mainly important for the history of the eighteenth century, when they "became the political bible" for the educated classes.[16]

Macaulay often disparaged political philosophy outright. If it was not pernicious, as, for example, in the case of James Mill's encouragement of doctrinaire oversimplifications, it was utopian and unrealistic, as with Plato, or irrelevant, as, for example, with Montesquieu or the state-of-nature theorists. There were exceptions, however. He esteemed Machiavelli. He must have recognized in Machiavelli some of the themes that he found so congenial in the writings of Halifax, whose thinking reflected Machiavellian teachings. He emphasized Machiavelli's practical experience, which served to correct his general speculations, giving them "that vivid and practical character which so widely distinguishes them from the vague theories of most political philosophers."[17] He esteemed Bacon for the same reason, not because he was a philosopher, but because he promoted science, which was not only more modern than philosophy in its aims but also more likely to achieve useful results. He also admired Adam Smith and Bentham for implementing the Baconian dream of practical philosophy.

However hard he might try, Macaulay could not completely avoid questions conventionally considered by political philosophers. He occasionally pondered the ends of government but was content with vague and conventional statements that governments should keep peace and arbitrate disputes so as to provide security for persons and property. In the tradition of Bacon and the Utilitarians, he acknowledged that "societies and laws exist only for the purpose of increasing the sum of private happiness."[18] Rather than establish priorities, he converted ends into means. In view of Macaulay's status in the history of liberalism and the importance of constitutionalism in his outlook, we might have expected him to hold liberty as a supreme end, yet he consistently and emphatically held that it was merely a means of promoting the security of persons and property.[19] He seemed to avoid questions that held no promise of yielding satisfactory answers. This was part of Bacon's appeal. Whereas Plato asked important questions for which there were no answers, Bacon narrowed the scope of inquiry but enlarged the expectations of useful results.

Macaulay, who was an omnivorous reader, read philosophic writers; but it was for their literary value or their ingenuity and, in the end, one suspects, to persuade himself once more that they had nothing to offer. He was not interested in their deeper moral reflections. His sister Margaret, who died when Macaulay was thirty-four, made a record of the way he would discuss metaphysical questions:

> Not that on many mysterious questions he would endeavour to bring me to any settled creed, but that he would show me the question in all its bearings, and far from — as many do, whose minds cannot rest in uncertainty — proposing for doubts which can never be removed explanations which will not bear a strict examination, he would go to the very bottom of the subject, talk it round and round on every side, and finding at last an impenetrable mystery — "thus far shalt thou go and no further" — he would show me it was not on the question alone we might then be considering that this uncertainty remained, when followed out to the end; but on all questions of morals, on all speculations upon this strange theatre upon which we have appeared, just to play a part and then vanish.[20]

This was not an acceptance of mystery so much as a belief in its unimportance. It was an attitude he never gave up. "How little I have troubled myself about metaphysics since I was a lad at college," he confessed in middle life, "and how profoundly sceptical I am about all the great metaphysical questions."[21] Still later he records in his journal that he was reading

> more of the articles on Metaphysics in the Encycl. Brit. What trash! What a waste of the powers of the human mind — I declare that I would rather have written John Gilpin than all the volumes of Fichte, Kant, Schelling and Hegel together. [And, a week later:] Encyl. Brit. — looked through that on Logic, with an increasing conviction of the utter worthlessness of the study, and an increasing contempt for such great men as Sir William Hamilton.[22]

Bacon he admired for his common sense; Bacon did not "meddle with those aenigmas which have puzzled hundreds of generations, and will puzzle hundreds more. He said nothing about the grounds of moral obligation."[23] It could be a description of Macaulay himself.

Macaulay's thinking was narrowed and lacked depth as a result of his reluctance to consider moral arguments apart from their political implications. This is illustrated in his observation on the regicides. They "had committed, not only a crime, but an error." On the removal of the gates from Somnauth: "Morally, this is a crime; politically, it is a blunder."[24] Observations such as these give an appearance of cynicism, and they stimulate doubt whether the moral or the political consideration is more important to Macaulay. The same question is raised by his arguments against slavery. Although slavery provoked something like moral outrage in him, Macaulay did not neglect the political dimension of the problem. Slavery was "a great moral and political evil," and furthermore, in seeking a remedy, it would be necessary to compromise one's principles in order to accomplish a politically acceptable remedy.[25] This type of argument made him appear insensitive to the moral dimension of a problem in the eyes of those for whom the moral dimension had primacy. This kind of criticism, though not directed specifically at Macaulay, was voiced by John Morley, who complained about the "present [1874] exaggeration of the political standard as the universal test of truth." Morley's criticism of the reluctance to be morally assertive was, he thought, a national failing. If it was, Macaulay shared it.[26]

The mixing of political with moral considerations and the resulting undermining of the moral argument is evident in Macaulay's justifications for reforms. He supported parliamentary reform because it was good in itself but also because it was dangerous to withhold it. Similarly, he justified liberty for its contribution to (among other things) the stability of the government. First of all, it dissipated passion. "That governments may be permanent, nations must be free. That public opinion may not burst every barrier, it must be allowed an open channel.... It is when the destroying element is pent up within the volcano that it convulses the ocean and the earth." Free expression is important for another reason: it reveals discontents, which can then be dealt with by timely concessions. "The danger of states is to be estimated, not by what breaks out of the public mind, but by what stays in it." There is nothing "more terrible than the situation of a government which rules without apprehension over a people of hypocrites, — which is flattered by the press and cursed in the inner chambers." A policy of restricting expression, instead of curing the disease, removes the outward symptoms that allow for diagnosis.[27]

The same subordination of moral to political norms can be found in his rationale for toleration. Of course persecution and religious disqualifications were wrong. The emphasis, however, is on the imprudence of intolerance—on the fact that it alienated the victims and turned them into potential revolutionaries. Persecution was not only vicious, it was foolish. The Puritans were made dangerously rebellious by the cruelties of the church and the government. The same argument held for the Jews in his own time; if their disabilities were removed, their loyalty would be secured. The same process might yet be made to operate in Ireland, despite the long history of persecution and exclusion. Macaulay appealed to Burke's authority for the argument that the Irish Catholics would resist Jacobinism if, through a policy of toleration, they were attached to the regime.[28]

Thus, Macaulay, though he did not disregard moral ends, preferred to defend them by pointing to the way their implementation contributed to the stability of the constitutional order and the social system. Considerations of morality and policy tended to become interchangeable. In making judgments he appealed "to the principles either of morality, or of what we believe to be identical with morality; namely, far-sighted policy."[29] However, although he thought them identical, he clearly preferred to think in terms of "far-sighted policy," and this obscured consideration of the moral dimension of policy. Thus in criticizing his political antagonists, he emphasized what was dysfunctional rather than what was immoral; and in defending policies, he emphasized what was useful rather than what was good. This was a shift of emphasis in the Whig tradition. Without abandoning the traditional Whig rationale for toleration and liberty, Macaulay, as a spokesman for a new generation of Whigs, added the amoral, functional argument.

His unwillingness to confront problems in moral and political philosophy without thinking preeminently of their practical political consequences suggested an insensitivity which in fact was a deep and exclusive commitment to practical politics. It also led critics with broader interests to accuse him of intellectual shallowness and philosophic vacuity. His critics are numerous and severe. To Matthew Arnold he was "the great apostle of the Philistines" who could not penetrate beneath the surface of events; "for what the French call the *vraie vérité,* he had absolutely no organ."[30] Gladstone took a similar position in an essay which, although not without appreciation for Macaulay's gifts and achievements, provides the most extensive and penetrating criticism of the character of Macaulay's mind. In Gladstone's view Macaulay was distinguished by a shallowness, a "want of depth," made worse by his having a closed mind—what Gladstone called an "invincible ignorance." There was a blandness, an unawareness of problems that was close to philosophic blindness. Macaulay was a man "for whom the mysteries of human life, thought, and destiny appear to have neither charm nor terror, and whose writings seem audibly to boast in every page of being bounded by the visible horizon of the practical and work-day sphere." This was exemplified in his insensitivity to the quality of Saint Augustine's *Confessions:* Macaulay

> had indeed no admiration, and but little indulgence, for any of these introspective productions. They lay in a region which he did not frequent; and yet they are among not only the realities, but the deepest and most determining realities, of our nature. We reckon his low estimate of this inward work as betokening the insufficient development of his own powerful mind in that direction.[31]

Macaulay's critics included Tories, especially those who, like Croker, had been the subject of his unsparing critical reviews. Yet many of the most penetrating and angriest of his critics were men who would have looked on Macaulay as being politically in approximate alignment with themselves. Their severity did not arise from political differences; rather, they were critical of his mode of thinking, the scope of his thought, and the insignificance he attached to pure intellectualism. Macaulay was, in other words, not sufficiently an intellectual. This theme informs Morley's judgment. For him Macaulay's work was commonplace; and, what went with this, it enjoyed popularity:

> He was in exact accord with the common average sentiment of his day on every subject on which he spoke. His superiority was not of that highest kind which leads a man to march in thought on the outside margin of the crowd, watching them, sympathizing with them, hoping for them, but apart. Macaulay was one of the middle-class crowd in his heart, and only rose above it by splendid attainments and extraordinary gifts of expression.

His defect was that he was not an intellectual, apart from society. Indeed, Morley was quite sure that had Macaulay been an Athenian citizen, "he would have taken sides with Anytus and Meletus in the impeachment of Socrates."[32]

John Stuart Mill—the prototypical intellectual—also was severe, and on similar grounds. According to Mill, Macaulay, though able, was a man "who has not even one of the ideas or impressions characteristic of this century and which will be identified with it by history—except, strangely enough, in mere literature." In other words, he was not with the avant-garde, which, for Mill, was located among the German and French intellectuals. "In politics, ethics, philosophy, even history, of which he knows superficially very much—he has not a single thought of either German or French origin, and that is saying enough." Mill finally says of Macaulay that "he is what all cockneys are, an intellectual dwarf—rounded off and stunted, full grown broad and short, without a germ of principle of further growth in his whole being."[33]

His critics were, in a sense, correct. Macaulay was intellectually unadventurous. For him, theoretical explorations were acceptable only if they had some connection with the world as it was experienced by most men. Thus Bentham's theorizing about the law was praiseworthy because it was an instrument for improving the legislation and the administration of the law. The literature of political economy, including the writings of Malthus on population, interested him because it contributed to practical improvement. In the same spirit he appreciated Machiavelli and, surprisingly, Hallam, whose speculations were "strikingly practical," teaching "us not only the general rule, but the mode of applying it to solve particular cases. In this respect they often remind us of the Discourses of Machiavelli."[34] In Bacon, too, it is his practicality that is admired; and Bacon, it will be recalled, praised Machiavelli on the same grounds.

Macaulay's severe condemnation of theorizing that was not also practical entered into his judgment of Carlyle, although personal animosity, contempt for Carlyle's style, political differences, and perhaps rivalry also played a part. On reading Carlyle's *Frederick,* Macaulay noted in his journal: "I never saw a worse book. Nothing new of the smallest value. The philosophy nonsense and the style gibberish."[35] The most extreme example of Macaulay's scorn in this respect was perhaps reserved for Coleridge: "What an overrated creature he was. And he to prate about *a whole* and the importance of unity of design. And he to blame severe and one sided criticism!—Was there ever such a heap of unconnected nonsense as this Biog[raphia Literaria]?"

Again, "It is quite inconceivable that if there were any meaning in his philosophy it should not peep out here or there through the clouds of gibberish. But I declare that, having read many hundreds of pages of his writing, I have not the slightest guess at what he means by an idea or by the reason as distinct from the understanding.... It is mere hocus pocus."[36] Here is Macaulay's intolerance of obscure language and even more of unnecessarily complex thought. He believed that anything worth saying could be expressed simply yet with perfect clarity, and he has been celebrated for these stylistic qualities. He was disappointed that "many readers give credit for profundity for whatever is obscure, and call all that is perspicuous shallow."[37]

In fact he was not simply antiintellectual, though some of his critics thought him so. He loved—indeed, lived for—books. He read while shaving, while dressing and undressing, while walking in the country and through crowded London streets. He died with a book in his hands. His journals to a great extent are a record of his reading and his judgments on it. But the books he read were not always treated with the seriousness intended by their authors. It was German philosophy that he read while dressing and undressing.[38] The arguments did not reach into that part of the mind in which one struggles to understand because the significance of the ideas is recognized. Perhaps this was because Macaulay would not acknowledge that ideas can be considered independently of the effect of politics on them or of their political consequences. Whenever the logic of ideas led to the adoption of a philosophic position that was incompatible with his playing the political role that he never abandoned (even when writing), Macaulay did not follow.

Since he directed his attention to the political texture of events (in his own time and historically), the realm of ideas was subordinated to politics. He drew upon that realm as it suited his political purposes, but he rarely explored it systematically. Furthermore, politics, as he kept insisting, did not follow logical patterns. Consequently it is difficult to identify Macaulay with a distinct philosophical outlook or school.[39] There were brief periods, it is true, when he appeared to be a Benthamite or a Baconian, but most of the time it is difficult to associate him with a particular intellectual outlook. He is sometimes associated with Utilitarianism;[40] yet he publicly and effectively criticized James Mill and the so-called Utilitarian theory of government. He is conventionally labeled a Whig, and in a way that implies that he should be seen as one who shared a Lockean understanding of politics; yet although he approved and appreciated the political and constitutional developments historically associated with Locke's name, there are many indications that he was dubious about the merits of Locke's speculations.

Still another example concerns the Scottish philosophers of the eighteenth century. Here, too, Macaulay was influenced by them without being an orthodox spokesman for them. The most notable representatives of this school were Adam Smith, Adam Ferguson Hume, Francis Hutcheson, and Henry Home (Lord Kames). One of the distinguishing features of their outlook was the belief that much of the institutional order of society is not the result of design, let alone of wisdom or reason. Examples of such undesigned, unanticipated outcomes are language or a libertarian constitution. In the words of Adam Ferguson,

> Every step and every movement of the multitude, even in what are termed enlightened ages, are made with equal blindness to the future; and nations stumble upon establishments which are indeed the result of human action, but not the execution of human design . . .; communities . . . admit of the greatest revolutions where no change is intended, and . . . the most refined politicians do not always know whither they are leading the state by their projects.[41]

This theme is also to be found in Macaulay's historical analysis, most notably in his concept of "noiseless revolutions," which bear a close resemblance to the kind of changes described by Ferguson. These were the long-term changes in institutions that resulted from the slow accumulation of small causes, certainly not from design. They were recognized by the historian, not foreseen by the politician.

An example of Macaulay's use of this conception of historical development is provided by his account of the decision in 1695 to allow the Licensing Act to lapse (it had put the press under the control of licensers). In the paper that vindicated the Commons' decision an abundance of reasons were offered. But, Macaulay said, the paper "proves . . . that they knew not what they were doing, what a revolution they were making, what a power they were calling into existence." All their objections to the licensing law were concerned with petty details, with the difficulties and annoyances connected with its administration. But "on the great question of principle, on the question whether the liberty of unlicensed printing be, on the whole, a blessing or a curse to society, not a word is said." Petty arguments achieved what Milton's *Areopagitica* had failed to do. Indeed, the great event passed almost unnoticed, yet it "has done more for liberty and for civilization than the Great Charter or the Bill of Rights." The outcome was nothing less than liberty of the press.[42]

That Macaulay had been influenced by the Scottish philosophers is not surprising. He had read many of them. He was also exposed to them at second hand, so to speak, in the *Edinburgh Review,* where Francis Jeffrey, who as a student had been exposed to their teachings, often discussed them and their views. And Macaulay was intimately familiar with Jeffrey's writings: "I have read, and re-read, his old articles till I know them by heart."[43] However, while the Scottish philosophers' understanding of historical change clearly made a powerful impression on Macaulay, he did not share it entirely. Here again it is difficult to identify him with an intellectual tradition. The Scottish philosophers held that beneficial outcomes are not always dependent on human intervention. This view is conventionally identified and ridiculed by reference to the "invisible hand," a phrase that Adam Smith used once, or perhaps twice, in *The Wealth of Nations.*[44] Smith and others of his school did allow for legislative regulation and interference. But Macaulay, by comparison, provided for massive political intervention in the historical process. This, after all, was the role of Macaulay's heroes: to manage crises (what he called "conjunctures") in order to help give shape to new institutions. The hero's achievement, it is true, depended on his skillful exploitation of opportunities that latently existed in the historical situation. Yet to recognize them required a power of discernment, and to exploit them required unique political skill. His heroes were not philosopher-kings; but neither were they agents of historical forces, unwittingly contributing to fortunate developments. In this important way Macaulay deviated from the Scottish tradition.

Macaulay accepted parts of the intellectual heritage as it was passed down from many different sources. From the Utilitarians, from Bacon, and from the eighteenth-century Scottish philosophers he took some ideas but rejected others. (And so it is inappropriate to label him simply a Utilitarian or a representative of the Enlightenment.) He eclectically combined ideas from these (and other) sources as a result of a process of selective exposure in which he incorporated some ideas from a given source without feeling logically compelled to accept all. This process is exemplified by his belief that society tends to move, alternately, between extremes of despotism and anarchy. Despite his speaking for the Moderns against the Ancients, this view may well have had its origin in his reading of ancient authors.

Such eclecticism was not self-conscious, as it had been for John Stuart Mill after his recovery from his mental crisis. Mill systematically exposed himself to a great variety of incompatible ideas, each representing, as he thought, partial or half-truths, his purpose being to lay the foundation for an ultimate synthesis. Macaulay, on the contrary, drew on his reading for illustration, for rhetorical purposes. He did not try to systematically combine the ideas of those by whom he was influenced. He did not take ideas that seriously. Indeed, he was not concerned with the origins of the ideas he did use; he was so preoccupied with the political and social context with which the ideas mingled and in which they were altered that they ceased to be part of logic and philosophy but became, instead, part of the living flow of events. Gladstone must have had this in mind when he said that Macaulay "remembered his own knowledge, in the modern phrase his own concepts, better than he retained, if indeed he ever had embraced, the true sense of the authorities on which the 'concepts' were originally framed."[45] Therefore, the fact that Macaulay's ideas can be traced back to their sources does not imply that he was a spokesman for the philosophic tradition from which the ideas were derived.

This applies to Macaulay's "Machiavellianism." There are affinities that can be discerned, but Macaulay hardly identified himself with Machiavelli, although he did exonerate Machiavelli from the immorality that others conventionally attributed to him. Among the similarities are their shared concerns with stability, leadership, the political use of religion, and the avoidance of destructive factionalism. Macaulay's preference for defining problems in political rather than moral terms also finds a parallel in Machiavelli. Even Macaulay's heroes, like Machiavelli's, are men with the qualities that will allow them to bring order out of chaos.[46] In any case, much of the Machiavellian flavor of Macaulay's outlook was, in the nineteenth century, no longer distinctive, for it was an almost inevitable accompaniment to the barely concealed secularism and the forthright modernism that characterized many Victorian intellectuals. Furthermore, Macaulay eagerly exposed himself to the writings of men by whom Machiavelli's influence was transmitted. Bacon was an intellectual descendant of Machia-velli's; and although Macaulay looked upon Bacon as primarily an advocate of induction, he was also exposed to the more specifically political (and Machiavellian) themes in Bacon's writ-ings. Halifax also was saturated with Machiavellian ideas. He "had digested Machiavelli"; indeed, in all his published writings he only once mentioned a political author by name, and that was Machiavelli.[47]

In view of Macaulay's depreciation of political philosophy and the difficulty in identifying him with any particular philosophic school, and since he held that statesmen should be guided by the results of historical inquiry, the search for the intellectual context of his thought should perhaps be directed to those with a similar outlook. This associates him with Halifax and Burke. All three of them were politicians who theorized about politics, but their theorizing was not sufficiently generalized to qualify as genuine philosophy. They were between what Macaulay called the man of theory, who sees nothing but general principles, and the man of business, who sees nothing but particular circumstances.

Halifax, Burke, and Macaulay, whose understandings of poli-tics can be associated with this genre, are in certain ways similar. All were connected with the Revolutionary settlement, either by directly contributing to its development or by deepening the national understanding of it, therefore giving it continuing signifi-cance in the political life of the nation. This predominance of the Revolutionary settlement and related practical concerns in their thought gave it an appearance of insularity that conceals its wider significance.

All three were reluctant to deal with principles of morals in relation to politics. Even Burke, although he made some forth-right pronouncements about natural law, was somewhat equivocal in his view. His position on natural law, which appears in his writings and speeches on India and Ireland, was obscured by his much more prominent critique of "metaphysical politicians" and their abstract mode of thinking. Halifax's reticence about the role and status of principles can be found (among other writings) in the section of his *Political Thoughts and Reflections* entitled "Of Fundamentals" (by which he meant principles):

> The word soundeth so well that the Impropriety of it hath been
> the less observed. But as weighty as the word appeareth, no
> Feather hath been more blown about in the World than this
> word, *Fundamental*.

It is one of those Mistakes that at some time may be of use, but it is a Mistake still . . .

Even in morality one may more properly say, There *should be* Fundamentals allowed, than that there *are* any which in Strictness can be maintained.[48]

Macaulay shared this equivocalness about moral principles but was less forthright about it.

Burke and Halifax also shared with Macaulay a nervousness about the security of the social order and the capability of the government to control its centrifugal tendencies in a manner compatible with constitutional values. All three saw men as sometimes having what Macaulay called "darker passions," and all thought such passions were easily provoked by the distresses of life, thus posing a threat to the regime. They all agreed that those passions could be easily agitated by zealous politicians, thus creating fanaticism, an insuperable obstacle to tolerance and conciliation. Finally, all three thought it the politician's most important function to reduce extremes, to promote consent, to reconcile. To this end they all urged adaptability in adjusting the constitution to changing circumstances. Even Burke took this position, arguing that "a constitution without the means of some change is without the means of its conservation."

By their support for far-reaching changes, justified on the ground that they would enlarge support and therefore help to preserve the existing constitutional and social order, they each confound those who would classify them as either liberal or conservative. Since each can reasonably be considered as representing in his speculations and conduct both liberal and conservative outlooks, these are not the most useful categories with which to classify them. Each of these men can, and has been, placed in both the conservative and liberal traditions. But they belong solely to neither.[49]

Macaulay's unqualified admiration for Halifax has been mentioned. Equally significant is his esteem for Burke. There is ample evidence throughout his own writings of his great familiarity with Burke's, and with Burke's career. He was reading Burke (the first of the *Letters on a Regicide Peace*) as early as 1822 in preparation for the prize essay on William III, where he calls him "the most brilliant and popular political writer of our country." He was anxious to write a long article on Burke for the *Edinburgh Review* and began work on it but then gave it up as unmanageable within the limitations of an article for a quarterly. A decade later he recorded "reading again most of Burke's works—Admirable—the greatest man since Milton."[50] Macaulay's close intellectual and temperamental tie to Burke was recognized by Disraeli, who referred to Macaulay in *The Young Duke* by adapting the words used by Goldsmith about Burke. Macaulay, Disraeli said, "like the individual whom he has most studied, will 'give up to party what was meant for mankind.'"[51]

Burke was, Macaulay said (referring to the late eighteenth century), "the greatest man then living." He had eloquence and was the only match in conversation for Dr. Johnson. In addition, "Burke was a man in whom compassion for suffering, and hatred of injustice and tyranny, were as strong as in Las Cases or Clarkson." Macaulay's admiration for Burke extended to almost all realms of activity: his speeches were splendid (though rhetorically not as skillful as Fox's); as a writer he ranked with Shakespeare, Milton, Dryden, and Johnson, that is, with "the greatest names of our literature"; and the quality of his thought was at the highest level—he was "superior to Fox in largeness of comprehension, in extent of knowledge, and in splendour of imagination." Splendid and varied were the treasures stored in Burke's mind.[52]

Yet Macaulay did not find Burke faultless. He remarked that Burke sometimes lost control of his passions and became zealous in showing animosity (a fault he shared with Macaulay himself). He was unfair in the impeachment proceedings against Hastings. "His indignation, virtuous in its origin, acquired too much of the character of personal aversion." This characteristic, by which he was "led into extravagance by a tempestuous sensibility, which domineered over all his faculties," was also the source of his "preaching a crusade against the French republic."[53] An even harsher judgment was made when Macaulay pointed to his "fierce and ungovernable sensibility," as a result of which "he generally chose his side like a fanatic"—a judgment softened only by the observation that he "defended [the side he chose] like a philosopher." Trevelyan, Macaulay's nephew and biographer, aware of these qualifications of Macaulay's esteem for Burke, yet testified to Macaulay's "sincere and entire sympathy with that great statesman."[54]

Macaulay's admiration for Burke may appear inconsistent with his celebration of modernity, his lack of strong religious feeling, and his indifference to the problem of establishing a moral basis for politics. For Burke was emphatically concerned about the moral foundation of the political order, and his belief in natural law was in part sustained by religious conviction. However, for his own reasons, Burke avoided giving prominence to these views; instead he typically emphasized the aspect of his thought that had affinities with Halifax and Macaulay, the side of his outlook that gave great prominence to conciliation, compromise, and the untrustworthiness of abstract approaches to politics, — all of which constituted prudence, which he called the first of political virtues. It was possible for Macaulay to neglect the aspect of Burke that made him a moral and political philosopher; indeed, many of the commentators on Burke since his time have deemphasized it. Macaulay's appreciation of Burke was — or was to become — the conventional nineteenth-century interpretation.[55] It was not his idiosyncratic interpretation that allowed him to find Burke congenial. His view was unusual only in the depth and intensity of his appreciation.

Once that side of Burke that emphasizes prudence, compromise, and conciliation is given prominence, there is little difficulty in finding continuities between him and Macaulay, and, for that matter, with Halifax as well.[56] Although Macaulay is less reverent than Burke, both saw religion as a restraint on the appetites and passions which, if removed, would unleash threats to public order that government could control only by becoming less libertarian. In each there was a hypersensitivity to threats to the established order and a belief that it was highly vulnerable. They shared a fear of fanaticism, although Macaulay was more prone to see this as a religious as well as a secular phenomenon. For the same reason both were suspicious of doctrinaire theorists; James Mill was Macaulay's culprit, just as the French philosophers of the mid-eighteenth century were Burke's. And Macaulay's characterizations of civil prudence — with emphasis on the need to balance conveniences and inconveniences, good and evil — clearly are paraphrases of Burke.[57]

The most remarkable congeniality between Burke and Macaulay is to be found in their analyses of the French Revolution. It is true that in their evaluations of that event they disagreed, for Macaulay often held that, despite its cruelty and injustice, its long-term consequences were to be welcomed. Yet even while he held this view, his analysis was remarkably similar to Burke's. As in Burke, there was the same emphasis on abstract and speculative theory, the same concern for prescription and about natural rights, the same contrast between England and France. Indeed, Macaulay's analysis is a paraphrase of Burke:

> They [the French] would not have reform; and they had revolution.... All the great English revolutions have been conducted by practical statesmen. The French Revolution was conducted by mere speculators. Our constitution has never been so far behind the age, as to have become an object of aversion to the people. The English revolutions have therefore been undertaken for the purpose of defending, correcting, and restoring, — never for the mere purpose of destroying. Our countrymen ... [i]n the very act of innovating ... have constantly appealed to ancient prescription; they have seldom looked abroad for models; they have seldom troubled themselves with Utopian theories; they have not been anxious to prove that liberty is a natural right of men; they have been content to regard it as the lawful birthright of Englishmen. Their social contract is no fiction. It is still extant on the original parchment, sealed with wax which was affixed at Runnymede.... Very different was the spirit of the Constituent Assembly.... All the past was loathsome to them. All their agreeable associations were connected with the future. Hopes were to them all that recollections are to us. In the institutions of their country they found nothing to love or to admire. [58]

One difference remains, however. According to Macaulay, the occasion for the Revolution was oppression. In an allusion to Burke, Macaulay shows that he thought this analysis did not contradict but rather supplemented Burke. "It was long the fashion to ascribe all the follies which [the revolutionaries] committed to the writings of the philosophers. We believe that it was misrule, and nothing but misrule, that put the sting into those writings." [59]

Given so similar an analysis, we should not be surprised that Macaulay responded to revolution much as Burke did. An indication of this is found in the article of 1827, in which Macaulay's warnings about the threat of revolution takes on Burkean dimensions. He pointed to discontents and the spirit of innovation; the vulnerability of the working classes to revolutionary ideas and the presence of revolutionary leadership among the intellectual middle classes; to the way an irreconcilable Tory policy (not an unreal possibility) would provoke all reformers and all those with discontents into a revolutionary posture. He then drew parallels between England under Charles I and France under Louis XV. And he concluded that there was an "extreme risk of revolution" and that, if it took place, there would be "a bloody and unsparing revolution—a revolution which will make the ears of those who hear of it tingle in the remotest countries, and in the remotest times."[60] This suggests what his response to the French Revolution would have been had he judged it in the 1790s. He acknowledged that "very great indulgence is due to those who, while the Revolution was actually taking place, regarded it with unmixed aversion and horror.... We can perceive that the evil was temporary, and the good durable." But, had he been living at that time, he too might have been so disgusted that he also would have thought the revolution the embodiment of insanity and crime.[61]

The main link between Macaulay and Burke was their shared attitude to continuity and change, tradition and reform, old and new, past and future. Both were willing to go to considerable lengths to make the changes that would preserve the essential features of a constitutional order. (To refer to the considerable lengths to which Burke would go is to remind ourselves of the liberal Burke who defended the American colonists, the persecuted Irish Catholics, and the oppressed in India, and who urged the adoption of administrative and constitutional reforms.) Like Macaulay, Burke could eulogize the constitution for allowing the "principle of renovation, and union of permanence and change"; "in all our changes we are never wholly old or wholly new...; [we] preserve unbroken the traditionary chain of maxims and policy of our ancestors ... and enough of the new to invigorate us and bring us to our true character."[62] Macaulay's eulogy of the way the events of 1689 were managed breathed the spirit of these words. His argument for timely concession as a way of avoiding revolution recalls Burke's argument for "timely reform."[63] And his defense of parliamentary reform in 1831-32 was an application of Burke's maxim that "a constitution without the means of some change is without the means of its conservation."

That Macaulay saw Burke as one who shared his own rationale for timely concession is revealed in his discussion of Irish affairs. Ireland's relations with England were marked by acrimony, distrust, hostility, and sometimes rebellion. But it need not have been this way. Had Catholic disabilities been removed, had the Catholic clergy been treated generously, had Catholic education been properly supported, there might have been, instead of distrust and rebellion, a union of "the hearts and affections of the people." Had these changes been effected as late as 1813 or even during the early 1820s, the union "would fully now [1844] have been as secure, and as far out of the reach of agitation, as the Union with Scotland." This had been Pitt's policy, whose "views and opinions agreed with, and were, I have no doubt, taken from those of Mr. Burke, a man of an understanding even more enlarged and capacious than his own."[64]

Finally, Macaulay gave Burke the highest praise when he pointed out that, unlike most of his contemporaries, Burke correctly discerned the character of the conflict between the people and the Parliament as it emerged during the late eighteenth century. Burke anticipated in this the correct analysis of the discontents that nourished the movement for parliamentary reform during the following fifty years.[65] Macaulay could therefore imply, during the debates on parliamentary reform in 1832, that Burke could have approved of the Reform Bill then before the House of Commons. Thus Burke was the model of the wise ancestor to whom Macaulay looked when, in supporting the Reform Bill, he advised his hearers to do, not what their ancestors had done, but what, in present circumstances, they would do.[66] The account of Burke's analysis of the discontents and conflicts that were to come into prominence during the nineteenth century showed that Burke anticipated the understanding of the "philosophical historian" (though Macaulay did not on this occasion use the phrase). This was the ability to discern the true character of events in a way that would be confirmed by historians generations later. It will be recalled that he commended Halifax in these terms.

In view of the differences between them, Burke's influence on Macaulay should not be exaggerated, especially as Macaulay was too much of an eclectic to be labeled simply a Burkean. Nor can a sharply defined intellectual tradition from Halifax to Burke to Macaulay be identified, for the distinguishing characteristics of these philosopher-politicians were formed by temperament as well as intellectual considerations, and, in addition, constitutional crises seemed to elicit the flexible, trimming responses for which they sought a principled rationale. Yet there is a tradition here, one that can accommodate men with radically different outlooks in normal times. But this tradition attracts those who are sensitive to crisis and who give priority to the problem of maintaining the legacy of rules and procedures and civilized habits that provide the framework within which party and even ideological politics is permissible.

Since Macaulay fits into this tradition, it is not surprising that he is difficult to place on the spectrum of modern political ideologies. He was not primarily concerned with the policy problems with which these ideologies are concerned; and his views on a question such as the free market and regulation, considered over his lifetime, were equivocal. He mainly wished to define and encourage a manner of conducting politics that protected the kind of constitutional and social system that reduced the risks of anarchy and despotism. Thus his main concern was with the legitimacy of the political system that achieved this, namely, the system that emerged from the constitutional struggles of the seventeenth and early ninteenth centuries. It will be recalled that he thought of the latter as approaching the former in historical significance. Whereas the earlier one put the Parliament in harmony with the monarchy, the latter took a major step toward establishing a harmonious relationship between people and Parliament. With this restoration of legitimacy, consent for the constitution was created anew, taking into account modern circumstances. Such problems were the greatest challenge to politicians. The ideologies of liberalism, or Toryism, or socialism assumed the stability and legitimacy of the political system. But Macaulay had not assumed it, and his political outlook developed during the post–French Revolutionary period and before the Reform Act established what he expected to become a new era of harmony and domestic peace. This was before the ideologies that dominated the mid-century had become sharply defined; indeed, some of them had only begun to emerge.[67] In this connection it should be repeated that although Macaulay was familiar with the categories of Left and Right, it is noteworthy that he very infrequently used these terms.

His trimming outlook, and with it his eclecticism, also makes it difficult to classify him as a liberal or a conservative. In the main he has, of course, been associated with liberalism, and those who think he was a spokesman for liberal ideas can point to his endorsement of values associated with individualism and a libertarian society, as well as his qualified support of laissez-faire economic policy. In addition, there are his enlightened attitude toward the role of religion in social and political life, his modernism, revealed in his welcoming of Baconian ideas and material progress, and his opinion that the French Revolution was on the whole and in the long run a salutary development. Yet, however much these ingredients qualify him as a representative of liberalism, they were combined with a conservatism of purpose that sharply differentiated his thinking from that of many other liberals whose policies he endorsed. This was made explicit in his rationale for the Reform Bill, a measure supported by all liberals, and many Radicals as well, and considered at the time to be a considerable and imaginative if not revolutionary change. Whereas liberals sought reform because it was improvement that reduced the gap between ideal and reality, Macaulay's main purpose was conservative: "Reform that you may preserve." His conservative intention is also revealed in his approval of the events of 1688–89 as a defensive, preserving, conservative revolution. Although the conservative element is pronounced, only a reminder of his qualifications as a liberal is sufficient to dismiss him from the conservative camp. Yet the presence of the conservative ingredient also makes it difficult to consider him as a typical spokesman for the liberal tradition. As one should expect for a trimmer, he was severely criticized by both those conservatives and those radical liberals who were sufficiently doctrinaire to be dissatisfied with what appeared to be the impurity of Macaulay's views.[68]

This mixture of outlooks is reflected in Macaulay's apparently contradictory attitudes to historical continuity and tradition. On the one hand, he valued continuity. Prescription was not a bad thing. Amidst the disputes of 1689, "eager and angry as both sides were, the speeches on both sides indicated that profound reverence for law and prescription which has long been characteristic of Englishmen, and which, though it runs sometimes into pedantry and sometimes into superstition, is not without its advantages." On the other hand, combined with his respect for historical continuity was his disapproval of what he thought was the Tory attitude to the past: the wish to perpetuate policies and institutions. This was "the error of minds prone to reverence whatever is old," an error particularly pernicious in a statesman.[69]

In these seemingly contradictory attitudes to the past Macaulay was seeking both continuity and flexibility, tradition and change.

Neither was good in itself. Both could contribute to the making of a viable society that enjoyed the support of the populace, that is, legitimacy, or, in traditional Whig terms, consent. Continuity was useful because it made possible the survival of those procedures and values that allowed the constitution to function in a libertarian yet orderly way. And just as continuity provided for stability of the regime, so also flexibility served the same purpose. That Macaulay was willing to go far in this direction is indicated by his approval of Sir John Maynard's position in the Convention of 1689, when he "scornfully thrust aside as frivolous and out of place all that black letter learning" that was an obstacle to resolving the problems created by the Revolution; [70] by his own role in the proceedings leading to the Reform Act; and by his willingness in 1835 to consider abolition of the House of Lords. The question whether continuity or flexibility was to predominate had to be settled by the politicians. The response depended on their prudent management — on their artfulness. It was one of William's achievements that he appreciated the importance of both continuity and change. Although the leader of a revolution, "he outraged no national prejudice. He abolished no ancient form. . . . Thus he imparted to innovation the dignity and stability of antiquity."[71] Macaulay would have had the politicians lean toward continuity and tradition; but if a crisis justified it, he would have them be flexible, not superstitiously adhering to what their ancestors had done in other circumstances, but by doing what their ancestors would have done in present circumstances.

The events of 1689 and 1832, in which continuity and change were combined and linked together as a means of providing stability, were almost perfect examples of the way a trimmer's purposes could be artfully achieved. Conflict and perhaps civil war are avoided, opponents are reconciled, and consent is given to new constitutional remedies. It is no accident that the one event was the apotheosis of Macaulay's *History* and the other of his political career.

List of Abbreviations and Short Titles

BM   British Museum

Diaries of the 7th earl of Carlisle. Diaries of Lord Morpeth, later 7th earl of Carlisle. Manuscript at Castle Howard, Yorkshire. My notes refer to vols. 2-37, 1844-60.

Edin. Rev.   *The Edinburgh Review*

"Essay on William III."   "Essay on the Life and Character of King William III." Macaulay's "prize essay" of 1822. Printed, with editorial comment by A. N. L. Munby, in the *Times Literary Supplement* (London) , 1 May 1969, pp. 468-69. Page numbers in the notes refer to this issue of the *TLS*.

Gladstone, *Gleanings.*   W. E. Gladstone, *Gleanings of Past Years, 1843-78.* 4 vols. New York: Charles Scribner's Sons, n.d. References in the notes are to vol. 2: *Gleanings of Past Years, 1844-78.*

Hansard.   *Hansard's Parliamentary Debates*, 3d series.

History.   Thomas Babington Macaulay, *The History of England from the Accession of James the Second.* Edited by Charles Harding Firth. 6 vols. London: Macmillan, 1913.

Journals.   Macaulay's Journals, in 11 volumes. Manuscript in Trinity College Library, Cambridge.

Misc. Wr.   *The Miscellaneous Writings of Lord Macaulay.* Edited by T[homas] F[lower] E[llis] . 2 vols. London: Longman, Green, Longman & Roberts, 1860.

Pinney, *Letters.*   *The Letters of Thomas Babington Macaulay.* Edited by Thomas Pinney. 2 vols. Cambridge, Eng.: At the University Press, 1974.

PRO   Public Record Office, London

Speeches   *Speeches of the Right Honourable T.B. Macaulay, M.P., Corrected by Himself.* London: Longman, Brown, Green, & Longman, 1854.

TBM   Thomas Babington Macaulay

Trevelyan, *Life*.   George Otto Trevelyan, *The Life and Letters of Lord Macaulay*. With a Preface by G. M. Trevelyan. World's Classics ed. 2 vols. London: Oxford University Press, 1932. First published in 1876.

Wallington   Wallington, Northumberland; administered by the National Trust. Its collection of books includes the largest surviving portion of Macaulay's library.

NOTE. — All manuscript letters in Trinity College Library, Cambridge, are in the Macaulay Papers, unless they are identified as parts of other collections.

Notes

CHAPTER 1. POLITICAL AND RELIGIOUS CONFLICT

1. *History,* 4, 1763; 5, 2597. References to the Cato Street Conspiracy are also to be found in "Barère's *Memoirs,*" *Edin. Rev., 79* (April 1844), 349, and in *Hansard, 15,* 260 (6 February 1833).

2. TBM to Zachary Macaulay, [14 September 1819], [September 1819], 21 November 1820, Pinney, *Letters, 1,* 131-34, 150. Selina Macaulay's Diary, entries of 15, 22 [June 1826], Huntington Library. He recalled that he "bore part in a furious contest between 'God save the King' and 'God save the Queen'" at the Town Hall, Cambridge, in 1820: Journals, vol. 11, fol. 309 (11 May 1858). "The trial of Sacheverell produced an outbreak of public feeling scarcely less violent than those which we can ourselves remember in 1820, and in 1831": "Life and Writings of Addison," *Edin. Rev., 78* (July 1843), 233.

3. "Essay on William III," p. 469.

4. *Ibid.,* pp. 468-69.

5. It is evident in his analysis of postrevolutionary politics in France, particularly during the Napoleonic era. This appears in his unfinished "History of France, from the Restoration of the Bourbons to the Accession of Louis Philippe." See above, pp. 42-43, and chap. 2, n. 69.

6. "The Present Administration," *Edin. Rev., 46* (June 1827), 261-62.

7. *Ibid.,* pp. 261-62, 264.

8. *Ibid.,* pp. 260, 262-63. "The events of that year [1820] ought to impress one lesson on the mind of every public man, — that an alliance between the disaffected multitude and a large portion of the middling orders, is one with which no government can venture to cope, without imminent danger to the constitution" (p. 263).

9. TBM to Hannah Macaulay, 13 September 1831, Pinney, *Letters, 2,* 99-100.

10. Macaulay did not find Canning's opposition to parliamentary reform an objection to supporting the coalition ministry; see "Present Administration," p. 256.

11. "Hallam's *Constitutional History*," *Edin. Rev., 48* (September 1828), 100, 168–69.

12. *Ibid.*, p. 168.

13. "Since these men [the Puritans] could not be convinced, it was determined that they should be persecuted. Persecution produced its natural effect on them. It found them a sect: it made them a faction. To their hatred of the Church was now added hatred of the Crown. The two sentiments were intermingled; and each embittered the other." The policy, however, was ineffective. It "had been severe enough to irritate, but not severe enough to destroy. They had been, not tamed into submission, but baited into savageness and stubbornness." The result demonstrated "how persecution protects churches and thrones.... A systematic political opposition, vehement, daring, and inflexible, sprang from a schism about trifles, altogether unconnected with the real interest of religion or of the state": *History, 1,* 50–52, 68; "Hallam," *Edin. Rev., 48,* 111.

14. *History, 1,* 101

15. "Milton," *Edin. Rev., 42* (August 1825), 339–40. Macaulay's judgment of the Puritans was mixed. He viewed them with distaste, yet acknowledged their many qualities; they were fanatics, yet they helped achieve so much of which he approved, although perhaps for the wrong reasons: *ibid.,* pp. 338–42; *History,1,* 141, 168; *3,* 1396.

16. "Present Administration," *Edin. Rev., 46,* 260–61.

17. In part this was a matter of "diversities of temper, of understanding, and of interest, which are found in all societies.... Not only in politics, but in literature, in art, in science ... even in mathematics, we find this distinction. Everywhere there is a class of men who cling with fondness to whatever is ancient.... We find also everywhere another class ... quick to discern the imperfections of whatever exists, disposed to think lightly of the risks and inconveniences which attend improvements.... In the sentiments of both classes there is something to approve. But of both the best specimens will be found not far from the common frontier": *History, 1,* 87–88.

18. *Speeches,* pp. 371, 391, 385; Trevelyan, *Life, 2,* 280; *Mirror of Parliament, 21,* 1274 (17 April 1833). "The person about whom I am uneasy is the working man.... Is he to go without religious instruction altogether? That we should all think a great evil to himself, and a great evil to society": *Speeches,* p. 385. Catholicism also performed these politically useful purposes, but it was its moderate, tepid character that recommended Protestantism; indeed, it resembled Macaulay's version of nineteenth-century Whiggism — a moderate position between two equally unpalatable extremes. "There is a vast interval, in which the human mind, it should seem, might find for itself some resting place more satisfactory than either of the two extremes [of atheism and Catholicism]. At the time of the Reformation, millions found such a resting place": "Ranke's *History of the Popes*," *Edin. Rev., 72* (October 1840), 258. Protestantism, as compared to Catholicism, was also commendable because it encouraged economic and intellectual progress (pp. 252–53).

19. It had a civilizing influence in the provinces; it taught "more truth with less alloy of error than would be taught by those who, if she were swept away, would occupy the vacant space"; and, if destroyed, her present members would either neglect religion altogether or "fall under the influence of spiritual mountebanks, hungry for gain or drunk with fanaticism": "Church and State," *Edin. Rev., 69* (April 1839), 278–79. Macaulay thought that Bunyan should not have been buried in Westminster Abbey, since it was a religious edifice and Bunyan had denied the validity of the sacraments and had preached and written against the church: TBM to Hannah Trevelyan, 14 October 1854, Trinity College Library.

20. Journals, vol. 11, fol. 392 (26 November [1858]); letter, recipient not identified, n.d. [1844]: Pierpont Morgan Library. On the other hand, in commenting on Bacon's statement that "atheism did never perturb states," Macaulay wrote, "The French Revolution is cited as proof to the contrary. But I agree with Bacon": copy of TBM's notes in Bacon's *Works*, 10 vols. (London, 1819), note to vol. 2, p. 293, line 2: Trinity College Library.

21. Journals, vol. 5, fol. 161 (2 November [1852]); vol. 11, fols. 115–16 (11 May [1857]); fol. 89 (22 February [1857]). Macaulay delighted in describing the Muggletonian belief that "the sun is only 4 miles from the earth, because the sun is in heaven, and the tower of Babel was intended to reach to Heaven, and could not be more than 4 miles high": Diary of 7th earl of Carlisle, vol. 36 (3 July 1858). The times, he said, "require a Middleton," and he was eager to play the part: TBM to Napier, 23 February 1843, Napier Papers, BM, Add. MSS 34623, fol. 458. Conyers Middleton was a rationalist theologian and controversialist of the early eighteenth century.

22. *History, 5*, 2402; see also *1*, 71. On Exeter Hall, see *Speeches*, p. 377; also p. 325; *Hansard, 51*, 832 (29 January 1840); Journals, 4, fol. 179 (22 July [1851]).

23. Journals, vol. 11, fol. 202 (28 October [1857]); vol. 3, fol. 64 (30 October [1850]); TBM to Mrs. Hannah Trevelyan, 17 January 1864, Trinity College Library. The Tractarians would "hold the faith of Rome with the endowments of the English Church": *Hansard, 57*, 764 (31 March 1841). However, in 1850, when there was an outburst of "Protestant fury" in response to the papal claims to infallibility, a deputation unsuccessfully tried to persuade him to move what he thought an intolerant resolution at a public meeting: TBM to Mrs. Hannah Trevelyan, 15, 23, 30 November 1850, Trinity College Library.

24. *History, 4*, 2082. *Edinburgh Evening Post*, 28 July 1847, p. 2; 31 July 1847, pp. 2–3. Of course this was not the only issue; see Trevelyan, *Life, 2*, 130. Cockburn thought the defeat had nothing to do with Maynooth, but that "the truth is, that Macaulay . . . is not popular. He cares more for his history than for the jobs of his constituents, and answers letters irregularly, with a brevity deemed contemptuous; and above all other defects, he suffers severely from the vice of over-talking, and consequently of under-listening [to deputations]": *Journal of Henry*

Cockburn, being a continuation of the Memorials of His Time, 1831-1854
(Edinburgh, 1874), *2*, 158-59 (entry of 25 July 1846); see also pp.
191-92. Even Adam Black, Macaulay's election agent, said he "had a
provoking lack ... of ... accommodating flexibility.... He was too
honest to conceal any of his opinions, or to abstain from arguing in
support of them, instead of listening deferentially to objections, and
cautiously saying that he would give them his best consideration":
Memoirs of Adam Black, ed. Alexander Nicolson (Edinburgh, 1885), p.
145. For a report of a constituent who was a frustrated member of a
deputation (and one of Macaulay's successors as Member for Edinburgh),
see Charles Cowan, *Reminiscences* (privately printed, 1878), p. 209.
However, the religious issue appears to have been the most important; see
Donald Southgate, *The Passing of the Whigs, 1832-1886* (London:
Macmillan, 1962), p. 160. Macaulay was not unique; the general
election was fought on religious grounds, with Maynooth as the major
stimulant to religious feeling; see Norman Gash, *Reaction and Reconstruction in English Politics, 1832-1852* (Oxford: Clarendon Press,
1965), p. 98.

25. Journals, vol. 6, fols. 115-16 (19 July [1853]); *History, 5*, 2142.

26. Trevelyan, *Life, 1*, 260-61. Actually he did not even profess belief,
for he said only, "I am a Christian." Of course he also held that a political
meeting was no place for theological discussion. What it meant to him to
be a Christian perhaps is indicated by his having especially commended
this observation of Conyers Middleton: "If to *live strictly* and to *think
freely;* to practice *what is moral,* and to believe *what is rational,* be
consistent with the *sincere profession of Christianity,* then I shall always
acquit myself like one of its *truest Professors*": A. H. L. Munby,
Macaulay's Library, Glasgow University Publications (Glasgow: Jackson,
1966), p. 20. Even more can be inferred from his observation that
"Middleton was not more of a believer than Gibbon. Middleton was
Gibbon in holy orders": written (in 1834) in margin, at *1,* 91, of William
Field, *Memoirs of the Life, Writings, and Opinions of the Reverend
Samuel Parr* (London, 1828) (from the collection of Macaulay's books at
Wallington). On his reserve regarding his own religious convictions, see
Trevelyan, *Life, 2,* 44; Gladstone, *Gleanings, 2,* 284.

27. Diary of the 7th earl of Carlisle, vol. 26, fol. 27 (13 May 1851); vol.
35, fol. 51 (8 May 1857). Carlisle noted that "Macaulay's unphilosophical
anti-credulity always appears to me excessive," although he also had in
mind Macaulay's reactions to claims regarding ghosts, clairvoyance, and
mesmerism.

28. This passage is a marginal comment appearing opposite the eighth
line from the bottom of page 290 of volume 2 of Macaulay's copy of
Bacon, *Works* (London, 1819): Copy of Notes, Trinity College Library.
One can also see a reflection of his own views in this comment on the
Athenians: "As civilization advanced, the citizens of that famous republic
became still less visionary, and still less simple-hearted. They aspired to
know, where their ancestors had been content to doubt; they began to
doubt, where their ancestors had thought it their duty to believe":

"History," *Edin. Rev.*, *47* (May 1828), 335. Compare the passage in *History, 1,* 16: "English thinkers aspired to know, or dared to doubt, where bigots had been content to wonder and to believe."

29. *History, 2,* 980. His nephew said Macaulay "was fond of indicating observations on human character, and on the conduct of life, which have about them a perceptible flavour of autobiography": George Otto Trevelyan, *Marginal Notes by Lord Macaulay* (London, 1907), p. 14.

30. Gladstone, *Gleanings, 2,* 284. G. M. Trevelyan suggests that Macaulay probably never formulated his religious convictions to himself and that "the term 'agnostic,' in the stricter sense of that misused word, might have fitted him": *Sir George Otto Trevelyan, A Memoir* (London: Longmans, 1932), p. 15.

31. Diary of the 7th earl of Carlisle, vol. 22, fols. 7-8 (5 October 1849).

32. Margaret Knutsford, *Life and Letters of Zachary Macaulay* (London, 1900), p. 338. While still sixteen, Macaulay sent an anonymous letter to his father's journal in which he defended novel-reading: "Observations on Novel Reading," signed "Candidus," *Christian Observer, 15* (December 1816), 784-87. Referring to the late eighteenth century, Macaulay said, "The very name of novel was held in horror among religious people. In decent families which did not profess extraordinary sanctity, there was a strong feeling against all such works": "Madame D'Arblay," *Edin. Rev., 76* (January 1843), 569; see also p. 536.

33. F.A. Hayek, Introduction to Henry Thornton, *An Enquiry into the Nature and Effects of the Paper Credit of Great Britain* (London: Allen & Unwin, 1939; 1st ed., 1802), pp. 22-23; James Stephen, "The Clapham Sect," in *Essays in Ecclesiastical Biography* (London, 1872). After reading Stephen's essay when it was first published in 1844, Macaulay recalled "having known, as far as a boy can know men, all the people to whom it relates, and ... retaining the most lively impressions of their looks, voices, and manners": TBM to Napier, 3 July 1844, Napier Papers, BM, Add. MSS. 34624, fol. 499.

34. Knutsford, *Life and Letters of Zachary Macaulay,* pp. 252-55.

35. "The Life and Writings of Sir William Temple" *Edin. Rev., 68* (October 1838), 123. Macaulay ridiculed the Sabbatarian strictness of "the most rigid Pharisee in the Society for the Reformation of Manners"— an allusion to the Evangelicals: *History, 6,* 3004. At every opportunity he ridiculed Quakers; for example he wrote to his brother Henry (26 May 1824): "If you are inclined to turn Quaker yourself, I am sure, I have no objection. The drab will become you. And you have already the demure look—the sharp eye to the main-chance, and the coolness—aye, Hal, and, if I remember right, the obstinacy too, necessary for supporting the character. The whine of the meeting thou hast not yet acquired. But what of that? The Spirit can impart gifts even more miraculous": Pinney, *Letters, 1,* l96-97. He also said, "If the Quakers were more numerous, he would exempt them from toleration, on account of their refusal to defend their country": Diary of 7th earl of Carlisle, vol. 26, fol. 35 (27 May 1851). His analysis of Penn's character and conduct was so harsh that it drew heavy criticism from Quakers seeking to defend Penn's

reputation. Macaulay' historical judgment of Penn has been shown to be incorrect. Trevor-Roper has suggested that, in addition to hating Quakers, Macaulay found them uncongenial because they "were unpolitical, which to Macaulay was a fault." In the case of Penn, who became involved in politics, the fault was aggravated, as he was naive and, worse, on the wrong side. See H. R. Trevor-Roper, Introduction to Macaulay, *The History of England* (New York: Washington Square Press, 1968), pp. 33-35.

36. William H. Wickwar, *The Struggle for the Freedom of the Press, 1819-1832* (London: Allen & Unwin, 1928), pp. 36-37; Ernest Marshall Howse, *Saints in Politics* (London: Allen & Unwin, 1952), p. 120; Knutsford, *Life and Letters of Zachary Macaulay,* p. 361; *Christian Observer, 19* (February 1820), 139. *Part the First, of an Address to the Public, from the Society for the Suppression of Vice, instituted, in London, 1802. Setting forth, with a list of members, the utility and necessity of such an institution, and its claim to public support* (London, 1803), pp. 58, 98. Zachary was one of approximately 520 members in 1803 and one of approximately 260 in 1825; see *Address to the Public,* pp. 5-20, and *Society for the Suppression of Vice* (London, 1825), pp. 13-20. On Evangelicals and the Tory party see G. Best, "The Evangelicals and the Established Church in the Early Nineteenth Century," *Journal of Theological Studies,* n.s. *10* (April 1959), 76-77.

37. Wickwar, *Struggle for Freedom of the Press,* p. 82. The Society pointed to the connection between atheism and treason: *Address to the Public,* p. 29 n. Although Carlile had been prosecuted for blasphemous libel, Zachary thought of him as being also guilty of sedition, i.e., as a political offender. A record of young Macaulay's views on this subject survives. In 1831, with Carlile still facing prosecutions, he described a conversation "about prosecutions for blasphemy, — and about [Rev. Robert] Taylor, and [Richard] Carlisle [*sic*], and the Rotunda. I was surprised at the way in which we divided on the matter. Sydney [Smith], Tom Moore, and [George] Lamb, were for prosecution, — at least in extreme cases, — Rice and I against prosecuting in any case. I somewhat doubtingly — Rice quite warmly and decidedly": TBM to Hannah Macaulay, 14 June 1831, Pinney, *Letters, 2,* 43-44. In Parliament he also said he would "not defend the present law relative to blasphemy.... I think that every man ought to be at liberty to discuss the truth and falsehood of religion, but not to force upon the unwilling eyes and ears of others sights and sound which are insulting to them": *Mirror of Parliament, 21,* 1272 (17 April 1833).

38. Zachary Macaulay to Hannah More, 8 May 1819, in Knutsford, *Life and Letters of Zachary Macaulay,* p. 349.

39. *Ibid.,* p. 352. Zachary also advocated repressive views in the *Christian Observer.* Although he retired as editor in 1816, he was said to have written during these years the "Public Affairs" section (from which the passages below are taken): *Letters of Hannah More to Zachary Macaulay, Esq., Containing Notices of Lord Macaulay's Youth,* ed. Arthur Roberts (London, 1860), p. 188. There is agreement between views published in the *Christian Observer* and in Zachary's personal

correspondence. On Peterloo, see *Chr. Obs., 18,* 621-22 (September 1819). On the Six Acts, see *Chr. Obs., 18,* 819-23 (December 1819). "We cannot express too great an abhorrence of the wickedness of those who take advantage of this distress to excite a spirit of disaffection to the institutions and government of the country": *Chr. Obs., 18,* 482 (July 1819). "The impiety, audacity, and scurrility of some of these men [Wooler, Burdett, Hunt, Cobbett] is almost without a parallel. It is an indignity to the national character to witness the atrocious publications which issue from the seditious press, and the placards which disgrace the walls of our metropolis and large towns": *Chr. Obs., 18,* 560. See also R. Coupland, *Wilberforce* (Oxford, 1923), pp. 55, 414, 421.

40. "Essay on William III," p. 469. A similar combination of analysis of seventeenth-century developments with reflections on early nineteenth-century analogues is to be found in the *Edinburgh Review* essay (1828) reviewing Hallam's *Constitutional History,* which ends with the suggestion that his contemporaries faced alternatives similar to those that had been available in the time of Charles I.

CHAPTER 2. CONCILIATORY POLITICS

1. "History," *Edin. Rev., 47* (May 1828), 362-67, "On Mitford's History of Greece" (November 1824), *Misc. Wr., 1,* 178; *History, 1,* 2. Macaulay complained that "the most numerous class is precisely the class respecting which we have the most meagre information": *History, 1,* 406. Macaulay's use of ballads in the absence of conventional evidence is an example of his search for the makings of noiseless revolutions. "It was in rude rhyme that their [the common people's] love and hatred, their exultation and their distress found utterance. A great part of their history is to be learned only from ballads": *History, 1,* 410. From ballads, Macaulay said, "trifling as they might at first appear, the signs of the times might often be collected": *Hansard, 15,* 1329 (28 February 1833).

2. *History, 5,* 2386. Of course this is illustrative of Macaulay's conception of noiseless revolutions and not an accurate historical analysis. Also see *History, 6,* 2840, 2853, 2877-78.

3. *History, 1,* 18. Other examples of noiseless revolutions were changes in the state of knowledge due to the growth of new sciences; the growth of parliamentary power; the gradual disappearance of the distinction between executive and legislative powers; and the invention and increasing use of printing: "The London University," *Edin. Rev., 43* (February 1826), 326; *History, 1,* 230; "Lord Nugent's *Memorials of Hampden,*" *Edin. Rev., 54* (December 1831), 510.

4. *Speeches,* p. 8 (2 March 1831).

5. *History, 1,* 37.

6. *Speeches,* p. 78 (16 December 1831), and p. 91 (28 February 1832).

7. "Hallam," *Edin. Rev., 48* (September 1828), 169.

8. *Speeches,* pp. 79-80.

9. "Life and Writings of Sir William Temple," *Edin. Rev., 68* (October 1838), 152-53.

10. Trevelyan, *Life, 1,* 442. In 1828 he formulated the analogy in similar terms: "The conflict of the seventeenth century was maintained by the Parliament against the Crown. The conflict which commenced in the middle of the eighteenth century, which still remains undecided, and in which our children and grandchildren will probably be called to act or to suffer, is between a large portion of the People on the one side, and the Crown and the Parliament united on the other": "Hallam," *Edin. Rev., 48,* 165.

11. "The Earl of Chatham," *Edin. Rev., 80* (October 1844), 526. The public mind was apathetic; "both factions were gradually sinking deeper and deeper into repose" (p. 529); "The mutual animosity of the Whig and Tory parties had begun to languish after the fall of Walpole" (p. 549).

12. "Thackeray's *History of the Earl of Chatham*," *Edin. Rev., 58* (January 1834), 544; "Chatham," *Edin. Rev., 80,* 535; *Speeches,* p. 498 (21 March 1849). A sign of the end of destructive conflict was the applause for Blackstone's *Commentaries* during the third quarter of the century in places where, in the memory of some, books had been burned for arguing on behalf of limited and mixed monarchy: "Mackintosh," *Edin. Rev., 61* (July 1835), 322. "The great battle for our ecclesiastical and civil polity had been fought and won. The wounds had been healed. The victors and the vanquished were rejoicing together. Every person acquainted with the political writers of the last generation, will recollect the terms in which they generally speak of that time. It was a glimpse of a golden age of union and glory—a short interval of rest, which had been preceded by centuries of agitation, and which centuries of agitation were destined to follow": "Hallam," *Edin. Rev., 48,* 164; see also pp. 162-63.

13. "Chatham," *Edin. Rev., 80,* 529.

14. Edinburgh election speech, 14 July 1846, in Adam Black, "Notes on Lord Macaulay's Parliamentary Connection with Edinburgh," *Biographies,* p. xxxiv. In the preface to the edition of his *Speeches* (1854), he noted (p. vii) that he was writing in quiet times; but he recalled the "fierce contentions" of the times when the speeches were given and explained that they included "expressions which, when society was convulsed by political dissension, and when the foundations of government were shaking, were heard ... with sympathy," whereas "now that the passions of all parties have subsided," they might be thought intemperate.

15. "Chatham," *Edin. Rev., 80,* 538. "The Revolution produced a description of abuses that were unknown in the time of the Stuarts; and the Reform Act ... like the Reformation of the Church and the Revolution, produced some new, and aggravated some old, evils": *Hansard, 48,* 468 (18 June 1839). "Progress is the very thing which makes the reform absolutely necessary": *Speeches,* p. 25 (5 July 1831).

16. "Chatham," *Edin. Rev., 80,* 539. "Between the time when our Parliaments ceased to be controlled by royal prerogative and the time when they began to be constantly and effectually controlled by public opinion there was a long interval.... The rules which had been originally designed to secure faithful representatives against the displea-

sure of the sovereign, now operated to secure unfaithful representatives against the displeasure of the people.... The evil was not diminished, nay, it was aggravated, by that Revolution which freed our country from so many other evils. The House of Commons was now more powerful than ever as against the Crown, and yet was not more strictly responsible than formerly to the nation": *History, 4,* 1801-2. See also "Hallam," *Edin. Rev., 48,* 163-65; "Walpole's Letters to Sir Horace Mann," *Edin. Rev., 58* (October 1833), 242-44.

17. *Speeches,* pp. 54, 2, 11, 69, 61 (2 March, 10 October, 16 December 1831); "Hallam," *Edin. Rev., 48,* 168-69; "The Time was now [1831] come when they might attach to the Constitution the whole of the middle classes of England, who, though they loathed corruption, and writhed under oppression, felt as much interest in upholding the Constitution as the highest nobleman in the country": *Hansard, 5,* 711 (3 August 1831). Macaulay also argued that to sustain the legitimacy of private property it was necessary to eliminate the abuses connected with it: *Hansard, 16,* 1386-87 (1 April 1833).

18. "Hallam," *Edin. Rev., 48,* 169.

19. *Speeches,* p. 8 (2 March 1831). "Let the Legislature depend on those who boldly declared ... the danger of rejecting Reform, rather than upon the smooth-tongued Conservatives; the former, he contended, were the only true Conservatives": *Hansard, 12,* 856 (10 May 1832).

20. "History," *Edin. Rev., 47* (May 1828), 362; "Mitford," *Misc. Wr., 1,* 176.

21. "Mitford," *ibid.,* pp. 176-77, 277; "Machiavelli" *Edin. Rev., 45* (March 1827) 265.

22. *Speeches,* p. 77.

23. "History," *Edin. Rev., 47* (May 1828), 365-67. In contrast to these pleas, his own *History,* although it did not neglect the social and economic context of political events, was emphatically political. Even his famous Chapter 3 on the state of England in 1685 did not serve the purpose he ascribed to social history in the early essays on the nature of historical inquiry. On Chapter 3 see Peter Gay, *Style in History* (New York: Basic Books, 1974), pp. 117-18.

24. *Speeches,* pp. 18, 69 (2 March and 16 December 1831); "Hallam," *Edin. Rev., 48,* 169. There are passages in which Macaulay indicates that he is aware that concessions will be postponed, making it necessary that decisions about them be made in haste. Bacon said, "It were good ... that men in their innovations would follow the example of time itself, which indeed innovated greatly, but quietly and by degrees scarce to be perceived." Macaulay, in his marginal note to this passage, wrote, "In practice reforms are so strongly opposed, that when at last they are made it is under the operation of causes which make it impossible to act slowly and cautiously": against line 3, page 311 of volume 2 of Bacon, *Works* (London, 1819), copy of TBM's notes, Trinity College Library.

25. *Speeches,* p. 34.

26. "Hampden," *Edin. Rev., 54* (December 1831), 511. Compare his recommendations on Irish church policy: "This, Sir, is true policy. When

you give, give frankly. When you withhold, withhold resolutely. Then what you give is received with gratitude; and, as for what you withhold, men, seeing that to wrest it from you is no safe or easy enterprise, cease to hope for it, and, in time, cease to wish for it.... I well know that you will refuse to make it [concession] now. I know as well that you will make it hereafter.... You will make it when its effect will be not to appease, but to stimulate agitation. You will make it when it will be regarded, not as a great act of national justice, but as a confession of national weakness": *Speeches,* pp. 399, 401 (23 April 1845). See also "Burleigh and His Times," *Edin. Rev., 55* (April 1832), 294-95.

27. "Hampden," *Edin. Rev., 54,* 512. "But gratitude is not to be expected by rulers [such as James] who give to fear what they have refused to justice": *History, 3,* 1109. "Concessions, therefore, which would once have extinguished nonconformity, would not now [1689] satisfy even one half of the nonconformists": *History, 3,* 1398. "'I will make no concession,' he often repeated; 'my father made concessions, and he was beheaded'": *History, 2,* 719.

28. "The Present Administration," *Edin. Rev., 46* (June 1827), 265. "It was because the French aristocracy resisted reform in 1783, that they were unable to resist revolution in 1789.... They would not endure Turgot: and they had to endure Robespierre." Macaulay asked those who opposed reform to look to France, where one could still see "signs of a great dissolution and renovation of society.... And why were those haughty nobles destroyed with that utter destruction?... Because they had no sympathy with the people, no discernment of the signs of their time; because ... they refused all concession till the time had arrived when no concession would avail": *Speeches,* pp. 34, 50 (5 July and 20 September 1831). For a slight qualification see "Dumont's *Recollections of Mirabeau,*" *Edin. Rev., 55* (July 1832), 571.

29. *Hansard, 51,* 820-21 (29 January 1840); *15,* 261 (6 February 1833).

30. *Hansard, 15,* 260-61 (6 February 1833); *Mirror of Parliament, 16,* 1650 (9 March 1840); TBM to Margaret Trevelyan, 26 September 1849, Trinity College Library. He supported Peel's bill to provide for the use of Chelsea pensioners to restore order in the event of disturbances; when in office (as secretary for war) he had prepared a similar bill: *Hansard, 71,* 745-47(15 August 1843). When there were disturbances in the manufacturing districts, he was willing "to make examples of Oastler and some of that set." He was pleased when he heard that the Chartist leaders Stephens and O'Connor were likely to be jailed in connection with disturbances: Journals, vol. 1, fol, 283 (28 December, [1839]); fol. 319 (7 January, [1840]). After one Edward Oxford attempted to assassinate the queen, Macaulay thought "there must be no weak indulgence in such a case": Journal entry for 10 and 11 June 1849, vol. 1, unfol., in *Macaulay: Prose and Poetry,* ed. G. M. Young (London, Hart-Davis, 1952), p. 804. "The real statesman is he who, in troubled times, keeps down the turbulent without unnecessarily harassing the well-affected": "Barère's *Memoirs,*" *Edin. Rev., 79* (April 1844), 312. On the other

hand, he disapproved of the severity with which the Edinburgh radicals of the 1790s were punished: TBM to Napier, 10 August 1844: Napier Papers, BM, Add. MSS 34624, fols. 554-55. And with regard to the trial of Cartwright, Wooler, and others in 1820, Macaulay observed, "crime enough I think, though I do not know that I should have prosecuted them": marginal comment on page 199, volume 2, of William Field, *Memoirs of the Life, Writings, and Opinions of the Reverend Samuel Parr* (London, 1828) (in Macaulay's copy at Wallington).

31. *Hansard, 15*, 1326-27 (28 February 1833). Greville reported that at this time Macaulay said (to Denison) "that if he had had to legislate he would ... have suspended the laws for five years in Ireland, given the Lord-Lieutenant's proclamations the force of law, and got the D. of W[ellingto]n to go there": *The Greville Memoirs, 1814-1860*, ed. Lytton Strachey and Roger Fulford (London: Macmillan, 1938), *2*, 363.

32. "Hallam," *Edin. Rev., 48*, 169; *Speeches*, pp. 34-35.

33. *History, 1*, 54. In contrast, William IV did not place himself at the head of the reforming party. By allowing the Reform Bill to receive royal assent by commissioners, he gave "proof of his impotent enmity to his ministers and his people.... I fear—I fear—that he has entered on the path of Charles and Louis. He makes great concessions: but he makes them reluctantly and ungraciously. The people receive them without gratitude or affection. What madness! to give more to his subjects than any King ever gave, and yet to give in such a manner as to get no thanks!": TBM to Hannah and Margaret Macaulay, 8 June 1832, Pinney, *Letters, 2*, 124.

34. *Speeches*, p.34. For a similar distinction see Burke, "Speech on Conciliation with America," *The Works of the Right Honourable Edmund Burke*, 12 vols. (London, 1887), *2*, 136.

35. *Speeches*, p. 57. There would be "a resistance by no means amounting to rebellion, a resistance rarely amounting to any crime defined by the law, but a resistance nevertheless which is quite sufficient to obstruct the course of justice, to disturb the pursuits of industry, and to prevent the accumulation of wealth" (p. 59). He thought it unlikely that insurrection could succeed if there was a professional army: "Hallam," *Edin. Rev., 48*, 126-27; *History, 1*, 27, 35. But even with such an army there could be resistance on the Irish model. The evidence on the degree of his nervousness in 1831-32 is mixed, and there are even conflicting reports (compare *Hansard, 12*, 857 [10 May 1832] with *Mirror of Parliament, 18*, 1987; whereas the latter reports, "save the country ... from ruins," *Hansard* had him urge, "save [the] country ... from a disastrous convulsion ... from confusion and anarchy"). In March 1831 he was "certain of victory, and of victory without commotion"; yet in September he had "uneasy forebodings" and claimed to know "how terrible the danger is"; however, in the same letter in which this concern is revealed, he also indicated that nothing more was needed than the creation of peers to relieve the crisis: TBM to T. F. Ellis, 30 March 1831; TBM to Hannah Macaulay, 13 September 1831: Pinney, *Letters, 2*, 9, 99-100. A sister reported that he spoke of dangers and "prophecies that

blood will flow in this city before the end of the week"; but it should be noted that she also said of Macaulay that his "imagination you know often exaggerates evils": Margaret Macaulay to Henry Thatcher, 30 September 1831, Pinney, *Letters*, *2*, 99 n. 1. How much of this was momentary panic, how much considered judgment? Fear of imminent disturbances is evident in some of his letters written during the period of the Reform Bill crisis, but it is not a pervasive or recurring theme. In June 1832, a month after the final passing of the Reform Bill, he emphasized the peacefulness of the events: "We, too [like the French], fought a great battle, but it was with moral arms.... Not one crime committed, not one acre confiscated, not one life lost, not one instance of outrage or attack on the authorities or the laws": report of speech at Leeds, in Frederick Arnold, *The Public Life of Lord Macaulay* (London, 1862), p. 101. Macaulay was referring to the events of May 1832; of course, as an account of the entire crisis it would be inaccurate. His assessment some years later recalled the panic but denied that it had revolutionary implications: "a most fearful and sanguinary revolution it would have been in any other nation than this. That revolution was effected here without civil disorder, and without the effusion of blood; but unquestionably the passing of the bill was attended with much excitement and danger": *Hansard*, *48*, 475 (18 June 1839). Although Macaulay was concerned about revolution in the event that concessions were not made, his fear of imminent violence and revolutions arising out of the crisis of 1831-32 is greatly exaggerated in John Clive, *Macaulay: The Shaping of the Historian* (New York: Knopf, 1973), pp. 154-56, 171-76. It is worth noting Macaulay's distinction in this observation on the state of feeling in 1688: "There was doubtless much discontent in England: but the interval was immense between discontent and rebellion": *History*, *3*, 1091.

36. *History*, *3*, 1311-12.

37. *Speeches*, pp. 26, 500, 508.

38. *History*, *3*, 1398; see also *ibid.*, *1*, 66-67.

39. "Temple," *Edin. Rev.*, *68*, 118.

40. Journals, vol. 11, fols, 338, 358, 370 (30 June, 12 August, 30 September [1858]). Macaulay had been able to observe Cobbett in the House of Commons in 1833-34.

41. *Speeches*, pp. 62-63. "In every age the vilest specimens of human nature are to be found among demagogues"; *History*, *2*, 580.

42. Journals, vol. 6, fol. 161 (9 November [1853]). He added "There is not a line in Tom [Paine] that any sixth rate radical and infidel might not write who would stoop to write it."

43. For example, *History*, *2*, 564, 622, 624, 669, 890; *3*, 1136, 1176, 1206-7, 1212, 1214, 1318; *4*, 1746, 1771, 1817.

44. *History*, *3*, 1206.

45. For example, "Macaulay thinks torture under regulations not so absurd as it has been thought—but he does not recommend it": Diary of 7th earl of Carlisle, vol. 28, fol. 64 (7 May 1852). Carlisle thought him (and also Charles Austin) "rather too strongly for hanging": Diary, vol.

17, fol. 18 (10 March 1848). When the Union Society considered the question (4 December 1822), "Whether a severe code of criminal law leniently executed be preferable to a lenient code rigidly executed," he spoke on behalf of the severe code: *Laws and Transactions of the Union Society* (Cambridge, 1834), p. 24. On the death penalty, compare his Penal Code for India: Frederick Arnold, *The Public Life of Lord Macaulay* (London, 1862), p. 220.

46. Trevelyan, *Life, 2,* 361; TBM to Mrs. Hannah Trevelyan, 10 August 1857, Trinity College Library.

47. *History, 4,* 1811.

48. *History, 1,* 220-22; *5,* 2130-32; *6,* 2936. Compare *History, 2,* 559: "But no sophism is too gross to delude minds distempered by party spirit."

49. *History, 2,* 1035-36; *Misc. Wr., 1,* 250.

50. *Speeches,* p.36 (20 September 1831); *Hansard, 54,* 1357 (19 June 1840).

51. *Speeches,* pp. 28-29 (5 July 1831). "How is it that such men [demagogues], formed by nature and education to be objects of mere contempt, can ever inspire terror? How is it that such men, without talents or acquirements sufficient for the management of a vestry, sometimes become dangerous to great empires? The secret of their power lies in the indolence or faithlessness of those who ought to take the lead in the redress of public grievances": *Speeches,* p. 63 (10 October 1831).

52. *Hansard, 11,* 457 (19 March 1832).

53. *Hansard, 51,* 827-28, 830 (29 January 1840); *54,* 1355-56 (19 June 1840).

54. "Hallam," *Edin. Rev., 48,* 99. Macaulay often pointed out that Pitt was not a supporter of the doctrines celebrated in Pitt clubs: "The pretending disciples of Mr. Pitt ... have renounced every one of his principles": *Hansard, 72,* 1183 (19 February 1844). "A Pittite means, in the phraseology of the present day, a person who differs from Mr. Pitt on every subject of importance. There are, indeed, two Pitts, — the real and the imaginary": "Present Administration," *Edin. Rev., 46,* 249. "This mythical Pitt ...": "William Pitt," *Misc. Wr., 2,* 373.

55. *Hansard, 60,* 757 (21 February 1842); also *70,* 798, 803-4 (7 July 1843).

56. *Hansard, 72,* 1176 (19 February 1844).

57. Journals, vol. 9, fols. 259-61 (14 May [1856]).

58. Trevelyan, *Life, 2,* 9, 212; *Speeches,* pp. 375, 377, 508, 516.

59. "The Present Administration, "*Edin. Rev., 46,* 260, 263. One can find Macaulay offering the opposite judgment in his 1824 speech to the Anti-Slavery Society: "When was it ever known that the mere exposure of theoretical evils excited a people to rebellion, while they were enjoying comfort and personal security?... More appeals are made to their [i.e., the people of England's] passions in a week than to those of the West Indian Slaves in a year. Yet who lives in apprehension of rebellion? Who, except in times of temporary distress, expects even a riot? Who does not know that, while their rights of property, person, and conscience, are

protected by law, and while they are well fed and clothed, Cobbett may
write away his fingers, and Hunt may talk away his lungs in vain!":
*Report of the Committee of the Society for the Mitigation and Gradual
Abolition of Slavery throughout the British Dominions* (London, 1824),
p. 72. But this is a most unusual view for him.

60. "The Late Lord Holland," *Edin. Rev., 73* (July 1841), 560-61.
"The Tories acted after their kind. Instead of removing the grievance
they tried to put down the agitation": *ibid.*, p. 560.

61. "Horace Walpole," *Edin. Rev., 58* (October 1833), 234.

62. *Speeches*, pp. 506-7. Compare "Essay on William III" (1822):
"Each is the cause and the effect of its antagonist.... Anarchy in turn
generated tyranny. Tyranny had now again produced resistance and
revolution." "And so, in politics, it is the sure law that every excess shall
generate its opposite; nor does he deserve the name of a statesman who
strikes a great blow without fully calculating the effect of the rebound":
"Barère," *Edin. Rev., 79* (April 1844), 347.

63. *Speeches*, p. 29; *History, 1*, 88. There was the "madness of the
innovator and the madness of the alarmist": "Pitt," *Misc. Wr., 2*, 364.
There were the "enemies of all order and the enemies of all liberty":
Speeches, p.76.

64. "Hampden," *Edin. Rev., 54*, 542, 545. The word "animate"
appears in the corrected edition of Macaulay's *Critical and Historical
Essays;* it replaces the word "moderate," which was obviously inappropriate.

65. *History, 1*, 97, 99.

66. "Milton," *Edin. Rev., 42* (August 1825), 336. Macaulay in his
generous estimate of Cromwell put forth what for his time was a novel
interpretation. On the limitations placed on Cromwell by circumstances,
see also "Hallam," *Edin. Rev., 48*, 142-43, 145. Cromwell was a fanatic,
but his fanaticism never led him to an impractical undertaking, nor did it
confuse him (p. 144); yet the most blamable act of his life was the
execution of Charles (p. 147), which, however, Macaulay blamed on his
followers (see also *History, 1*, 107). "The coarse fanaticism ... concealed
the yet loftier genius of Cromwell [which was] destined to control a
mutinous army and a factious people, to abase the flag of Holland, and
arrest the victorious arms of Sweden, and to hold the balance firm
between the rival monarchies of France and Spain": "History," *Edin.
Rev., 47*, 362. However, it was not all praise. He was one of "the great
mixed Characters of ancient and modern times" (along with Alexander,
Caesar, Elizabeth, Peter, and Napoleon): TBM to Zachary Macaulay, 5
October 1822, Pinney, *Letters, 1*, 180. Cromwell's Irish policy "was
simple—strong, fierce, hateful, cruel; it might be comprised in one
word ... —extirpation": *Hansard, 72*, 1174 (19 February 1844). See
also "John Dryden," *Edin. Rev., 47* (January 1828), 1.

67. *History, 1*, 108-9, 115.

68. "Essay on William III," p. 469; "Present Administration," *Edin.
Rev., 46*, 265-66; "Mirabeau," *ibid., 55*, 555.

69. "The History of France, from the Restoration of the Bourbons to

the Accession of Louis Philippe," pp. 17, 28-29: Longman Archives at University of Reading. I am grateful to Longman Group Ltd. for permission to quote from this. The essay mainly deals with theNapoleonic regime and the brief restoration in 1814. Apparently it was never published or completed; all the same, at least part of what had been written was put into page proofs, which is what has survived. On the covers it was given the title "Fragments of a History of France." G. O. Trevelyan reported that the proofs had been found in the Spottiswoode printing office in about 1866, but they seem subsequently to have disappeared. The essay was intended for the Cabinet Cyclopaedia, edited by Dionysius Lardner, but it is not among the 133 volumes in the British Museum's books in this series. Macaulay initially thought of writing on French politics for the *Edinburgh Review*. About to set off for Paris in August 1830, he proposed "an article on the politics of France since the Restoration, with characters of the principal public men, and a parallel between the present state of France and that of England." Having the agreement of the editor, Macvey Napier, he turned down a proposal from Lardner that he write a book-length sketch of the Revolution, only to find that Napier had submitted to Brougham's demand that Brougham's own article on France be published instead of Macaulay's. Macaulay's annoyance led to his threat to stop contributing to the *Edinburgh Review*. In October 1830 he made an agreement with Lardner to write "an account of the political changes of France since the Restoration and of this late revolution for his Cabinet Cyclopaedia." Although he hoped to complete the book by Christmas 1830, he was still working on it as late as October 1831. Trevelyan, *Life, 1,* 155. TBM to Napier, 19 August, 16 September, 16 October 1830; 14 March, 29 October 1831: Pinney, *Letters, 1,* 281-82, 298-300, 311; *2,* 8, 107.

70. "History of France," pp. 50, 71. Macaulay noted that the republican party allied itself to the soldiers, in opposition to the monarchy: pp. 67-71. Although Napoleon's regime was a despotism that established order after the chaos of Revolution and was therefore counterrevolutionary, Macaulay recognized that in certain ways it also provided continuity with the Revolution. Thus, "though not a free government, [it] was a revolutionary government. He had derived his title from the revolution: his power ... had lasted just long enough to consolidate the work of the revolution; to fortify the new social system by an alliance with law, order, and religion.... In his person the revolution had assumed the character of legitimacy" (pp. 44-45). However, "If the plans of Napoleon had succeeded ... it is scarcely possible to estimate the amount of evil which he would have produced. He would have renewed, perhaps for centuries, the expiring lease of tyranny. He would have substituted for the feudal monarchy of the Bourbons a monarchy on the more simple pattern of the east.... A new generation would have grown up skillfully trained and broken in to slavery.... The government would have ... a vast official hierarchy ... with an oppressed people beneath and a solitary tyrant at the summit; and the human intellect would have languished" (p. 34).

71. *Ibid.,* pp. 55-62, 67-72.

72. "Mirabeau," *Edin. Rev., 55* (July 1832), 557–58, 560–61, 571; "Mackintosh," *Edin. Rev., 61,* 275–76. In the Cambridge Union he spoke (18 February 1823) in defense of the proposition that Mirabeau's political life was deserving of approbation; and (15 April 1823) in opposition to the proposal that foreign interference with the internal affairs of France in 1792 was justifiable: *Laws and Transactions of the Union Society,* pp. 25–27. See also "Mill's Essay on Government," *Edin. Rev., 49* (March 1829), 183; "Burleigh and His Times," *Edin. Rev., 55,* 277–78.

73. "Milton," *Edin. Rev., 42,* 331, 333; "Hallam," *Edin. Rev., 48,* 138; "Hampden," *Edin. Rev., 54,* 533. "The most just and salutary revolution must produce much suffering.... Even the wisest cannot, while it is still recent, weigh quite fairly the evils which it has caused against the evils which it has removed. For the evils which it has caused are felt; and the evils which it has removed are felt no longer": *History, 3,* 1318. "Though nobody supposed violence is good, what good cause has escaped being disfigured and injured by violence? The Christian religion itself ...": *Mirror of Parliament, 10,* 554 (13 December 1830). In his unfinished "History of France" he wrote, "The time of transition, even from a bad to a good government, is generally a time of greater misery than the time which precedes it. England was surely in a worse state during the civil war than while the star chamber sate [*sic*], and while the ship-money was exacted. France was in a worse state during the five years which followed the meeting of the states-general, than under madame de Pompadour, or madame du Barri" (pp. 47–48).

74. "Mirabeau," *Edin. Rev., 55,* 560; *History, 4,* 1533: "The violence of revolutions is generally proportioned to the degree of maladministration which has produced them. It is therefore not strange that the government of Scotland, having been during many years far more oppressive and corrupt than the government of England, should have fallen with a far heavier ruin. The movement ... was in England conservative, in Scotland destructive." "The violence of those outrages will always be proportioned to the ferocity and ignorance of the people: and the ferocity and ignorance of the people will be proportioned to the oppression and degradation under which they have been accustomed to live. Thus it was in our civil war": "Milton," *Edin. Rev., 42,* 331.

75. TBM to Zachary Macaulay, 5 October 1822, Pinney, *Letters, 1,* 179. The slavery question provoked another assertion that was made in the same spirit: "The fire of London has always been considered as a blessing, because it extinguished the seeds of the plague.... The political world, in the same manner, often derives great advantage from those fierce and destroying visitations, which lay in the dust for ever the dark and infected haunts where a great moral malady has fixed itself in irremediable malignity. Still we most earnestly desire that a change ... should be produced by the mildest means": "On West Indian Slavery," *Knight's Quarterly Magazine, 1* (1823), 93. Since his father was passionately opposed to both slavery and revolution, one wonders whether Macaulay was not trying to provoke him.

76. "History of France," p. 48.

77. *Ibid.*, p. 37; Journal Letter, [21-22 September 1830]: Pinney, *Letters, 1,* 305.

78. Trevelyan, *Life, 2,* 357-58; Journals, vol. 11, fol. 409 (29 December [1858]).

79. "Mirabeau," *Edin. Rev., 55,* 557. See also "Mackintosh," *Edin. Rev., 61,* 274-78.

80. "History of France," p. 50.

81. Diary of 7th earl of Carlisle, 3 April 1852; vol. 28, fol. 49.

82. Journal Letter, [21-22 September 1830]: Pinney, *Letters, 1,* 301, 305.

83. Journals, vol. 11, fol. 409 (29 December [1858]); "Essay on William III," p. 469. There is a passage where Macaulay describes 1688 as being comparable to the French Revolution: *Hansard, 11,* 458 (19 March 1832). But such a passage is not included in the *Mirror of Parliament, 17,* 1299 (19 March 1832).

84. "Present Administration," *Edin. Rev., 46,* 263; *Speeches,* pp. 469-70, 472, 475, 490, 505. "This strange and awful year is ending better than a few months ago there seemed reason to expect. England, Scotland, even Ireland, are quiet. In France and Germany the friends of order are getting the upper hand": TBM to Charles Macaulay, 27 November 1848, Booth Papers, University of London.

85. Journals, vol. 2, fols 358-59 (22 July [1850]) . Of course one cannot precisely draw a line marking the time when Macaulay felt less insecure about the foundations of society. Whereas he felt uneasy in April 1848, by November he was reassured: *History, 3,* 1311, n. 1. At the time of Louis Napoleon's coup he thought England "quite beyond the reach of infection now. The risk was something in 1848. But since 1848 we have become perceptibly wiser": Journals, vol. 4, fols. 318-19 (2 December [1851]). And the same confidence is evident in his judgment of Madame De Lieven's estimate of English conditions: "She calls this [Great] exhibition [of 1851] a bold—a rash experiment. She apprehends a terrible explosion—'You may get through it safe; and if you do you will give yourself more airs than ever.' And this woman is thought a political oracle in some circles. There is just as much chance of a revolution in England at present as of the falling of the moon": Journals, vol. 4, fols. 75-76 (1May [1851]). These observations indicate his prevailing mood; they do not mean he was never uneasy after 1851 or confident before.

CHAPTER 3. HISTORY AND CIVIL PRUDENCE

1. *History, 2,* 886-87. In the privacy of his journal Eldon is described more fully: "An old fool in everything but law. The utter poverty and wretchedness of his political views is amazing." "Finished [reading H. Turpin's] Ld. Eldon.... I think worse than ever of Eldon. He was a habitual liar, a hypocrite, a traitor to his confederates—altogether a thorough specimen of a canting greedy pettifogging Knave": Journals, vol. 2, fols. 173, 200-201 (16 December [1849], 10 January [1850]). The

two judgments are not inconsistent. Macaulay, describing the lawyer or judge, said that one who "witnessed the skill with which he analyses and digests a vast mass of evidence, or reconciles a crowd of precedents which at first sight seem contradictory, scarcely know him again when, a few hours later, they hear him speaking on the other side of Westminster Hall in his capacity of legislator. They can scarcely believe, that the paltry quirks . . . can proceed from the same sharp and vigorous intellect which had excited their admiration under the same roof, and on the same day": "Croker's Edition of Boswell's *Life of Johnson*," *Edin. Rev., 54* (September 1831), 31–32.

2. "Milton," *Edin. Rev., 42* (August 1825), 326; "Mackintosh," *Edin. Rev., 61* (July 1835), 283.

3. "Mill's Essay on Government," *Edin. Rev., 49* (March 1829), 161, 168.

4. *Ibid.*, pp. 166, 168–69, 186; "Utilitarian Theory of Government," *Edin. Rev., 50*, (October 1829), 112.

5. "Mill's Essay on Government," *Edin. Rev., 49,* 168, 186–87.

6. *Ibid.*, pp. 161, 186. Both Dr. Johnson and the legal profession provided examples. "How it chanced that a man [i.e., Dr. Johnson] who reasoned on his premises so ably, should assume his premises so foolishly, is one of the great mysteries of human nature. The same inconsistency may be observed in the schoolmen of the middle ages. Those writers show so much acuteness and force of mind in arguing on their wretched *data,* that a modern reader is perpetually at a loss to comprehend how such minds came by such *data*. Not a flaw in the superstructure of the theory which they are rearing, escapes their vigilance. Yet they are blind to the obvious unsoundness of the foundation. It is the same with some eminent lawyers. Their legal arguments are intellectual prodigies, abounding with the happiest analogies and the most refined distinctions. The principles of their arbitrary science being once admitted . . . these men must be allowed to be perfect masters of logic. But if a question arises as to the postulates on which their whole system rests, — if they are called upon to vindicate the fundamental maxims of that system which they have passed their lives in studying, these very men often talk the language of savages, or of children": "Croker's Boswell," *Edin. Rev., 54,* 31.

7. "Mill's Essay on Government," *Edin. Rev., 49,* 174; "Mackintosh," *Edin. Rev., 61,* 286. "If . . . we are to deduce the theory of government from principles of human nature, in arriving at which principles we have not taken into the account the manner in which men act when invested with the powers of government, then those principles must be defective. They have not been formed by a sufficiently copious induction": "Utilitarian System of Philosophy," *Edin. Rev., 49* (June 1829), 290.

8. "Utilitarian Theory of Government," *Edin. Rev., 50,* 109. Macaulay thought one ought not to be preoccupied with labels that concealed the variation in reality. In contrast to James Mill, his use of the language of class did not prevent him from recognizing the differentiation and variety of motive and outlook among those encompassed by a single label. For example, he was sensitive to the way mobility affected the composition of

social classes and the relations among them. He took note of the absence of exclusiveness in the aristocracy; the links between the nobility and the commonality; and "the salutary intermixture of classes." "Our democracy was, from an early period, the most aristocratic, and our aristocracy the most democratic in the world; a peculiarity which has lasted down to the present day, and which has produced many important moral and political effects": *History, 1,* 32-34. These observations suggest comparisons with Tocqueville. See Tocqueville, *Ancien Régime,* pt. II, chap. 9.

9. "Utilitarian Theory of Government," *Edin. Rev., 50,* 109.

10. *Ibid.,* p. 124; "Mill's Essay on Government," *Edin. Rev., 49,* 185. Macaulay described the reasoning of mathematicians in similar terms: "They are accustomed to look only for one species of evidence; a species of evidence of which the transactions of life do not admit. When they come from certainties to probabilities, from a syllogism to a witness, their superiority is at an end. They resemble a man who, never having seen any object which was not either black or white, should be required to discriminate between two near shades of grey. Hence, on questions of religion, policy, or common life, we perpetually see these boasted demonstrators either extravagantly credulous, or extravagantly sceptical [*sic*]": "The London University," *Edin. Rev., 43* (February 1826), 329. Referring to Macaulay's attack, J. S. Mill said his father "felt it keenly at the time, but with a quite impersonal feeling, as he would have felt anything that he thought unjustly said against any opinion or cause which was dear to him": J. S. Mill, Introduction to *Analysis of the Human Mind* by James Mill (London, 1869), p. xvii. James Mill at the time said the *Edinburgh Review* "has not fought with very formidable weapons. It has made its best use of stink-pots, but I am not much the worse for them ...; the empty-headed coxcomb ... only abuses what he does not understand": James Mill to Etienne Dumont, 13 July 1829, Bibliothèque publique et universitaire, Geneva. Mill did not reply to Macaulay, at least not directly and immediately; however, see Alexander Bain, *James Mill* (London, 1882), pp. 225-33. Macaulay's critique had a powerful influence on J. S. Mill's intellectual development: J. S. Mill, *Autobiography,* World's Classics ed. (London, 1958), pp. 133-36. "The *Logic* ... was destined to take a different course. Its future was to be moulded by Macaulay's criticism of his father's *Essay on Government*": Oskar A. Kubitz, *Development of John Stuart Mill's "System of Logic,"* Illinois Studies in the Social Sciences, *18,* nos. 1-2 (Urbana, March-June 1932), 31; see also pp. 31-37.

11. *History, 3,* 1277. "We must remember that arguments are constructed in one way, and governments in another": *History, 4,* 1978.

12. "Hallam," *Edin. Rev., 48* (September 1828), 100.

13. *History, 3,* 1261; *4,* 1711.

14. "Life and Writings of Sir William Temple," *Edin. Rev., 68* (October 1838), 118; "Hallam," *Edin. Rev., 48,* 99. Of course, some of his contemporaries were doctrinaire because of religious views; see Macaulay's pleas for flexibility and his complaints about the uncompro-

mising politics of the Scottish Dissenters: J. B. Mackie, *Life of Duncan McLaren* (London, 1888), *1*, 212-13, 217, 219-20, 249-50, 257-59, 266.

15. "Utilitarian Theory of Government," *Edin. Rev., 50,* 124; "Mill's Essay on Government," *Edin. Rev., 49,* 160.

16. *Autobiography,* World's Classics ed., p. 91.

17. "Mill's Essay on Government," *Edin. Rev., 49,* 160; "Utilitarian System of Philosophy," *ibid.,* pp. 275, 279, 295-96, 298-99.

18. "The Present Administration," *Edin. Rev., 46* (June 1827), 261-63; Trevelyan, *Life, 1,* 228; see also above, p. 12. Macaulay was most worried by the potential danger of the Benthamite Radicals in 1827; yet even in 1829, when he had "no apprehensions of danger to the institutions of this country from the Utilitarians," he also said, "Some of them have, however, thought fit to display their ingenuity on questions of the most momentous kind, and on questions concerning which men cannot reason ill with impunity": "Utilitarian System of Philosophy," *Edin. Rev., 49,* 275, 298.

19. There was also a personal dimension to the criticism, at least to its bitterness, although Macaulay evidently began working on the critique before this consideration became relevant. His sister Margaret reported that "his articles against Mr. Mill he wrote because he had heard that Mr. Mill had said on hearing something of it, 'What! Macaulay—I will crush him to atoms.' He [Macaulay] said to-day, 'I always forgive them as soon as I have taken my revenge, I have quite forgiven Mill for what he said'": (entry of 27 November 1831): [Margaret Macaulay], *Recollections by a Sister of T. B. Macaulay* (1834) (London: Privately printed, 1864), pp. 59-60. "In discipleship or reaction [to the Utilitarians] no young mind of the thirties could escape their influence": G. M. Young, *Victorian England: Portrait of an Age,* 2d ed. (London: Oxford University Press, 1964), p. 8.

20. J. S. Mill, *Autobiography,* World's Classics ed., pp. 64-65: "The effect he [Charles Austin] produced on his Cambridge contemporaries deserves to be accounted an historical event; for to it may in part be traced the tendency towards Liberalism in general, and the Benthamic and politico-economic form of it in particular, which showed itself in a portion of the more active-minded young men of the higher classes from this time [early 1820s] to 1830.... Through him I became acquainted with Macaulay." F. D. Maurice recalled that when he first went to Cambridge in 1825, "Among the younger and cleverer undergraduates of the day, especially in Trinity, Benthamism was the prevalent faith"; during the late twenties, however, anti-Utilitarianism became fashionable: R. Robson, "Trinity College in the Age of Peel," *Ideas and Institutions of Victorian Britain: Essays in Honour of George Kitson Clark,* ed. R. Robson (London: Bell, 1967), p. 327 and n. 3.

21. Trevelyan, *Life, 2,* 353. Austin is recalled by John Moultrie as one for whom

> ... truth deduced
> By logical conclusion, close, severe,

> From premises incontrovertible —
> This was the mistress of his fond desire —
> His first, his only love;
>
> .   .   .   .
>   . . . in all things he appear'd
> A strict utilitarian; —yet the Man
> Was nobler than his creed . . . .

"The Dream of Life," *The Dream of Life; Lays of the English Church; And Other Poems* (London, 1843), 94–95.

22. [J. S. Mill], "Mr. [James] Mill," in Edward Lytton Bulwer, *England and the English* (London, 1836; 1st ed., 1833), 2, 326. Macaulay for a brief period had taken part in the London Debating Society in which J. S. Mill and several of James Mill's disciples had a prominent part. Macaulay alluded to what he may have found there when referring to such slogans as the social contract and the greatest-happiness principle: "Both the one expression and the other sound very well in debating clubs; but in the real conflicts of life, our passions and interests bid them stand aside and know their place": "Utilitarian System of Philosophy," *Edin. Rev., 49,* 295. It is most probable that Macaulay's articles were responsible for the discussion on 8 January 1830 in the London Debating Society of the question, "That the Utilitarian System of Philosophy is pernicious and absurd" ['Utilitarian' is misprinted 'Unitarian' and corrected by an unidentified hand]: *Fourth Supplement to the Laws and Transactions of the London Debating Society* (London, 1831), pp. 12–13.

23. "Mill's Essay on Government," *Edin. Rev., 49,* 185.

24. "Utilitarian System of Philosophy," *Edin. Rev., 49,* 275.

25. "Mitford," *Misc. Wr., 1,* 160–61. When preparing an antislavery speech for a Union debate in 1823, Macaulay studied Mill (presumably his *Encyclopaedia Britannica* article "Colony") for arguments on the economic dimensions of the issue: TBM to Zachary Macaulay, 4 January 1823, Pinney, *Letters, 1,* 183–84.

26. "Mitford," *Misc. Wr.,* 160–62. For a discussion of Macaulay's opinions on democracy, see above, pp. 125–36.

27. While in India as a member of the Governor-General's Council (1834–38) Macaulay drafted a penal code for India. Indian affairs provided an occasion for reconciliation. Macaulay's appointment was supported by Mill (in his capacity as an official of the East India Company). They dined together amicably; Macaulay publicly praised Mill's *History of British India,* saying that, although not free from faults, it was the greatest historical work in English since Gibbon; and he professed himself a sincere mourner on hearing of Mill's death in 1836: Trevelyan, *Life, 1,* 311, 324, 343, 421; T. F. E[llis], Preface, *Misc. Wr., 1,* ix–xiii; *Hansard, 19,* 513 (10 July 1833); "Mackintosh," *Edin. Rev., 61,* 286–87. See also Eric Stokes, *The English Utilitarians and India* (Oxford: Clarendon Press, 1959), pp. 184–233.

28. "Utilitarian System of Philosophy," *Edin. Rev., 49,* 274; "Mirabeau," *Edin Rev., 55* (July 1832), 552–53; *Speeches,* p. 533 (1 June

1853); C. D. Dharker, *Lord Macaulay's Legislative Minutes* (London: Oxford, 1946), pp. 140-41. In various places Macaulay ranked Bentham with Galileo, Locke, and Adam Smith; and since he also thought of Bacon as a founder of the science of legislation, presumably Bentham was to be ranked with him as well: "Lord Bacon," *Edin. Rev., 65* (July 1837), 104. *History, 3,* 1389; *Misc. Wr., 2,* 71 (which was written soon after Bentham's death; the second paragraph eulogizes him). A passage in the second of the articles criticizing James Mill (*Edin. Rev.,* "Utilitarian System of Philosophy," *49,* 278) suggests the possibility that Macaulay had met Bentham. All his praise was withdrawn in 1849; after reading Bowring's biography of Bentham, Macaulay, using one of his favorite adjectives, recorded his judgment: "Trash—by a trashy man and about a trashy man—How Bentham ever imposed on me at all I cannot now understand; and yet he imposed on me less than on any other person, I think, who entered life at the same time with me and in the same circumstances. The truest words that he uttered are those which he used, as Bowring tells us, to repeat in old age

> An old old driveller am I,
> Which nobody nobody can deny.

I only wish that I had spared James Mill more and used the whipcord more unsparingly against old Jeremy": Journals, vol. 2, fol. 119 (21 October [1849]). Yet Macaulay went on reading Bentham and about him: Journals, vol. 11, fols. 28, 99 (27 July [1856]; 27 March [1857]). He also praised him in the speech of 1 June 1853.

29. "Mackintosh," *Edin. Rev., 61,* 281-82; for other examples of his use of the language of science see "Mitford" (1824), *Misc. Wr., 1,* 160, and "History," *Edin. Rev., 47* (May 1828), 353; "Present Administration," *Edin. Rev., 46,* 247.

30. *History, 1,* 396-98. All the books of philosophers known in the Middle Ages "were not worth a page of the Novum Organum"; Bacon was "the prince of all philosophers": *Speeches,* pp. 463, 464.

31. "Lord Bacon," *Edin. Rev., 65,* 92, 87-94.

32. *Ibid.,* pp. 73-75, 79. Macaulay was highly critical of Temple's part in the controversy over the comparative merits of ancients and moderns: "Temple," *Edin. Rev., 68,* 180-84.

33. "Bacon," *Edin. Rev., 65,* 80. "To make men perfect was no part of Bacon's plan. His humble aim was to make imperfect men comfortable" (p. 78). The inadequacy of Macaulay's defense of Bacon is revealed in the passage in which he identifies the "object [of Baconian philosophy as being] . . . the good of mankind, in the sense in which the mass of mankind always have understood, and always will understand the word *good*" (p. 73). He was heavily criticized. Gladstone rejected Macaulay's neglect of Aristotle and his depreciation of the intellectual enterprise in which the ancients were engaged, and he called Macaulay's characterizations of the ancients "really outrageous exaggerations": *Gleanings, 2,* 307-13. Whereas Macaulay eulogized Bacon in connection with the growth of the scientific outlook, he was severely critical of his politics and

character. This part of the article also provoked a reply, including a two-volume defense of Bacon against the accusations of corruption, servility, ingratitude, and ambition: James Spedding, *Evenings with a Reviewer, or Macaulay and Bacon* (London, 1881; privately printed in 1848).

34. "Bacon," *Edin. Rev., 65,* 82-83. "The sciences are always in a state of progression . . .; the alterations made by a modern editor in an old book on any branch of natural or political philosophy are likely to be improvements. Many errors have been detected by writers of this generation [an allusion to Bentham in his *Defense of Usury*] in the speculations of Adam Smith": "Croker's Boswell," *Edin. Rev., 54,* 15.

35. "Mill's Essay on Government," *Edin. Rev., 49,* 188-89. "Hence it is, that, in generalization, the writers of modern times have far surpassed those of antiquity": "History," *Edin. Rev., 47* (May 1828), 358.

36. *History, 3,* 1388-89. "The science of Government was essentially an experimental science—that is, that its conclusions were so wholly the creatures of experience, and its application so dependent upon ever-changing circumstances, that nought could be predicated of them of universal applicability. Political doctrines were not like the axioms and definitions of the geometer—of intrinsic truth, wholly uninfluenced by time and place; [they] . . . were necessarily as changing as the circumstances on which all experience was founded. . . . It was observed by [Lord Plunkett], that history not read in a philosophical manner was merely an old almanack": *Hansard, 11,* (19 March 1832), 451.

37. "Mill's Essay on Government," *Edin. Rev., 49,* 161; "Utilitarian Theory of Government," *Edin. Rev., 50,* 101-2.

38. *Speeches,* pp. 394-96; see also *Hansard,* 70, 808-9 (7 July 1843).

39. *Hansard, 91,* 1019-20 (19 April 1847).

40. Duncan Forbes, *The Liberal Anglican Idea of History* (Cambridge: At the University Press, 1952), p. 126; reference is made to Leslie Stephen, *English Utilitarians* (London, 1900), *2,* 86, where a similar observation is made. The enthusiasm for the idea of science led Macaulay to label as general laws what were in fact maxims; see above, pp. 66-67. On the physician metaphor, see "Mill's Essay on Government," *Edin. Rev., 49,* 189; "Utilitarian System of Philosophy," *Edin. Rev., 49,* 285, 290; *History, 3,* 1351; "Hallam," *Edin. Rev., 48,* 98, where comparison is to the anatomist; "Mackintosh," *Edin. Rev., 61,* 282; and *Speeches,* p. 396, where he asks, "are not the principles of experimental philosophy the same in politics as in medicine?"

41. "History," *Edin. Rev., 47,* 340-41; "Utilitarian System of Philosophy," *Edin. Rev., 49,* 290-91.

42. *History, 3,* 1389.

43. *History, 2,* 720; also see *Speeches,* pp. 172, 232. Hallam judged according to the "maxims of civil prudence": Thomas P. Peardon, *The Transition in English Historical Writing, 1760-1830* (New York, 1933), p. 211.

44. "Mirabeau," *Edin. Rev., 55,* 560-61; see also pp. 562-63. "The violence of revolutions is generally proportional to the degree of the

maladministration which has produced them"; thus the Revolution of 1688 was more destructive in Scotland than in England: *History, 4,* 1533. See also above, chap. 2, n. 74.

45. *History, 3,* 1182.

46. "Hallam," *Edin. Rev., 48,* 152; *History, 1,* 168. Also "... the general law of human nature. Both in individuals and in masses violent excitement is always followed by remission, and often by reaction": "Hastings," *Edin. Rev., 74* (October 1841), 249. See also "Mackintosh," *Edin. Rev., 61,* 288–89, 301. Referring to the anti-Puritan reaction of the Restoration, he said that "extreme relaxation is the natural effect of extreme restraint, and that an age of hypocrisy is, in the regular course of things, followed by an age of impudence": *History, 1,* 392.

47. "Mirabeau," *Edin. Rev., 55,* 559.

48. In 1848 he said that the new government in Paris was "refuting the doctrines of political economy in the way that a man would refute the doctrines of gravitation by jumping from the Monument": Diary of 7th earl of Carlisle, vol. 17, fol. 11b (4 March 1848).

49. "For in the political, as in the natural world, there may be an equality of momentum between unequal bodies, when the body which is inferior in weight is superior in velocity": *History, 4,* 1982. "In the Italian States, as in many natural bodies, untimely decrepitude was the penalty of precocious maturity": "Machiavelli," *Edin. Rev., 45* (March 1827), 267–68. See also "Hallam," *Edin. Rev., 48,* 164–65, and "Southey," *Edin. Rev., 50* (January 1830), 562–63. Yet on at least one occasion he denied that he was formulating a general law: "Ranke," *Edin. Rev., 72* (October 1840), 258.

50. "History," *Edin. Rev., 47,* 341, 358; "Machiavelli," *Edin. Rev., 45,* 289; Trevelyan, *Life, 1,* 399.

51. *Speeches,* pp. 172–73. Macaulay described one instance in which an undesirable policy was defended with what was alleged to be "a fundamental principle of political science": *History, 6,* 2736.

52. "Hallam," *Edin. Rev., 48,* 111; see also "Mackintosh," *Edin. Rev., 61,* 315.

53. *Speeches,* p. 8.

54. "Mackintosh," *Edin. Rev., 61,* 283–84.

55. *History, 1,* 22–23. Another example of history being misused for partisan purposes was provided by the controversy in 1697 over the standing army. "History was ransacked": *History, 6,* 2736–37.

56. "History," *Edin. Rev., 47,* 359. "Hume, from whose fascinating narrative the great mass of the reading public are still contented to take their opinions, hated religion so much, that he hated liberty for being allied with religion—and has pleaded the cause of tyranny with the dexterity of an advocate, while affecting the impartiality of a judge": "Milton," *Edin. Rev., 42,* 325.

57. "History," *Edin. Rev., 47,* 360–61; "Mitford," *Misc. Wr., 1,* 174.

58. *History, 2,* 886–87. Whatever he might think of Macaulay's practice, Butterfield could hardly object to this statement; see above, pp. 110–12.

59. "Mackintosh," *Edin. Rev.*, *61*, 282-84.

60. *History*, *1*, 22.

61. "History," *Edin. Rev.*, *47*, 361; however, compare p. 340, where Macaulay is quite condescending toward Thucydides. Only later did he fully revise his judgment: "The ancient writers, now that I go back to them at thirty-four ... having seen something of the world, having been a spectator and an actor in politics, appear quite new to me. I find in such a writer as Thucydides or Demosthenes, ten thousand things worthy of notice which never struck me in my college days.... I did not much like Thucydides formerly. I have now no hesitation in pronouncing him the greatest historian that ever lived": TBM to Richard Sharp, 11 February 1835, Munby Papers, Trinity College Library.

CHAPTER 4. THE POLITICAL TEACHING OF THE *History*

1. "Hallam," *Edin. Rev.*, *48* (September 1828), 97.

2. "History," *Edin. Rev.*, *47* (May 1828), 340.

3. *Ibid.*, p. 338; see also "Burleigh and His Times," *Edin. Rev.*, *55* (April 1832), 272.

4. "Hallam," *Edin. Rev.*, *48*, 97.

5. "History," *Edin. Rev.*, *47*, 365. These passages, combined with his professed wish to make his writing popular and "amusing," have led critics to assume that this was an end in itself for Macaulay and that history, for him, was only a branch of literature. For example, see R. L. Schuyler, "Macaulay and His History—a Hundred Years After," *Political Science Quarterly*, *63* (June 1948) 191. This assumption makes it difficult to appreciate his rhetorical purpose, to which literary qualities were subordinated.

6. "History," *Edin. Rev.*, *49*, 367. History "impresses general truths on the mind by a vivid representation of particular characters and incidents": "Hallam," *Edin. Rev.*, *48*, 96. James Fitzjames Stephen recognized that "the greater part of Lord Macaulay's opinions on politics are characteristically embodied in his narratives": *Essays by a Barrister* (London, 1862), p. 100.

7. "History," *Edin. Rev.*, *47*, 331, 339, 352; "Hallam," *Edin. Rev.*, *48*, 97. The distinction between philosophy and poetry in the context of an evolutionary theory of literature that is attributed to Macaulay is interestingly discussed in Ronald Weber, "Singer and Seer: Macaulay on the Historian as Poet," *Papers on Language and Literature*, *3*, no. 3 (Summer 1967), 210-19, and in René Wellek, *A History of Modern Criticism: 1750-1950*, vol. 3: *The Age of Transition* (London: Cape, 1966), pp. 126-31.

8. "History," *Edin. Rev.*, *47*, 331. This passage does not justify sneering at Macaulay's arrogance and vanity, for it is to be understood in the context of his early writings about history, which were written twenty-one years before he published the first two volumes of the *History* and about ten years before he planned an ambitious historical work. See Weber,

"Singer and Seer," p. 218, where it is observed that for Macaulay history is superior to any kind of imitative literature.

9. "History," *Edin. Rev., 47,* 331-34, 353, 358-61. For a later change in his estimate of Thucydides see chap. 3, n. 61.

10. H. R. Trevor-Roper, Introduction to Macaulay, *History of England* (New York: Washington Square Press, 1968), p. xli; "Mackintosh," *Edin. Rev., 61* (July 1835), 266.

11. Journals, vol. 2, fol. 208 (18 January 1850).

12. J. L. Laughton, *Memoirs of the Life and Correspondence of Henry Reeve* (London, 1898), *1,* 342. His portraits and character sketches are realistic, not necessarily correct. Since Bagehot it has been customary to criticize Macaulay for being psychologically simplistic and insensitive. Occasionally, however, he is credited with "psychological insight": see J. P. Kenyon, Introduction to Halifax, *Complete Works* (Harmondsworth: Penguin, 1969), p. 23.

13. George Levine, *The Boundaries of Fiction: Carlyle, Macaulay, Newman* (Princeton: Princeton University Press, 1968), pp. 81-82; Gladstone, *Gleanings, 2,* 338-39. For sensitive and illuminating discussions of Macaulay's style, see Jane Millgate, *Macaulay* (London: Routledge, 1973), passim, and John Clive, *Macaulay: The Shaping of the Historian* (New York: Knopf, 1973), passim.

14. Given this understanding of Macaulay, one must disagree with W. A. Madden's argument that in Macaulay there is a radical separation of past and present, that Macaulay retreated to a remote, "unreal" past that had "little to do" with the historical progress that created the Victorian present. Far from trying "to draw his readers' attention away from the immediate context," including fears and hopes of revolution, as Madden argues, it was Macaulay's purpose to point to the interconnections between past and present and to the immediate relevance of past to present. See W. A. Madden, "Macaulay's Style," in *The Art of Victorian Prose,* ed. George Levine and William Madden (New York: Oxford, 1968), pp. 141, 149-50. I would also disagree with George Levine's view that Macaulay was complacent and that he "deliberately anaesthetized himself against the present": *The Boundaries of Fiction,* pp. 81, 87.

15. This view disagrees with Trevor-Roper's suggestion that Macaulay, in the tradition of C. J. Fox, Mackintosh, and Hallam, merely implemented a Holland House plan to establish a Whig response to Hume: H. R. Trevor-Roper, Introduction to Macaulay, *Critical and Historical Essays* (London: Collins, 1965), pp. 11-15. Another edition of Mackintosh's book was published a year earlier, in 1834, as *History of the Revolution in England in 1688: Comprising a View of the Reign of James II: From His Accession, to the Enterprise of the Prince of Orange, by the Late Right Hon. Sir James Mackintosh; and Completed, to the Settlement of the Crown, by the Editor* [William Wallace]. *To which is prefixed, A Notice of the Life, Writings, and Speeches of Sir James Mackintosh* (London, 1834). The edition of 1835 was published without Wallace's continuation and biographical notice because of complaints about them, which stemmed in large part from Macaulay's review of the 1834 edition.

On his return from India Macaulay faced the possibility of a duel with Wallace because of the severity of his review. Macaulay refused an offer from Lardner to complete Mackintosh's manuscript: Dionysius Lardner to John Allen, 15 October 1832, Holland Papers, BM, Add. MSS 52190, unfol. In the end Lardner was not the publisher. When reprinted in *The Miscellaneous Works of the Right Honourable James Mackintosh,* edited by R. J. Mackintosh, 3 vols. (London, 1846), as *Review of the Causes of the Revolution of 1688,* the text of Mackintosh's history was altered. Chapter organization was changed, and chapter 11 was eliminated, part of it being printed separately (at *1,* 541 ff.). Mackintosh's *History of England,* which at the time of his death he had carried to 1536, is less relevant than his *Reign of James II* for a comparison with Macaulay.

16. Macaulay said that the death of George IV would be the best halting place, but he clearly thought of the Reform Act as the culmination: Trevelyan, *Life, 1,* 442. Sumner to Hillard, 1 October 1838, in Edward Pierce, *Memoirs and Letters of Charles Sumner* (London, 1878), *1,* 364. With the passage of years he altered his goal, and in 1857 he saw the accession of the House of Hanover as his "extreme goal": see *What Did Macaulay Say about America?,* ed. H. M. Lydenberg (New York Public Library, 1925), p. 23. In the last, posthumously published volume of the *History* there is a statement about William III that Macaulay may have written with his own *History* in mind. He wrote that William in 1702 (the year of his death) "felt that his time was short, and grieved, with a grief such as only noble spirits feel, to think that he must leave his work but half finished": *History, 6,* 3000.

17. On lesser questions their views are not identical. They agree on Jeffreys' character and role, but Mackintosh is more generous in his judgment of Jeffreys' intellect. Mackintosh thought the birth of the Prince of Wales in 1688 not spurious and attributed the widespread belief that it was to a weakness of human nature; Macaulay, on the other hand, while hesitantly agreeing about the birth, was puzzled by James's failure to provide reliable witnesses to the event. Mackintosh's analysis of James II — his policy and his character — was more complex than Macaulay's.

18. Mackintosh, *Reign of James II* (1835), pp. 162–64. Macaulay, *History, 2,* 876–78; "Southey's Edition of the *Pilgrim's Progress,*" *Edin. Rev., 54* (December 1831), 457–58; *Misc. Wr., 2,* 227, 230–31, 233. See also Macaulay's portrait of the enthusiast, written in the style of the seventeenth-century character literature, but which appears to use Bunyan as a model: "Ranke's *History of the Popes,*" *Edin. Rev., 72,* (October 1840), 248–49.

19. *Reign of James II,* p. 26; see also p. 350. Macaulay, *History, 2,* 526, 528.

20. *Reign of James II,* p. 168; Macaulay, *History, 4,* 1991–95; "Mackintosh," *Edin. Rev., 61,* 270.

21. *History, 3,* 1311; see also "Mackintosh," *Edin. Rev., 61,* 289.

22. *Reign of James II,* pp. 4, 303, 320, 345. Of course Macaulay was aware of the context of Continental politics as it affected William, but his

purpose in writing the *History* led him to subordinate this aspect of the situation. Consequently, Mackintosh's more balanced view is probably more in keeping with modern scholarship as represented by Godfrey Davies, "The Treatment of Constitutional History in Macaulay's *History of England*," *Huntington Library Quarterly, 2* (1938-39), 197. See also John Carswell, *The Descent on England* (London: Barrie & Rockliff, 1969); Sir Charles Firth, *A Commentary on Macaulay's "History of England"* (London: Cass, 1964; 1st ed., 1938), p. 354. Yet compare Macaulay, "Essay on William III," p. 469; *History, 5,* 2216.

23. "Essay on William III" (1822), p. 469.

24. Macaulay was quite sensitive to the difficulties of revolutionary regimes in consolidating their power. "Nothing is harder than to overturn an old government, and nothing easier than to overturn a new one": "The History of France, from the Restoration of the Bourbons to the Accession of Louis Philippe," p. 18: Longman Archives at the University of Reading. I am grateful to Longman Group Ltd. for permission to quote from this. Macaulay often analyzed opposition to new regimes as counterrevolutions; see, for example, *History, 3,* 1318; *5,* 2123, 2337-38; "Lord Mahon's *War of the Succession*," *Edin. Rev., 26* (January 1833), 516.

25. *History, 4,* 1828-29.

26. "Essay on William III," p. 469; Macaulay so much assumed the alternation of extremes to have been the norm that he said, "We cannot think it altogether impossible that a house might have been packed which would have restored the days of Mary. We certainly do not believe that this would have been tamely borne. But we do believe that, if the nation had been deluded by the King's [i.e., James's] professions of toleration, all this would have been attempted, and could have been averted only by a most bloody and destructive contest, in which the whole Protestant population would have been opposed to the Catholics. On the one side would have been a vast numerical superiority. But on the other side would have been the whole organization of government, and two great disciplined armies, that of James and that of Louis. We do not doubt that the nation would have achieved its deliverance. But we believe that the struggle would have shaken the whole fabric of society, and that the vengeance of the conquerors would have been terrible and unsparing": "Mackintosh," *Edin. Rev., 61,* 309.

27. "Mackintosh," *Edin. Rev., 61,* 319; *History, 3,* 1311-12; see also *6,* 2730. On his judgment of the Long Parliament, see above, p. 149, and n. 70 in chap. 4. Of course Macaulay praised William for other achievements and qualities; see, for example, *History, 3,* 1354; *4,* 1848; *5,* 2348, 2358, 2362-63, 2391. And, contrary to general belief, he was not always uncritical; see, for example, *History, 5,* 2120, 2128, 2206; *6,* 2859, 2883, 2958-62, 2967-68; *Hansard, 72,* 1174-75 (19 February 1844) (on William's cruel policy in Ireland).

28. "Essay on William III," p. 469. Firth, *Commentary on Macaulay's "History,"* pp. 344, n. 1; 350. A rare exception, where Macaulay refers to William as "the Whig King": "Lord Mahon's *War of the Succession*," *Edin. Rev., 56,* 534.

29. *History, 3,* 1234, 1324; *4,* 1666. See also *4,* 1772, 1790; *5,* 2138.

30. *History, 3,* 1380.

31. *History, 4,* 1545-46.

32. *History, 6,* 2646-47.

33. *History, 2,* 840; *3,* 1380; see also *4,* 1545.

34. *History, 6,* 2646; *3,* 1292.

35. *History, 6,* 2882; *3,* 1184; see also *3,* 1216, 1238.

36. *History, 3, 1354;* see also *5,* 2347-48.

37. "Essay on William III," p. 469.

38. *History, 4,* 1676. The phrase is reminiscent of his famous characterization of Sydney as "the Smith of Smiths": TBM to Zachary Macaulay, 21 July 1826, Pinney, *Letters, 1,* 213. Sir Charles Grey was "the bore of bores": TBM to Whewell, 7 April 1843, Whewell Papers, Trinity College Library, Add. MS a.68[61]. Someone else—one Joy—was characterized in the same way: Journals, vol. 6, fol. 4 (10 December [1852]). Goldsmid, alas, was "the Jew of Jews": TBM to Margaret Cropper, 3 February 1834, Pierpont Morgan Library.

39. *History, 3,* 1328. Macaulay eulogized Halifax as early as 1838 (in the essay on Sir William Temple) and portrayed him as a worthy and skillful person as early as 1835 ("Mackintosh," *Edin. Rev., 61,* 279-81). But in 1828, in a passage describing an occasion that would have been accompanied by praise of Halifax had it been written a decade later, Macaulay did not mention Halifax; and elsewhere in the same essay, when he did mention or allude to him, it was to place him in a large class of corrupt men ("Hallam," *Edin. Rev., 48,* 154, 159). In his unfinished "History of France" Macaulay attributed characteristics of the trimmer's role, in varying degrees, to Lainé (pp. 36-37), Talleyrand (pp. 38-39, 55), and Constant. He described Constant in 1814 in terms similar to some of those he later used for Halifax in 1688: like Halifax with James II, Constant supported the monarch "as long as the conflict remained undecided"; when the monarch was expelled, "he gave in his adhesion to the imperial government [of Napoleon], and took an active part in the formation of the new constitution." Consequently he was accused of inconsistency. "History will probably pronounce that his conduct, though inconsistent in seeming, was perfectly consistent in substance; that he was faithful to the interests of the state, and indifferent to the names and titles of its rulers" (p. 77). During dinner conversation in 1845 Macaulay "highly praised the Marquis of Halifax (Charles 2nd) & his pamphlets": Diary of 7th earl of Carlisle, vol. 6, fols. 63-64 (12 March 1845). Macaulay owned a manuscript copy of Halifax's "Character of a Trimmer" in an unknown, apparently seventeenth-century hand; it is at Wallington. The shift in Macaulay's estimate of Halifax is a notable exception to what R. L. Schuyler has called Macaulay's "lack of mental flexibility" and his "habit of forming historical opinions on partial and insufficient evidence and adhering to them tenaciously thereafter": "Macaulay and His History," *Political Science Quarterly, 63* (June 1948), 187.

40. *History, 5,* 2484; *3,* 1328, 1050; see also *3,* 1226, 1274. For a skeptical, even cynical, interpretation of Halifax's politics see J. R. Jones, *The Revolution of 1688 in England* (London: Weidenfeld & Nicolson, 1972), pp. 242-44.

41. "The Character of a Trimmer," in *The Complete Works of George*

Savile, First Marquess of Halifax, ed. Walter Raleigh (Oxford: Clarendon Press, 1912), p. 48.

42. "The Life and Writings of Sir William Temple," *Edin. Rev., 68* (October 1838), 169-70; *History, 1,* 234; *3,* 1168; see also *3,* 1384. For a rare exception, where Macaulay refers to Halifax as a Whig statesman, see *Hansard, 70,* 808 (7 July 1843).

43. "Temple," *Edin. Rev., 68,* 169-70; *History, 1,* 234-35; *3,* 1232. "The brow, the eye, and the mouth of Halifax indicated a powerful intellect and an exquisite sense of the ludicrous; but the expression was that of a sceptic, of a voluptuary, of a man not likely to venture his all on a single hazard, or to be a martyr in any cause. To those who are acquainted with his countenance it will not seem wonderful that the writer in whom he most delighted was Montaigne": *History, 3,* 1050-51.

44. *History, 3,* 1107, 1169, 1220, 1328.

45. *History, 3,* 1169, 1328; see also *3,* 1221, 1226. According to J. P. Kenyon, Halifax defected to William only when this provided the best opportunity to achieve peace and when he concluded that William would support the most moderate solution: Introduction to Halifax, *Complete Works,* ed. J. P. Kenyon, p. 19.

46. *History, 2,* 870-71; *3,* 1370. "There is one and only one deep stain on the memory of this eminent man. It is melancholy to think that he, who had acted so great a part in the Convention, could have afterwards stooped to hold communication with Saint Germain's [where the exiled James held court].... It was by the ingratitude and malice of the Whigs that he was driven to take shelter for a moment among the Jacobites": *History, 5,* 2484. Of course, this was not unusual. Also, his "speculative turn of mind rendered him a bad adviser in cases which required celerity": "Temple," *Edin. Rev., 68,* 170.

47. *History, 1,* 232; *3,* 1389; *5,* 2484.

48. *History, 1,* 234-35; *3,* 1419; *4,* 1776; "Temple," *Edin. Rev., 68,* 169. Kenyon also refers to Halifax's fear of a renewal of civil war (Introduction to Halifax, *Complete Works,* pp. 14, 18). Kenyon appreciates Macaulay's "perceptive analysis" of Halifax and suggests that its quality is to be explained by the presumption that "Macaulay saw in Halifax his own reflection" (p. 24).

49. *Reign of James II,* pp. 8-9; see also pp. 174, 216-17, 244.

50. *Ibid.,* pp. 9-10; see also p. 348.

51. According to Kenyon, Macaulay was responsible for "a dramatic revision of Halifax's reputation," whereas his most prominent predecessors, Hallam and Mackintosh, echoed Hume's and Burnet's unfavorable judgments: Introduction to Halifax, *Complete Works,* p. 23. H. C. Foxcroft admitted that to Macaulay's "championship Lord Halifax owes what little popular recognition he has attained": *The Life and Letters of Sir George Savile, Bart., First Marquis of Halifax* (London, 1898), *1,* vi.

52. "This was not an ordinary meeting or an ordinary crisis. It seemed to me that a great era had arrived, and that, at such a conjuncture ...": *Speeches,* p. 421 (2 December 1845) (on the Corn Laws). Of course he did not only use the term in his special way; he also used it for any crisis

whose resolution might lead to novel developments. In this more normal sense he used the word with great frquency; see, for example, *History, 5,* 2308, 2352, 2383, 2414, 2450, 2488, 2560, 2579, 2608; the examples could be multiplied many times. H. Butterfield alludes to the significant use of this term, although without discussing it or mentioning Macaulay: *The Whig Interpretation of History* (London: Bell, 1951), p. vi.

53. "At this conjuncture [when Napoleon threatened invasion], as at some other great conjunctures in our history, the conjuncture of 1660, for example, and the conjuncture of 1688, there was a general disposition among honest and patriotic men to forget old quarrels"; and "those terrible conjunctures which confound all ordinary distinctions": "William Pitt," *Misc. Wr., 2,* 363, 372. See also p. 314.

54. *History, 1,* 131, 133-34.

55. *History, 2,* 1037-38; see also p. 1001; "Essay on William III," p. 469 (where he shows that, without using the word, he already had the idea). "The two parties [Tories and Nonconformists] whose strife had convulsed the empire during half a century, were united for a moment; and all that vast royal power which three years before had seemed immovably fixed, vanished at once like chaff in a hurricane": "Mackintosh," *Edin. Rev., 61,* 311. "Both the Restoration and the Revolution were accomplished by coalitions.... The Cavalier would, at the former conjuncture, have been able to effect nothing without the help of the Puritans who had fought for the Covenant; nor would the Whig, at the latter conjuncture, have offered a successful resistance to arbitrary power, had he not been backed by men who had a very short time before condemned resistance to arbitrary power as a deadly sin": *History, 4,* 1666. "Never, within the memory of man, had there been so near an approach to entire concord among all intelligent Englishmen as at this conjuncture": *History, 3,* 1206.

56. *History, 1,* 22; *3,* 1304-10, 1312. Since the Revolution defended the rule of law, it was "conservative ...; the English complained, not of the law, but of the violation of the law. They rose up against the first magistrate merely in order to assert the supremacy of the law": *History, 4,* 1533. Mackintosh also used the phrase "defensive revolution," defining it as one in which "the sole purpose is to preserve and secure the laws, has a fixed boundary, conspicuously marked out by the well-defined object which it pursues, and which it seldom permanently over-reaches; and is thus exempt from that succession of changes which disturbs all habits of peaceable obedience, and weakens every authority not resting on mere force": *Reign of James II,* p. 302. Earlier still, Macaulay had character- ized English revolutions as "defending, correcting, and restoring": "Mirabeau," *Edin. Rev., 55* (July 1832), 572. Similar phraseology can be found in Burke (see *The Works of the Right Honourable Edmund Burke* [London, 1887], *3,* 225; *4,* 80). The idea derives from the characteriza- tion of James as the aggressor against the established constitution, but Macaulay enlarged the notion to give it an extralegal dimension, whereby the defensive character of the Revolution was not only a matter of defend- ing the ancient constitution (see below, n. 101) against papist aggression

but also involved the continuity of institutions and the preservation of the public feeling that gave them legitimacy.

57. "Essay on William III," p. 469. "Politic statesmen have always been desirous to disguise innovations as much as possible under ancient names and badges. Where this is judiciously done institutions which are in fact new may speedily acquire all the authority of age": "History of France," p. 18.

58. *History, 1,* 89.

59. *History, 3,* 1261. One resource the statesman can use is the absence of strong feeling in the great majority. In the sixteenth century the zealous Catholics and the zealous Protestants were less than a twentieth of the nation. "The remaining nineteen-twentieths halted between the two opinions; and were not disposed to risk a revolution in the government, for the purpose of giving to either of the extreme factions an advantage over the other...; the nation, undetermined in its opinions and feelings, resigned itself implicitly to the guidance of the government": "Burleigh," *Edin. Rev., 55,* 286-87. In a different context, Macaulay wrote of "the indifferent, a large portion of every society": *History, 4,* 1943. He approved of a similar observation in a marginal note in *Oeuvres Complètes de P. L. Courier* (Brussels, 1828), *2,* 20: "There is a vast middle party which sometimes falls to the one side and sometimes to the other."

60. *History, 3,* 1276; see also pp. 1261, 1274, 1277.

61. *History, 3,* 1431; *1,* 108.

62. *Memoirs of the Life of the Right Honourable Sir James Mackintosh,* ed. Robert J. Mackintosh (London, 1835) , *2,* 455-56. Since Mackintosh aspired to interpret historical situations in terms of general causes that operated independently of political leadership, he shows himself to be more an heir to eighteenth-century Scottish intellectual influences than Macaulay. Mackintosh identified two types of history. The first emphasizes narrative, the presentation of particular situations from the past, which becomes a way of explaining maxims of policy. This was to be Macaulay's kind of history, with its emphases on the wisdom or foolishness, the good sense or bigotry, of people, both leaders and followers, all of whom intervene and affect the course of historical development. Mackintosh's second type of history developed in consequence of men's philosophizing: "they discover, not only that history may be made the vehicle of maxims of policy, and refined observations on the secret motives of action, but that it may also rise to those more extensive views, by which the revolutions of states are discovered rather to flow from general causes, than to be the work of the wisdom or folly of individuals. That these views of the state of the world are most important, must be universally admitted." This latter type of history was the kind, he said, for which alone "he could have any shadow of talent": *Memoirs, 2,* 456.

63. Mackintosh's explanation of persecution is more complex than it is for Macaulay, for whom it is a matter of bigotry. See *Reign of James II,* pp. 86-89. On the growth of disaffection under James and the development of a revolutionary situation, see *ibid.,* pp. 182, 215, 239, 251, 253,

258, 277-78, 280, 282, 286-89, 310, 341. Mackintosh mentions (pp. 46, 265) James's maxims about concession, but Macaulay's intimation of the lesson to be learned is missing.

64. "Mackintosh," *Edin. Rev.*, *61*, 271 (where "plums" is rendered "plumbs"). Mackintosh also avoids the extraction of lessons from history by criticizing those who "pursue their single maxim," for example, about concession: *Reign of James II*, p. 265.

65. *History*, *5*, 2571-74. There is also a sketch of Locke's character; Somers' generosity to Locke is mentioned; a reference to his view on toleration of Catholics; his dedication of the *Essay concerning Human Understanding* to Pembroke is mentioned; there is a note on his alleged connection with the Licensing Act; and there are observations on how some who had read Locke with approval were yet intolerant and oppressive in Ireland: *History*, *2*, 538-39, 670; *4*, 1806, 2078, 2082; *5*, 2396, 2482; *6*, 2774. Elsewhere Macaulay occasionally mentions Locke, usually in unrevealing ways. Perhaps the most favorable of these references appear at "Dryden," *Edin. Rev.*, *47* (January 1828), 3; "Horace Walpole," *Edin. Rev.*, *58* (October 1833), 233; *Hansard*, *51*, 834 (29 January 1840). Although Locke is not often mentioned in the *History* or used in its interpretation of events, it is worth noting that in early 1850, at a time when Macaulay was writing the part of the *History* that deals with the change from the Convention into Parliament in 1689, he was reading "a good deal of Locke": Journals, vol. 2, fol. 216 (27 January 1850).

66. Macaulay also said (29 May 1839), "I mean by a Whig, not one who subscribes implicitly to the contents of any book, though that book may have been written by Locke": *Speeches*, p. 183. Cf. Mackintosh, *Reign of James II,* chap. 10. Mackintosh's views, particularly those in this chapter, were criticized in R. Plumer Ward, *An Historical Essay on the Real Character and Amount of the Precedent of the Revolution of 1688: In Which the Opinions of Mackintosh, Price, Hallam, Mr. Fox, Lord John Russell, and the Merits of Sidney, are critically considered* (London, 1838), vol. 1, passim. See also below, chap. 7, n. 16.

67. Henry Hallam, *The Constitutional History of England from the Accession of Henry VII to the Death of George II,* 9th ed. (London, 1857), *3*, 49, 81, 112. On Halifax's skills, see *ibid.*, *2*, 428, 437. Hallam also suggested that Halifax did not take part in the invitation because he feared "the reproach of history" (*ibid.*, *3*, 81); Macaulay, it should be noted, said Halifax anticipated the verdict of history.

68. *Ibid.*, *2*, 55.

69. *Ibid.*, *3*, 199-200. Clarendon, he said, was a Tory, but Hobbes was not; Hoadley was a Whig, but Milton was not (pp. 199-200). Hallam acknowledged that the parties during the exclusion crisis were exceptions to his general characterizations (*ibid.*, *2*, 439). He thought his character-izations valid even for the period beginning with the Long Parliament, when the labels were not yet in use (*ibid.*, *3*, 199).

70. *Ibid.*, *2*, 102. See also p. 293. Hallam was not uncritical of the Long Parliament, even at its beginning: see pp. 103, 112-13. In his review of Hallam's *Constitutional History* Macaulay defended the Long

Parliament after 1641; but in his *History,* although he said that
Parliament, "in spite of many errors and disasters, [was] entitled to the
reverence and gratitude of all," the importance of the Long Parliament
was subordinated to that of the Revolution of 1688: "Hallam," *Edin.
Rev., 48* (September 1828), 112, 120; *History, 1,* 87.

71. Hallam, *Constitutional History, 3,* 83, 110. The case of Magdalen
College was an exception (p. 83).

72. *Ibid., 2,* 102. On the reign of Charles II, see *2,* 313-14 and *3,* 1.

73. *Ibid., 3,* 66, 86, 90, 102, 111.

74. *Ibid., 3,* 147. For praise of William, see pp. 107, 116, 119, 133,
148; for criticism, see p. 140.

75. *Ibid., 2,* 430; *3,* 92, 98, 107, 121. The Commons in the convention
Parliament "proceeded not by the stated rules of the English government,
but the general rights of mankind. They looked not so much to Magna
Charta as the original compact of society, and rejected Coke and Hale for
Hooker and Harrington" (*ibid., 3,* 98). The Revolution, Hallam said,
vindicated the exclusionists, who were to be condemned, not for their
intentions, but for their impracticality (*ibid., 2,* 455; *3,* 100).

76. *Ibid., 3,* 201-2.

77. *Ibid.,* pp. 114-15; see n. 91 in chap. 4.

78. Macaulay thought that Hallam was practical and not credulous
about the myths of politics; also he was "eminently judicial," indeed, "we
do not scruple to pronounce the Constitutional History the most impartial
book that we ever read": "Hallam," *Edin. Rev., 48,* 98-100. In view of
Hallam's unconcealed partisanship, it is worth speculating about what
Macaulay might have meant in calling him impartial. Hallam condemned
both Stuart despotism and the Commonwealth, and this distinguished
him from both Hume and pro-Commonwealth historians such as Godwin.
This intermediate position perhaps explains Macaulay's eulogy of his
impartiality. Among other things, Macaulay differed with Hallam on his
evaluation of the Long Parliament, the justice of the parliamentary
position in the Civil War, on the nineteen propositions, on the motives of
Charles I, and on Cromwell's character and achievements: *ibid.,* pp.
120, 124-25, 131, 140-48. Although Macaulay in the 1820s had some
sympathetic judgments for the Commonwealth, in his *History* those views
were absent: *History, 1,* 112-16.

79. "On Mitford's *History of Greece,*" *Misc. Wr., 1,* 176. In additon, of
course, historical inquiry should discern noiseless revolutions: see above,
pp. 21-24, 28-29.

80. *Hansard, 2,* 1196 (2 March 1831). Compare Mackintosh, *Vindiciae
Gallicae* (London, 1791), pp. 346-47: "Blind admirers of Revolutions
take them for implicit models. Thus Mr. Burke admires that of 1688; but
we, who conceive that we pay the purest homage to the authors of that
Revolution, not in contending for what they *then* DID, but for what they
now WOULD DO, can feel no inconsistency in looking on France, not to
model our conduct, but to invigorate the spirit of freedom, we permit
ourselves to imagine how Lord Somers, in the light and knowledge of the
eighteenth century, how the patriots of France, in the tranquillity and
opulence of England, would have acted."

81. *History, 6,* 2736. The passage refers to Somers, who elsewhere is

called "the foremost man of his age in civil wisdom" (p. 2878) and "the first of living English jurists and statesmen" (p. 2994). Macaulay as a politician claimed, as he said of an issue in 1840, to see it "as it will be judged by future ages": *Hansard, 51,* 832 (29 January 1840).

82. Macaulay's inaccuracies have been most systematically and comprehensively identified in Charles Firth, *A Commentary on Macaulay's "History of England."* His most vigorous critic on grounds of accuracy was John Paget, whose *The New "Examen,"* first published in 1861, was brought out again (London: Haworth, 1934) with an Introduction by Winston Chruchill, who was gratified by Paget's criticism of Macaulay's harsh portraits of Marlborough. For a critique of Paget, see James Moncreiff, "Macaulay's *History of England,*" *Edin. Rev., 114* (October 1861), 288-306.

83. I believe that J. R. Jones speaks for professional historians when he refers to "the obsolescence of the type of questions which he [Macaulay] asked": *The Revolution of 1688 in England,* p. 7. What Macaulay would have thought of the judgments of professional historians is perhaps expressed in Francis Jeffrey's response to a criticism of the first two volumes of *The History:* "If what he has written is not History—so much the worse, I think, for History": Jeffrey to Brougham, 21 January [1850]: University College Library, London, Brougham Papers, 10520. Macaulay was offered the Chair of Modern History at Cambridge in 1849: Trevelyan, *Life 2,* 197; although he refused, for practical reasons, his refusal symbolizes his rejection of academic history. One can find contemporary critiques of professional history that are congenial to Macaulay's understanding of the relation of historical inquiry to the practice of politics: see, for example, E. A. Reitan in *Burke Newsletter, 11,* no. 2 (Winter 1969-70), 1463-70. Although he did not intend it as a defense of Macaulay, Trevor-Roper's inaugural lecture is also relevant: *History, Professional and Lay* (Oxford: Clarendon Press, 1957). See G. M. Trevelyan, *Clio, A Muse and Other Essays* (London, 1930), pp. 141-70, for a defense of history as political education.

84. H. C. Foxcroft, "The Limitations of Lord Macaulay," *Fortnightly Review,* n.s. *72* (1902), 826-30. This charge can be extended to include oversimplification of issues. Thus Gay notes that "The profusion of parallel clauses in Macaulay's writings suggests that he perceived history as a succession of dilemmas, debates, and combats." Although this may not allow for an adequate explanation of events, by making "history . . . a vast antithesis" Macaulay was able to serve his didactic purpose. See Peter Gay, *Style in History,* p. 111.

85. In a recent book on the Revolution (J. R. Jones, *The Revolution of 1688 in England*) Somers is mentioned once and Halifax is not given a very significant role. In contrast, for Macaulay these men exemplified the art of civil prudence. Compare R. L. Schuyler's remark, "Historians really ought not to have clients or heroes," in "Macaulay and His History—A Hundred Years After," p. 186. It is worth noting that J. R. Jones, in severely criticizing Macaulay, declares that Macaulay thought the Revolution inevitable (p. ix). If this was so, it might be asked, why did Macaulay attribute wisdom and prudence and superb political skill to William and Halifax? Why were they given heroic status? The professional

historian's delineation of complexity in character and situation and his unwillingness to use categories and labels that have clear and direct meaning for the politician and citizen is displayed at its best in Stephen B. Baxter, *William III* (London: Longmans, 1966).

86. Arthur Marwick, *The Nature of History,* Macmillan Student Editions, Open University Set Book (London: Macmillan, 1970), p. 45. Foxcroft could not comprehend Macaulay's admiration for Halifax, since she thought Macaulay was "incapacitated, by the prejudice of party and by the limitations of an intellect robust rather than subtle, from due appreciation of his merits": *Life of Halifax, 1,* vi.

87. "Essay on William III," p. 469.

88. *Ibid.* Although appreciating his great talents, Macaulay was severe in his judgment of Shaftesbury. "Shaftesbury was the very reverse of a trimmer": "Temple," *Edin. Rev., 68* (October 1838), 169.

89. TBM to Russell, 3 January 1849, Russell Papers, PRO, 30/22/7E, fols. 129–30. Russell liked the *History* but took exception on this point. Mackintosh was much less severe than Macaulay on the Whigs of the 1670s and early 1680s: Mackintosh, *Reign of James II,* p. 340, and *Miscellaneous Works,* pp. 2, 13, 34–35. In the 1839 election speech Macaulay spoke approvingly of all Whigs, but he used the word "in no narrow sense," identifying as Whigs such varied parties as those who stood up to Elizabeth on monopolies, the earliest parliamentary opposition to James I, and the party that forced Charles I to give up ship money. His extravagance in this speech was so great that these statements can be discounted, especially as they are repeatedly contradicted by more considered statements made elsewhere (especially in the *History*): *Speeches,* pp. 182–84.

90. *History, 3,* 1407.

91. *History, 4,* 1772. On the Whigs' desire for vengeance, see also *3,* 1182, 1313, 1328; *4,* 1649, 1666, 1673, 1712, 1773, 1795, 1829. Macaulay's adjectives vary. The Whigs were also "uncompromising" (*3,* 1182, 1191, 1289; *4,* 1772); "intolerant" (*1,* 507, 511; *4,* 1774, 2082); and "resentful," "vehement," "intemperate," "vindictive," "malevolent," "zealous," and "violent" (*3,* 1276, 1330–31, 1370; *4,* 1671, 1673–75, 1772, 1793, 1804, 2016, 2078).

92. *History, 4,* 1772; see also *6,* 2661–66, 2761. While working on the Convention Parliament for volume 3, Macaulay wrote in his journal, "I shall not be thought partial to the Whigs": Journals, vol. 4, fol. 320 (3 December [1851]). Guizot reported having heard that Macaulay was subjected to "animated reproaches" from "ardent Whigs" for his severity in judging the Whigs of 1692. Guizot also thought him more impartial in dealing with the reign of William III than with earlier periods; "the justice of the historian surmounted the habits of the politician": F. Guizot, *An Embassy to the Court of St. James's in 1840* (London, 1862), p. 144.

93. *History, 4,* 1673, 1829; see also *3,* 1191, 1289. Macaulay also noted the Whigs' hatred of Halifax: *3,* 1370; *4,* 1774, 1776. Yet, despite all this, Leslie Stephen said of Macaulay, "the tenets of the Whig party were

for him the last word of political wisdom" and that he never "rises above the party view of politics": quoted with approval by T. F. Henderson, Introduction to Macaulay, *History* (London, 1907), p. xv. See also Marwick, *The Nature of History*, pp. 44-45, where it is said that "in a limited party sense Macaulay was a 'Whig historian': to his historical work he brought the bias of a practising Whig politician and his writings, in an obvious way, are an example of history as propaganda"; and, further, "overt party bias . . . attached to Macaulay." C. H. Firth also regarded Macaulay as a Whig advocate: "The Development of the Study of Seventeenth Century History," *Transactions of the Royal Historical Society*, 3d ser., 7 (1913), 41, 45. On the other hand, the difficulties in labeling Macaulay a Whig historian have been recognized; see William G. Carleton, "Macaulay and the Trimmers," *American Scholar, 19,* (1949), 73-82. Carleton notes Macaulay's defense of trimmers' policies, his disapproval of extremists who undermined the Revolutionary settlement, and his concern with consent.

94. *History, 3,* 1276; see also p. 1284. Conventional Whig doctrine is treated more favorably, however, at p. 1323 and in "Mackintosh," *Edin. Rev., 61,* 319-20.

95. *History, 4,* 2078, 2080, 2082. Yet it has been said that Macaulay was "doctrinaire in his Whiggism": H. R. Trevor-Roper, Introduction to Macaulay, *Critical and Historical Essays*, p. 17.

96. *History, 3,* 1319.

97. *Ibid.,* pp. 1046-47.

98. *Ibid.,* pp. 1109, 1318-19; *4,* 1666; see also *3,* 1054, 1102, 1105, 1261, 1306, 1329; "Mackintosh," *Edin. Rev., 61,* 312; "Present Administration" (1827), *Edin. Rev., 46,* 249, where he asserted that "the Revolution itself was the fruit of a coalition between parties." Compare a recent estimate of Macaulay: "He viewed the Revolution of 1688 as did the average Whig reader of his day"; "To some extent historical events, too, had to be forced into the same mechanical pattern and they are judged by Macaulay as men are judged, according to whether they aided or thwarted the Whig cause. It was quite impossible for him to see that the Tories were largely responsible for the Revolution of 1688 although the facts stared him in the face": J. H. Plumb, "Thomas Babington Macaulay," *Men and Places* (Penguin, 1966), pp. 279, 287-88.

99. H. Butterfield, *The Whig Interpretation of History,* passim, and *The Englishman and His History* (Cambridge: At the University Press, 1944), chaps. 3-5.

100. *Whig Interpretation,* p. 30; see also *The Englishman and His History,* pp. vi, 73, 78, 80. It should be noted that Butterfield in 1944, by acknowledging the political usefulness of the Whig interpretation, qualified his 1931 condemnation of it. "We may say that 'wrong' history was one of our assets . . .; whatever [the Whig interpretation] may have done to our history, it had a wonderful effect on English politics": *The Englishman and His History,* p. 7. In this passage (and elsewhere in the book) Butterfield wrote not only as a professional historian; thus he acknowledged the tension between professional history and history written

to perpetuate the historical memories and political understandings that sustain a particular polity.

101. *History, 5,* 2090. "No candid Tory will deny that these [constitutional] principles had, five hundred years ago, acquired the authority of fundamental rules. On the other hand, no candid Whig will affirm that they were, till a later period, cleared from all ambiguity. . . . The line which bounded the royal prerogative, though in general sufficiently clear, had not everywhere been drawn with accuracy and distinctness. There was, therefore, near the border some debatable ground": *History, 1,* 24-25. Thus Trevor-Roper has observed, "'The Macaulay view' as supposed by his modern opponents—the view that there was, in the seventeenth century, an accepted constitution which the tyrannical Stuarts broke and the virtuous Whigs defended—he never held, and one only has to read him to know it": "Macaulay and the Glorious Revolution" in *Men and Events* (New York: Harper, 1957), p. 251. For references (or allusions) to the ancient constitution, see *History, 1,* 71; *6,* 2730-31; "Milton," *Edin. Rev., 42,* 327-28; "Hallam," *Edin. Rev., 48,* 124-28, 142. The passage quoted acknowledges Hume's position. For Hume's view of the legal basis of the dispensing power, see his *The History of England from the Invasion of Julius Caesar to the Revolution in 1688* (London, 1802), *8,* 244-47, 256-57 (chap. 70); for Hume's position in relation to the ancient-constitution controversy, see Duncan Forbes, Introduction to David Hume, *The History of Great Britain: The Reigns of James I and Charles I* (Pelican, 1970; 1st ed., 1754), pp. 24-33.

102. *History, 2,* 887. Cf. "Mackintosh," *Edin. Rev., 61,* 286. For an argument that Restoration and eighteenth-century politicians ought not to be judged by standards of nineteenth-century England, see "Hallam," *Edin. Rev., 48,* 158; "Walpole," *Edin. Rev., 58,* 242-43. See also *History, 5,* 2290.

103. Butterfield, *Whig Interpretation,* p. 41.

104. *History, 2,* 886; *5,* 2089. These passages (and the fuller statements from which they are taken, and including the statement at *1,* 21-22) are completely consistent with Butterfield's position. Also see "Mackintosh," *Edin. Rev., 61,* 283, where Macaulay refers to the two errors, one of judging the present by the past, and the other, judging the past by the norms of the present. "The former of these errors we have often combated, and shall always be ready to combat: the latter, though rapidly spreading, has not, we think, yet come under our notice. . .; the latter is . . . symptomatic of a shallow understanding and an unamiable temper." Surprisingly, Acton, in asserting the historian's duty to use morality in passing judgment on the past, clearly alludes to (without citing) Macaulay as one who expresses the opposing and predominant view: "The men who . . . made history what it has become . . . set up the principle that only a foolish Conservative judges the present time with the ideas of the past; that only a foolish Liberal judges the past with the ideas of the present": "Inaugural Lecture on the Study of History" (1895), in *Lectures on Modern History,* ed. John N. Figgis and Reginald V. Laurence (London, 1918), p. 24. The allusion is to Macaulay's *History, 2,*

886, quoted above, p. 71. That Macaulay does not exemplify Butterfield's Whig interpretation has been recognized by Vincent E. Starzinger, *Middlingness: "Juste Milieu" Political Theory in France and England, 1815-48* (Charlottesville: University Press of Virginia, 1965), pp. 128-31. Finally, historians like Brodie and Hallam would seem to exemplify Butterfield's Whig historian much better than Macaulay.

105. "Present Administration," *Edin. Rev.*, 46, 261-65; *Hansard, 11*, 462 (19 March 1832); *51*, 834 (29 January 1840); *84*, 894 (10 March 1846). Apparently Macaulay was not alone in this; the importance of seventeenth-century events in the nineteenth-century historical memory has been emphasized by John Vincent, *The Formation of the Liberal Party, 1857-1868* (London: Constable, 1966), p. xxix. For an example, see *Three Early Nineteenth Century Diaries,* ed. A. Aspinall (London: Williams & Norgate, 1952), p. 255. See also "Nineteenth-Century Cromwell," *Past and Present,* no. 40 (July 1968), pp. 187-91.

106. "Essay on William III," p. 469. "I do not apprehend the dangerous issue which I fear will ultimately arrive to-morrow, or next year, or perhaps five years hence; but I say, that it is impossible that this country can safely follow up a system which has the effect of arousing and provoking the violent passions of multitudes, while at the same time, it promotes division, rivalry, and animosity, amongst the two great classes of proprietors in the country": *Hansard, 60,* 757 (21 February 1842). Macaulay was of course not the only one with such apprehensions; see Norman Gash, *Reaction and Reconstruction in English Politics 1832-1852* (Oxford: Clarendon Press, 1965), p. 117.

CHAPTER 5. TRIMMING AND DEMOCRACY

1. "The Present Administration," *Edin. Rev., 46* (June 1827), 260-67. Greville reported a conversation with Macaulay: "He had not been prepared for the tranquillity and contentment that he found on his return to England": *The Greville Memoirs, 1814-1860,* ed. Lytton Strachey and Roger Fulford (London: Macmillan, 1938), *4*, 77 (entry of 14 July 1838).

2. Lansdowne alluded to Macaulay's alarm: "I cannot help thinking that both Macaulay and McCullagh [*sic*] ... exaggerate somewhat the [case?] as respects England, the other Ireland, not the intensity, but the duration of the present disturbance of the public mind": Lansdowne to Russell, n.d. [endorsed 24 April 1848], Russell Papers, PRO, 30/22/7B, fol. 342.

3. *Hansard, 84,* 893-95 (10 March 1846); see also *ibid., 58,* 886 (27 May 1841). In defending the Army Estimates (when he was secretary for war), he held that he was "no alarmist ...; this nation ... would not, without a powerful struggle, surrender itself into the hands of men elated by extravagant hopes; but, at the same time, when I consider the wealth of our great cities, I cannot say that it is utterly impossible that a mob, exacerbated and infuriated by dishonest leaders, might inflict calamities that might lead to a crisis which the ingenuity and good fortune of years

could scarcely succeed in effacing": *Mirror of Parliament,* 2d ser., *16,* 1650 (9 March 1840). Also see *Hansard, 91,* 1008, 1012 (19 April 1847), where he draws on the history of riots to make credible his portrayal of the risks, as he argues that without education "there is at every period a risk of a *jacquerie.*" The nightmare of civil war was also made explicit in the *History, 1,* 27-28: "The effect of the constant progress of wealth has been to make insurrection far more terrible to thinking men than maladminis- tration. Immense sums have been expended on works which, if a rebellion broke out, might perish in a few hours …; if the government were subverted by physical force, all this movable wealth would be exposed to imminent risk of spoliation and destruction."

4. For examples of his referring to Bacon on straws in the wind see "Hallam," *Edin. Rev., 48* (Spetember 1828), 168; *Hansard, 15,* 1329 (28 February 1833); *67,* 1256 (21 March 1843); see also *60,* 755 (21 February 1842). Despite all this, critics continue to refer to Macaulay's optimism and complacency; for example, "he knew about what Carlyle called 'the-condition-of-England-question,' but his optimism, which remained unshaken, was strengthened by his historical studies": R. L. Schuyler, "Macaulay and His History," *Political Science Quarterly, 63* (June 1948), 191. His gloomier statements, which should be considered in connection with his observations on historical cycles, provide background for his famous New Zealander who, at some future date, would stand on a broken arch of London Bridge to sketch the ruins of St. Paul's: "Ranke's *History of the Popes,*" *Edin. Rev., 72* (October 1840), 228. See also "Mitford's History of Greece," *Misc. Wr., 1,* 179-80.

5. "Essay on William III," p. 469. See Vincent Starzinger, *Middling- ness: "Juste Milieu" Political Theory in France and England, 1815-48* (Charlottesville: University Press of Virginia, 1965), pp. 127-35. Although it focuses on what Starzinger calls "middlingness" and barely mentions trimming, his provocative book correctly distinguishes a genre of political thinking, has the merit of recognizing the character of Macaulay's intentions, and avoids misleading characterizations of him based on attributions of ideological doctrines that at most were peripheral to his political outlook. In addition to Macaulay, it deals with Brougham, Royer-Collard, and Guizot. William Carleton ("Macaulay and the Trimmers," *American Scholar, 19* [1949], 73-82), although focusing on Macaulay as a historian and not as a politician, identifies Macaulay's trimming sympathies in the *History.* William Madden discusses Macaulay's wish to avoid the absurdity of extremes in "Macaulay's Style," in *The Art of Victorian Prose,* ed. G. Levine and W. Madden (New York: Oxford, 1968), pp. 131-33.

6. "Moore's *Life of Sheridan,*" *Edin. Rev., 45* (December 1826), 32-33, 35-36. Jeffrey inserted into this review his response to the accusation made by James Mill (*Westminster Review, 1* [1824], 218) that the Whigs and the *Edinburgh Review* were vacillating, inconsistent, compromising— that they had a trimming, "see-saw" policy; much as Halifax did in 1688, Jeffrey welcomed the label "trimmer" and provided a rationale for the conduct it described; see esp. "Moore's *Life of Sheridan,*" pp. 32-33.

Jeffrey dealt with the same theme on other occasions—for example, in "State of Parties, 1810," *Contributions to the Edinburgh Review,* 2d ed. (London, 1846), *3,* 258-59, 267; in a note written for this second edition, Jeffrey said the article was "not *all* rhetorical or assuming: And the observations on the vast importance and high and difficult duties of a *middle party,* in all great national contentions, seem to me as universally true, and as applicable to the present position of our affairs, as most of the other things I . . . reproduce" (p. 258 n.). Their affinity of outlook may have been among Jeffrey's reasons for wanting Macaulay to succeed him as editor in 1830; however, he could not overcome Brougham's opposition: Selina Macaulay's Journal, 20 February 1830, Huntington Library.

7. [Margaret Macaulay], *Recollections by a Sister of T. B. Macaulay* (1834), (London: Privately printed, 1864), p. 96.

8. *Hansard, 60,* 755-56 (21 February 1842); *Speeches,* p. 424 (2 December 1845).

9. The passage that follows in the text is the most notable example of this usage. See also *Hansard, 70,* 797 (7 July 1843); "Hallam," *Edin. Rev., 48,* 98. Of course he was familiar with this usage in connection with French politics: TBM to Zachary Macaulay, 21-22, September 1830, Pinney, *Letters, 1,* 303; "Mirabeau," *Edin. Rev., 55* (July 1832), 568; "Barère," *Edin. Rev., 79* (April 1844), 346; "Mackintosh," *Edin. Rev., 61* (July 1835), 277 and 308, where an English parallel is mentioned. Implied references to the categories of Left and Right perhaps might be found in "Hallam," *Edin. Rev., 48,* 168-69; "Lord Mahon's *War of the Succession," 56,* 534-38; *History, 3,* 1261; *Hansard, 58,* 195 (11 May 1841). For ambiguous usages, see "Hallam," *Edin. Rev., 48,* 100; *History, 1,* 89; *4,* 2017. However, Macaulay did not make the assumption of linear change by which the Left-Right distinction often is sustained.

10. TBM to Spring Rice, 11 August 1834, John Rylands Library, Eng. MS 1187/1. Gash uses this passage to support his suggestion that Macaulay was visualizing the Liberal party of the future: Norman Gash, *Reaction and Reconstruction in English Politics, 1832-1852* (Oxford: Clarendon Press, 1965), pp. 165-66.

11. TBM to Spring Rice, 8 February 1836, quoted in *Bodleian Library Record, 1* (1941), 248.

12. He said he was "already weaned from that ambition which was the bane of [Mackintosh's] life. The part of a political leader is not one to which I aspire. I have had longings of that sort. But they are over": TBM to (Russell?), incomplete, n.d. (*c.* January 1842), Russell Papers, PRO, 30/22/48, fol. 258.

13. He added, "The determination of the government to resist that change as a government will prevent you from obtaining the services of a great number of very able men, who generally agree with you, whose opinions are by no means violent, but who consider that question as one of vital importance": *Bodleian Library Record,* 1 (1941), 248-49. The secret ballot was made an open question in 1839, and Macaulay defended this position: *Hansard, 48,* 466-69 (18 June 1839); *51,* 816 (29 January

1840). But he was not always unequivocally for the ballot; in 1830 he was undecided; in 1831–32 he was favorable to it but most reluctant to press for its establishment; and by 1848 he was doubtful about it: TBM to Napier, 27 November 1830, Napier Papers, BM, Add. MSS 34614, fol. 439; *Speeches,* p. 65; TBM to G. Rawson, 2 September 1831, Pinney, *Letters, 2,* 93; Frederick Arnold, *The Public Life of Lord Macaulay* (London, 1862), pp. 116–17; TBM to Russell, 23 April 1848, Russell Papers, PRO, 30/22/7B, fols. 331–35. However, in 1852 he said he had "always been favourable" to it: *Speeches,* pp. 519–20.

14. TBM to Spring Rice, 8 February 1836, quoted in *Bodleian Library Record, 1* (1941), 249; TBM to Hannah Macaulay, 13 July 1833, Pinney, *Letters, 2,* 270. Of course Macaulay had urged the creation of peers in May 1832: *Hansard, 12,* 850–54 (10 May 1832).

15. *Bodleian Library Record, 1* (1941), 249, 251; Trevelyan, *Life, 1,* 408; *2,* 8–9; *Hansard, 12,* 853 (10 May 1832).

16. TBM to Hannah Macaulay, 29 December 1838, Trinity College Library. TBM to Zachary Macaulay, 14 August 1827, Pinney, *Letters, 1,* 226; Trevelyan, *Life, 2,* 263–64; *Greville Memoirs, 4,* 77. "To condemn coalitions in the abstract, is manifestly absurd. . . . Those who will not stoop to compliances which the condition of human nature renders necessary, are fitter to be hermits than to be statesmen": "Present Administration," *Edin. Rev., 46,* 248.

17. *Greville Memoirs, 4,* 77.

18. *Ibid.*; TBM to Spring Rice, 8 February 1836, *Bodleian Library Record, 1* (1941), 248. He acknowledged that Peel could more effectively carry a measure of tariff reform than the Whigs: TBM to Ellis, n.d. [December 1845], Trinity College Library.

19. "Chatham," *Edin. Rev., 80* (October 1844), 526. Compare above, p. 155.

20. *History, 1,* 88–89 (1849).

21. TBM to Fanny Macaulay, 29 January 1839, Trinity College Library. He acknowledged some conservatism when explaining why he was declining an offer from the earl of Carlisle to stand for the pocket borough of Morpeth. Macaulay said "that he should not like to avow that change, unless as a Member for a large (?) constituency, and for that his health unfitted him. The only thing that could make him wish to come back to Parlt would be if the Puseyites attacked the Queen's supremacy": Diary of 7th earl of Carlisle, vol. 28, fol. 50 (3 April 1852). Compare Macaulay's reference in 1832 to "the new cant word, a decided 'Conservative'": *Misc. Wr., 2,* 78. On Robinson's recollection of Macaulay's use of the label "progressive," see *Henry Crabb Robinson on Books and Their Writers,* ed. Edith J. Morley, 3 vols. (London: Dent, 1938), *1,* 393.

22. *Speeches,* p. 538. When the queen, seeking Russell's participation in the Aberdeen coalition in 1852, informed him that she sought a government "at once conservative and reforming," Macaulay said he "could improve the Queen's letter neither in substance nor in language, and that she had expressed my sentiments to a tittle": Trevelyan, *Life, 2,*

263. In 1847 he said, "You call me a Liberal, but I don't know that in these days I deserve the name. I am opposed to the abolition of standing armies. I am opposed to the abrogation of capital punishment. I am opposed to the destruction of the National Church. In short, I am in favour of war, hanging, and church establishments": quoted in *Proceedings of the Literary and Philosophical Society of Liverpool,* no. 60 (1907), pp. 1-2. Perhaps symptomatic of his mood was his "theory for being always in favor of dominant and successful races—Spaniards against Indians, Anglo-Saxons agst Spaniards, Russians agst Poles, Virginians agst negroes": Diary of 7th earl of Carlisle, vol. 20, fol. 20 (17 March 1849). Also, on the occasion of the Ashton trial, "I am always for the man in possession": Journals, vol. 6, fol. 128 [9 August 1853]. By 1855 he could write that "the genius of Toryism" was its concern about "destroying at a blow institutions which had stood through ages, for the purpose of building something more symmetrical out of the ruins": *History,* 5, 2288. During the late 1850s he was uncertain about his political affiliations; he knew that he did not want a coalition with the Left; and he was embarrassed by his affinity with Tories. "I see that Ld Ellenborough made a speech exactly expressing all that I thought. A mad world!": Journals, vol. 11, fols. 462, 505-6 (1 April, 7, 8, June [1859]); TBM to Selina Macaulay, 29 January 1855, Trinity College Library. "There really are scarcely any public questions left on which the Ministers differ from the Whigs; and if personal resentments can be quieted, there may soon be a union of parties": Journals, vol. 11, fols. 279-80 (20 March 1858).

23. In another connection he said, "Perfect consistency, I admit, we are not to expect in human affairs. But, surely, there is a decent consistency which ought to be observed": *Hansard, 77,* 1289 (26 February 1845).

24. *Speeches,* p. 3 (2 March 1831); "Mitford" (1824), *Misc. Wr., 1,* 160. See also *Hansard, 11,* 456-57 (19 March 1832).

25. "Utilitarian System of Philosophy," *Edin. Rev., 49* (June 1829), 275.

26. "Mitford," *Misc. Wr., 1,* 160-62. The passage from which these statements are taken is also quoted at pp. 56-57, above. The formulation is strikingly similar to James Mill's in his "Essay on Government." Referring to writings and speeches of a later date, a severe critic (probably Roebuck) said, "We could point to passages almost copied verbatim from the pages of Mill and Bentham—passages, which, during the controversy in the *Edinburgh,* had been the subject of his animadversion" ("Mr. Macauley [*sic*], a Legislator for the Hindoos," *Tait's Edinburgh Magazine, 4* [January 1834], 488). In 1857 Macaulay said he was "certain that I never wrote a line, and that I never, in Parliament, in conversation, or even in the hustings ... uttered a word indicating an opinion that the supreme authority in a state ought to be intrusted to the majority of citizens told by the head, in other words, to the poorest and most ignorant part of society": *What Did Macaulay Say about America?*

Text of Four Letters to Henry S. Randall, ed. H. M. Lydenberg (New York Public Library, 1925), pp. 23-24.

27. "Mill's Essay on Government," *Edin. Rev., 49* (March 1829), 182; see also speech of 2 March 1831, in *Speeches,* pp. 3-4.

28. "Mackintosh," *Edin. Rev., 61* (July 1835), 287, 289.

29. *History, 5,* 2284. Most of Macaulay's statements on this subject concern improvement, not progress, and they are descriptions of observable conditions, not (what is often said by his critics) dogmatic assertions about a doctrine or theory of progress. On the other hand, Macaulay was influenced by the view of the Scottish Enlightenment that societies pass through stages from rudeness to refinement; this, however, is distinct from belief in a doctrine of progress; see Duncan Forbes, Introduction to Hume, *History of Great Britain* (Penguin, 1970), p. 38.

30. "Mackintosh," *Edin. Rev., 61,* 282, 287-88; "History," *Edin. Rev., 47,* 362-63; see also *History, 1,* 418.

31. "Southey's *Colloquies on Society,*" *Edin. Rev., 50* (January 1830), 557-61; see also *History, 1,* 414, 417.

32. "Southey," *Edin. Rev., 50,* 562-63. "Macaulay wished he could spend a day of every century in London since the Romans, tho' of the 2 he would rather spend a day in it 1800 years hence than 1800 years ago, as he can less easily conceive it. We agreed there never can have been 30 years in which all mechanical improvements have made so much progress as in the 30 last": Diary of 7th earl of Carlisle, vol. 28, fol. 20 (14 February 1852).

33. J. H. Plumb, *Men and Places* (Penguin, 1966), p. 282; H. R. Trevor-Roper, Introduction to Macaulay, *History of England* (New York: Washington Square Press, 1968), p. xxix; Pieter Geyl, "Macaulay in His Essays," *Debates with Historians* (New York: Meridian, 1958), pp. 43-44.

34. "The truth is that the evils are, with scarcely an exception, old. That which is new is the intelligence which discerns and the humanity which remedies them": *History, 1,* 412.

35. *Hansard, 11,* 455 (19 March 1832); see also *Speeches,* p. 428: "So visible was the misery of the manufacturing towns that a man of sensibility could hardly bear to pass through them. Everywhere he found filth and nakedness, and plaintive voices, and wasted forms, and haggard faces." On Ireland, see *History, 4,* 2076-82; *5,* 2362; *6,* 2697; *Hansard, 13,* 54 (24 May 1832); *72,* 1172 (19 February 1844).

36. "Bacon," *Edin. Rev., 65* (July 1837), 79-81.

37. *Speeches,* pp. 3, 265. "I believe that there are societies in which every man may safely be admitted to vote.... There are countries in which the condition of the labouring classes is such that they may safely be intrusted with the right of electing Members of the Legislature" (p. 3). From the hustings in 1839 he suggested that technological progress, free trade, and emigration to new countries would bring—indeed, was bringing—"a great and most blessed social revolution." This development would allow England to make her "institutions more democratic than they are, not by lowering the franchise to the level of the great mass of the community, but by raising, in a time which will be very short when

compared with the existence of a nation, the great mass up to the level of the franchise": *Speeches,* pp. 517, 519.

38. *Speeches,* p. 499; "Chatham," *Edin. Rev., 58,* 533; *History, 1,* 2; *3,* 1318; "It would be a great error to infer from the increase of complaint that there has been any increase of misery": *History, 1,* 406. Macaulay was not all complacency: He heard reports of distress and of prosperity. "There was much truth in both descriptions, but, at the same time, there was much fiction.... He could not agree in either of those extreme opinions.... We had vast resources, but ... [there was] the most appalling misery": *Hansard, 11,* 454–55 (19 March 1832).

39. *Speeches,* p. 264; see also pp. 3–4, 74, where the same theme is to be found in speeches of 1831 but in a context of argument less dubious about the long-run hopes of allowing the working classes to take part in politics. When, as a member of the Privy Council, Macaulay took part in the examination of one Edward Oxford, who had attempted to assassinate the queen, he did not attribute this incident to the Chartists but suspected that German agents "have played off on this young villain ... some delusion which has infatuated him. I should not wonder if they had worked him up by democratic stimulants for a purpose by no means democratic": from Macaulay's Journal for 10 and 11 June 1840, in *Macaulay: Prose and Poetry,* ed. G. M. Young (London, 1952), p. 804.

40. *Speeches,* 262, 265, 268 (3 May 1842); "Mill's Essay on Government," *Edin. Rev., 49,* 181; see also "Utilitarian System of Philosophy," *Edin. Rev., 49,* 284.

41. *Speeches,* pp. 264, 268; *History, 1,* 28. Chartists were "persons who profess doctrines subversive of all order and all property": *Hansard, 60,* 755 (21 February 1842); they were also "dishonest leaders" who stimulated "extravagant hopes" and by whom a mob was "exacerbated and infuriated": *Mirror of Parliament,* 2d ser. *16,* 1150 (9 March 1840).

42. To his mother he wrote (15 April 1828), "You have been there [the Old Town, Edinburgh]. But you have not seen the town—and no lady ever sees a town. It is only by walking on foot through all sorts of crowded streets at all hours that a town can be really studied to good purpose": Pinney, *Letters, 1,* 241. His account of the bill abolishing the privileges of Whitefriars and the Savoy is flavored by his own observations in London: there still "stood this labyrinth of squalid, tottering houses, close packed, every one, from cellar to cockloft, with outcasts whose life was one long war with society. The most respectable part of the population consisted of debtors who were in fear of bailiffs. The rest were attorneys struck off the roll ... sharpers, receivers of stolen goods ... and tawdry women, blooming with paint and brandy, who, in their anger, made free use of their nails and their scissors, yet whose anger was less to be dreaded than their kindness. With these wretches the narrow alleys of the sanctuary swarmed. The rattling of dice, the call for more punch and more wine, and the noise of blasphemy and ribald song never ceased during the whole night": *History, 6,* 2690.

43. "Fourierism, or Saint Simonianism, or Socialism, or any of those other 'isms' for which the plain English word is 'robbery' ": *Speeches,* p.

517. He also referred to a hypothetical "convention of socialists which proclaims all property to be robbery": *History, 5,* 2287; see also *Hansard, 16,* 1387 (1 April 1833).

44. *Speeches,* p. 268; TBM to H. S. Randall, 23 May 1857, in *What Did Macaulay Say about America?,* p. 24.

45. Journals, vol. 4, fols. 319-21 (3, 4, December [1851]); vol. 11, fols. 323-24 (28 May [1858]). Hobhouse reported a conversation with Macaulay: "He was all for Louis Napoleon": Broughton [John Cam Hobhouse], *Recollections of a Long Life,* ed. Lady Dorchester, 6 vols. (London, 1911), *6,* 290. "I think the existing government [of France] as good as any that is likely to rise in its place": TBM to Selina Macaulay, 5 April 1853, Trinity College Library. "Something is to be said for the man who sacrifices liberty to preserve order. Something is to be said for the man who sacrifices order to preserve liberty. For liberty and order are two of the greatest blessings which a society can enjoy; and, when unfortunately they appear to be incompatible, much indulgence is due to those who take either side": *History, 4,* 1711.

46. TBM to Randall, 23 May 1857, quoted in *What Did Macaulay Say about America?,* pp. 24-25. It might be argued that he had this view already in 1829: see the cryptic statement, "As for America, we appeal to the twentieth century": "Mill's Essay on Government," *Edin. Rev., 49,* 183. "When I left college it was the fashion of young liberals—I cannot say that it was ever exactly mine—to consider the American institutions as the very model of all good government. Now I find that even the most liberal men hold them exceedingly cheap.... I was never fanatical for them; and am not now disposed to be fanatical against them": Journals, vol. 1, fol. 282 (27 December [1839]). In 1822, at the Cambridge Union, Macaulay proposed and opened the question, "Does the Constitution of England or that of the United States of America tend more to promote the happiness of the people?" Macaulay spoke in favor of the English constitution: *Laws and Transactions of the Union Society* (Cambridge, 1834), p. 21. However, his sister Hannah, recalling family legend, reported that in the early 1820s (she was born in 1810), Charles Austin "inoculated him with his great admiration for American institutions": "Memoir of Macaulay by Hannah, Lady Trevelyan," fol. 29, Trinity College Library.

47. "Utilitarian System of Philosophy," *Edin. Rev., 49* (June 1829), 286.

48. *Greville Memoirs, 4,* 77.

49. *Speeches,* p. 32; see also p. 260; *Hansard, 11,* 459 (19 March 1832); *48,* 475 (18 June 1839).

50. He was at this time in favor of the secret ballot: see above, n. 13. He was opposed to pecuniary qualifications for MP's. He was opposed to annual or even triennial parliaments but was willing to shorten their duration to five years. He opposed the proposal that MP's be paid and that electoral districts be made equal and uniform but was willing to compromise on these matters too: *Speeches,* pp. 173, 259-60, 520.

51. *Speeches,* p. 512; see also p. 517. The extent of his willingness to

allow extensions of the suffrage of course varied (though he never favored universal suffrage); in 1840 and 1859 he was resistant, and in 1848 he was yielding: *Hansard, 51,* 818 (29 January 1840); Journals, vol. 11, fol. 444 (1 March [1859]); TBM to Russell, 23 April 1848, Russell Papers, PRO, 30/22/7B, fols. 331-35.

Chapter 6. Trimming and Whiggism

1. Herbert Butterfield, *The Englishman and His History* (Cambridge: At the University Press, 1944), pp. 79, 83-102, 112-38, and passim; see also W. H. Auden, Introduction to *Selected Writings of Sydney Smith* (New York: Farrar, Straus & Cudahy, 1956), pp. xvi-xvii.

2. *The Englishman and His History,* pp. 83, 138. It also has been said that Halifax's political creed is "the creed of John Bull": Walter Raleigh, Introduction to *The Complete Works of George Savile, First Marquess of Halifax* (Oxford, 1912), p. xiv.

3. *The Englishman and His History,* p. 73; see also pp. 84, 94, 97-98. Butterfield, while recognizing Whiggism as politically useful, remains critical of the Whig interpretation of history; however, the two are functionally interconnected (*ibid.*, pp. 2, 7, 72, 78-80, 120-23; see also Butterfield, *The Whig Interpretation of History* [London: Bell, 1971], passim).

4. Walter Bagehot, *The English Constitution,* World's Classics ed. (London: Oxford, 1955), pp. 126-27; *The Works and Life of Walter Bagehot,* ed. R. Barrington (London, 1915), *7,* 38-39. See also John Morley, *On Compromise* (London, 1874), p. 4.

5. *The Englishman and His History,* p. 92.

6. Rapin de Thoyras, *Dissertation sur les Whigs et les Torys* (London, 1717), pp. 46-50, 75-79, 87-88; see also pp. 22-24.

7. *Ibid.*, pp. 48-51, 77-78, 91; see also p. 81.

8. *The Englishman and His History,* p. 94.

9. Referring to Butterfield's qualification, W. R. Fryer writes, "He was highly justified in sounding such a note of caution respecting Rapin's appraisal of the Whig leadership in the heyday of Stanhope and the younger Sunderland. Indeed, had he been writing nearer the present time he might well have sounded an even louder note of caution, for the Whigs of Rapin's period, as they now appear in the pages of J. H. Plumb's Ford Lectures (1967), seem to merit a character violently in contrast with that which Rapin gave them": W. R. Fryer, "English Politics in the Age of Burke: Herbert Butterfield's Achievement," *Studies in Burke and His Time, 11,* no. 3 (Spring 1970), 1523-24.

10. Austin Mitchell, *The Whigs in Opposition, 1815-1830* (Oxford: Clarendon Press, 1967), p. 10; J. S. Watson, *The Reign of George III,* (Oxford: Clarendon Press, 1960), p. 361; W. R. Fryer, "The Study of British Politics between the Revolution and the Reform Act," *Renaissance and Modern Studies, 1* (1957), 105. Although closer to the notion of mediation held by Fox than to Macaulay's, Mackintosh provided perhaps

the most striking anticipation of Macaulay's conception of trimming in *A Letter to the Right Honourable William Pitt, on Apostasy from the Cause of Parliamentary Reform* (London, 1792), pp. 24, 33, 38, 43. It is notable not only for its use of the language of trimming but because Mackintosh, when writing his *History*, failed to introduce this theme (see chap. 4, above). That Mackintosh did not think the trimming theme of great importance is indicated by his statement (1818) that Burke's *Thoughts*, with its celebration of the principles of 1688, was "a work which was, is, and in its general principles must ever continue to be, the creed of English Whigs": quoted in Archibald S. Foord, *His Majesty's Opposition* (Oxford: Clarendon Press, 1964), p. 321. James Mill's charge of "see-saw" was directed against the eighteenth-century Whig rhetoric about mediation.

11. Alan Beattie, ed., *English Party Politics* (London: Weidenfeld & Nicolson, 1970), *1*, 23-27, 63-66. Beattie's selections from party rhetoric may be used as a sample; and there is hardly a hint of the trimming theme in his extracts from Whig writings and speeches.

12. Donald Southgate, *The Passing of the Whigs, 1832-1886* (London: Macmillan, 1962), p. xiv; "Mackintosh," *Edin. Rev., 61* (July 1835), 319-20; Beattie, *English Party Politics, 1,* 12.

13. "We are no admirers of the political doctrines laid down in Blackstone's Commentaries. But if we consider that those Commentaries were read with great applause in the very schools where, within the memory of some persons then living, books had been publicly burned by order of the University of Oxford for containing the 'damnable doctrine' that the English monarchy is limited and mixed, we cannot deny that a salutary change had taken place": "Mackintosh," *Edin. Rev., 61,* 322. Also, "doctrines favourable to public liberty were inculcated alike by those who were in power, and by those who were in opposition" (*ibid.*, p. 321). Locke's *Two Treatises of Government* in the 5th edition was reprinted for the sixth time in 1764; a 10th edition of the *Works* appeared in 1801.

14. Norman Gash, *Reaction and Reconstruction in English Politics* (Oxford: Clarendon Press, 1965), pp. 112, n. 3, 159; G. F. A. Best, "The Protestant Constitution and Its Supporters, 1800-1829," *Transactions of the Royal Historical Society,* 5th ser. *8* (1958), 110; Croker in *Hansard, 11,* 469 (19 March 1832).

15. Southgate, *Passing of the Whigs,* p. 12; Watson, *Reign of George III,* p. 441; G. M. Trevelyan, *Lord Grey of the Reform Bill* (London, 1920), pp. 29, 43.

16. E. Halévy, *History of the English People in the Nineteenth Century,* vol. 2: *The Liberal Awakening, 1815-1830,* 2d rev. ed. (London: Ernest Benn Ltd., 1949), pp. 34-35; George S. Veitch, *The Genesis of Parliamentary Reform* (London: Constable, 1965), p. 348; William H. Wickwar, *The Struggle for Freedom of the Press, 1819-1832* (London: Allen & Unwin, 1928), pp. 148-51; Michael Roberts, *The Whig Party, 1807-1812* (London: Cass, 1965), pp. 173-83, 235-39, 275-78.

17. Walter E. Houghton, *The Victorian Frame of Mind, 1830-1870*

(New Haven: Published for Wellesley College by Yale University Press, 1957), p. 54; see also pp. 55-57; R. K. Webb, *Modern England: From the Eighteenth Century to the Present* (New York: Dodd, Mead, 1968), p. 131, n. 1.

18. "Speech at Taunton," in *Works of the Rev. Sydney Smith* (London, 1854), p. 563.

19. The phrase was used with reference to the Whigs by Acton, but with a different purpose; and he identified different attributes; see Gertrude Himmelfarb, *Lord Acton: A Study in Conscience and Politics* (London: Routledge, 1952), p. 71.

20. Lord Holland, quoted by Macaulay in "The Late Lord Holland," *Edin. Rev., 73* (July 1841), 561.

21. Southgate, *Passing of the Whigs,* pp. 22, 194; Gash, *Reaction and Reconstruction,* pp. 6, 161-62, 169, 183-84; see also p. 121.

22. Nor was it an amalgam of these older ingredients of the heterogeneous Whig tradition with features of those nineteenth-century ideologies which became prominent only after Macaulay's political outlook took shape. Therefore, it is necessary to dispute the characterizations of his Whiggism that are typically made. For example, "His Whiggism in the historical field consisted of a belief in religious toleration and parliamentary government": G. M. Trevelyan, *Clio, A Muse* (London: Longmans, 1930), p. 169; or, he adopted "Whiggery, the politics of compromise and expedience, of property and free trade, and of progress": George Levine, *The Boundaries of Fiction: Carlyle, Macaulay, Newman* (Princeton: Princeton University Press, 1968), p. 80; or, we are told that, for Macaulay, "Whiggism was progress" and that he believed in laissez-faire and thus thought that problems would be solved automatically: H. R. Trevor-Roper, Introduction to Macaulay, *Critical and Historical Essays* (London: Collins, 1965), pp. 9, 13; and we hear that he was a spokesman for the "new liberalism": Houghton, *Victorian Frame of Mind,* p. 6. These statements say too little and they say too much. They ignore the distinctively trimming character of Macaulay's Whiggism; and they attribute to him doctrinal preferences associated with mid-century ideologies which he, who was as antiideological as Burke, was unwilling to acknowledge. His alleged belief in the automaticity of laissez-faire is hardly compatible with the great variation in his views of a free market, nor is it compatible with his belief in the necessary intervention of politicians to guide the process of change; and his observations on progress, which in any case did not constitute a doctrinal belief, require qualification in the light of his persistent apprehensions about destructive conflict and instability.

23. Quoted in Himmelfarb, *Acton,* pp. 208-9. Bagehot's observations—that Whigs were "heedless of large theories and speculations ... with a clear view of the next step" and that "Whiggism is not a creed, it is a character"—are also relevant. Macaulay (and Jeffrey) can be seen as making Whiggism into a creed, although this word suggests a doctrinal rigidity that is incompatible with Macaulay's purpose. Bagehot's characterization is applicable to many leading Whig politicians but not, as he

thought, to Macaulay and Jeffrey. See "The First Edinburgh Reviewers" (1855) in *The Works and Life of Walter Bagehot*, ed. R. Barrington, *2*, 62.

24. John Clive (*Macaulay: The Shaping of the Historian* [New York, 1973], pp. 41-44, 61, 95) has deemphasized Zachary's legendary Toryism, suggesting that he became more hopeful of support for the antislavery cause from Whigs than from Tories and that his liberal views were so emphatic that one cannot properly call him a Tory. However, this does not fit with Zachary's wish to avoid mixing antislavery agitation with other political issues; Zachary was unwilling to risk losing Tory support for his favorite cause by allowing liberal views on other issues to be promoted at an antislavery meeting. "You know that men of all . . . varieties of political creed from the highest tory, and the fiercest corn monopolist, and the most resolute enemy to parliamentary reform, profess to concur in the condemnation of Slavery. . . . It seems expedient to do nothing connected directly with the anti-slavery cause . . . which seem to call for a concurrence in matters which would impinge on prejudices however unreasonable": Zachary Macaulay to Brougham, 14 August 1830, University College London, Brougham Papers, 10571. This is in keeping with TBM's statement that slavery "is a question which does not promote the objects, or rest upon the support, of any faction. It is a question which has united men of all sects and parties; which has combined Tories with Reformers . . .": "On West Indian Slavery," *Knight's Quarterly Magazine, 1* (June 1823), 85. Furthermore, Trevelyan thought of Zachary as a Tory (*Life, 1*, 63-65, 87), as did Zachary's daughter Hannah, who said Macaulay's views on going up to Cambridge "were very much those of his Father and his set. I suppose what was then considered very liberal Toryism. As time went on and my Father found that only the very liberal section of Parliament would support his Anti Slavery views, he gradually more and more became a decided Whig, but I can well remember about 1820 the family views were Tory" ("Memoir," fol. 29: Trinity College Library). There can be no doubt about the conservatism of many of his opinions, especially his fear of radicalism and his wish to repress it: see pp. 18-19 and n. 39 in chap. 1.

25. TBM to Zachary Macaulay, [September 1819], [13? November 1820], Pinney, *Letters, 1*, 132-34, 148. Trevelyan, *Life, 1*, 88-89. Disapproval of the government's policy did not necessarily make him a partisan of the queen. Two Trinity contemporaries had differing recollections of his views on the queen: Pinney, *Letters, 1*, p. 148, n. 2. Trevelyan states that Macaulay and his father were partisans of the queen: *Life, 1*, 91. But with regard to Zachary, Knutsford presents evidence that does not support this: Margaret Knutsford, *The Life and Letters of Zachary Macaulay* (London: Arnold, 1900), pp. 351, 361, 364, 365. Macaulay had a rather iconoclastic attitude toward the coronation ceremony in 1821: TBM to Zachary Macaulay, 9 August 1821, Pinney, *Letters, 1*, 159.

26. Lionel A. Tollemache, "Mr. Charles Austin," *Fortnightly Review*, n.s. *17* (1875), 323. Trevelyan, *Life, 1*, 71-72. On Charles Austin at this

time, see J. S. Mill, *Autobiography*, World's Classics ed. (London, 1958), pp. 64-66.

27. Trevelyan, *Life, 2,* 353; see also *ibid., 1,* 73, where Macaulay is described as "plying Austin with sarcasms upon the doctrine of the Greatest Happiness." See also above, p. 56.

28. Tollemache, "Mr. Charles Austin," p. 326. It would appear that Austin was a religious skeptic at this time, not only by reputation, but as indicated by the style and mode of argument, including his criteria of evaluation, in his Hulsean Prize essay: *The Argument for the Genuineness of the Sacred Volume, as generally received by Christians, Stated and Explained* (Cambridge, 1823). However, the nominal and explicit orthodoxy of his essay should be noted. He was later reported to have said he could have written a much better essay on the other side: Tollemache, "Mr. Charles Austin," p. 332. He was also described as a reformer who "declared war against all existing institutions in a mild constitutional fashion. The war was never a very bitter one": *Pall Mall Budget,* 2 January 1875, p. 21.

29. TBM to Zachary Macaulay, [September 1819], 31 August 1821, Pinney, *Letters, 1,* 132, 161-62.

30. Recollection of Henry Sykes Thornton in Dorothy Alston, "Some Personal Recollections of Lord Macaulay," *London Mercury, 18* (May 1928), 60. The author reported that Thornton "carefully remembered and preserved" this and other recollections, but no date is attributed to them. "The two young men were not much occupied with politics; they read the newspapers 'almost daily' . . . ; Macaulay's love of discussion would have prevented his taking any definite side" (p. 62). Thornton's father (also Henry) was a banker and an MP and was associated with Zachary in various Evangelical enterprises. Henry Sykes Thornton's journal, used by Alston, has not been found.

31. Tristram Merton [i.e., Macaulay], "On West Indian Slavery," *Knight's Quarterly Magazine, 1,* pt. 1 (June 1823), 85.

32. *Laws and Transactions of the Union Society, revised and corrected to March, 1834. To which is annexed A List of Members and Officers, from its formation in 1815, and a List of the periodical and other Works taken in by the Society* (Cambridge, 1834), pp. 20-21, 23.

33. Richard Perry, *Contributions to an Amateur Magazine, in Prose and Verse, with a Preface, and Additional Notes,* 2d ed. (London, 1861), p. 311 (Perry entered Trinity in the same year as Macaulay); Derwent Coleridge, "Memoir," in *The Poems of Winthrop Mackworth Praed* (New York, 1885), *1,* 34-35 (Coleridge also was a Trinity contemporary); [Charles Knight], *Knight's Quarterly Magazine, 1* (June-October 1823), 16 (where the reference is to Macaulay's pseudonym "Merton"); *St. James's Chronicle,* 8 October 1864, pp. 764-65.

34. *Laws and Transactions of the Union Society,* pp. 25-27.

35. "Mitford," *Misc. Wr., 1,* 159, 168.

36. *Ibid.,* pp. 160-61. See above, chap. 5, pp. 126-27 and n. 26. It was reported that at one time he had been intimately acquainted with Benthamites; see "Mr. Macauley [*sic*], a Legislator for the Hindoos,"

Tait's Edinburgh Magazine, 4, (January 1834), 486.

37. Trevelyan, *Life, 1,* 72 n. The statement was made to John Hampden Gurney (1802-62), a Trinity College contemporary (B.A. 1824). Trevelyan did not give the source or the precise date.

38. "Milton," *Edin. Rev., 42* (August 1825), 324, 325, 329, 331, 334. See Clive, *Macaulay,* chap. 4, for the argument that historical interpretations, especially in the essay on Milton, reveal enduring political attitudes. But Clive infers too much from this essay; and on the basis of it, but contrary to much other evidence, he attributes to Macaulay long-standing convictions that he did not have. Compare Macaulay's statement in 1843, that the essay on Milton "contains scarcely a paragraph such as his matured judgment approves"; although he was condemning the essay's style, he also appears to be referring to its substance: Preface to *Critical and Historical Essays* (London, 1895; 1st ed., 1843), *1,* viii. See above, pp. 149, 154, and nn. 41 and 60, this chapter.

39. Mill, *Autobiography,* p. 107; *Henry Crabb Robinson on Books and Their Writers,* ed. Edith J. Morley, 3 vols. (London: Dent, 1938), *1,* 341.

40. "Mitford," *Misc. Wr., 1,* 160.

41. Compare Clive, *Macaulay:* Macaulay's purpose was "to see Milton from within the context of the politics of the 1820's, and to pay homage to him as one of the chief representatives of a well-defined political tradition" (p. 81), i.e., the Commonwealth tradition as described by Caroline Robbins in *The Eighteenth Century Commonwealthman* (Cambridge, Mass.: Harvard University Press, 1961). "This tradition of radical Whiggism . . . is very much alive in Macaulay's Milton essay" (Clive, p. 87). According to Clive, Macaulay, by praising Milton, was "taking sides against the Establishment"; it was a way of "declaring one's allegiance to the 'good old cause,' to the popular, the anti-aristocratic, side" (p. 89). The Milton essay was a "political manifesto" (p. 81) that identified Macaulay with "the most radical" kind of Whiggism (p. 87). See also my "Macaulay's Politics," *Reviews in European History, 1* (September 1974), 206-14.

42. "A Conversation between Mr. Abraham Cowley and Mr. John Milton, touching the Great Civil War. Set down by a Gentleman of the Middle Temple" (August 1824), *Misc. Wr., 1,* 104, 123.

43. "Milton," *Edin. Rev., 42,* 341, 343. Also, Milton "was not a Puritan. He was not a freethinker. He was not a Cavalier. In his character the noblest qualities of every party were combined in harmonious union" (*ibid.,* p. 342).

44. "A Conversation between . . . Cowley and . . . Milton," *Misc. Wr., 1,* 123; these words are attributed to Milton in the imaginary conversation. Compare the 1822 prize essay: "The blind veneration for antiquity, however it may be despised . . . should be judiciously indulged. The leaders of revolutions, instead of considering how much it may be possible to change, should reflect how much it may be safe to spare": "Essay on William III," p. 469. There are other close parallels between the two essays.

45. "Milton," *Edin. Rev.*, *42*, 333; "A Conversation between ... Cowley and ... Milton," *Misc. Wr.*, *1*, 122-23.

46. "Milton," *Edin. Rev.*, *42*, 335-36.

47. *Laws and Transactions of the London Debating Society, with a list of the Members, Corrected up to November 1st, 1826* (London, 1826), pp. 15, 20. Macaulay is listed as a member (p. 24), but his name does not appear as a speaker. John Stuart Mill in his *Autobiography* (World's Classics ed., pp. 107-8) implies that Macaulay had not taken part.

48. Mill described with satisfaction how debate "was a *bataille rangée* between the 'philosophic Radicals' and the Tory lawyers," and remarked that "our debates were very different from those of common debating societies, for they habitually consisted of the strongest arguments and most philosophic principles which either side was able to produce, thrown often into close and *serré* confutations of one another" (*Autobiography*, pp. 108-9). Mill's description refers in the main to debates that took place after Macaulay ceased attending, but it is assumed that Macaulay had an opportunity to discern the spirit in which the enterprise would be conducted. Macaulay had already met Mill, then in his most doctrinaire period, through Charles Austin (*ibid.*, p. 65). These encounters provided some of the basis for Macaulay's characterizations of the young Benthamites in his articles of 1827 and 1829-30.

49. Canning also made it clear to prospective Whig colleagues that parliamentary reform was not to be brought forward. Canning also opposed repeal of the Test and Corporation Acts. He had been a contributor to the *Quarterly Review;* see P. J. V. Rolo, *George Canning* (London: Macmillan, 1965), pp. 11, 131, 152, 155, 186. For Macaulay's response to Canning's opposition to parliamentary reform, see "Present Administration," *Edin. Rev., 46* (June 1827), 256.

50. G. M. Trevelyan, *Lord Grey of the Reform Bill* (London, 1920), pp. 123, 201-8. Brougham thought Grey's objections "proceeded on the old Fox feelings towards him": Henry Brougham, *The Life and Times of Henry Lord Brougham* (New York, 1871), *2*, 365. Mackintosh supported the coalition, and Sydney Smith opposed it.

51. She added, "In the latest account of the numbers I have yet seen Mr. [William John] Bankes was three above Sir N. Tyndall [*sic*] so that Tom's vote will not come at all amiss": Selina Macaulay's Journal, 10 May 1827, Huntington Library. Tindal was successful, by a vote of 479 to 378; but when Macaulay decided to go to Cambridge, he probably knew only about the first day's voting as reported in the *Times:* Bankes, 102, and Tindal, 99 (this report was incomplete, for the first day's result was Bankes, 173, and Tindal, 174). Both were Tories, but Bankes was opposed to Catholic emancipation: see Macaulay's "The Country Clergyman's Trip to Cambridge: An Election Ballad," *Misc. Wr., 2,* 413-16. It is not clear how important the Catholic question was in Macaulay's vote. Whereas Bankes was vociferously anti-Catholic, Tindal also professed this view in an election circular; and the *Times* reported that Tindal had voted and would vote again against Catholic emancipation: *Times,* 8 May 1827, p. 3; 10 May, p. 3; 14 May, p. 2; 19 May, p. 3; *Cambridge*

Chronicle and Journal, 4 May 1827, p. 3; 11 May, p. 3. Tindal had been in Parliament since 1824 and had been appointed solicitor-general by Liverpool in 1826. Macaulay, while on the Northern Circuit, had met him at Sydney Smith's; he called him one of the "best lawyers, best scholars, and best men in England": TBM to Zachary Macaulay, 26 July 1826, Pinney, *Letters, 1,* 215.

52. Brougham, who had an important initiative in arranging for Whig participation, saw the coalition as a way of promoting gradual and moderate reform. He was critical of Macaulay's article, which had appeared in the issue immediately preceding: "State of Parties," *Edin. Rev., 46,* (October 1827), 415, 419, 421-22, 431-32. It has been suggested that, if Canning had not died in 1827, he might have dominated a coalition (including the Whigs) that might have held together. "The new 'liberal' party which could thus have emerged would have had a greater Tory bias and would surely have known more enemies to the left": Rolo, *Canning,* pp. 5, 60. Had this happened, what would Macaulay's political affiliation and reputation have been?

53. "Hallam," *Edin. Rev., 48* (September 1828), 100. Hallam, like Macaulay, is judged quite differently by professional historians. See above, pp. 101-4 and n. 78 in chap. 4.

54. "Mill's Essay on Government," *Edin. Rev., 49* (March 1829), 173.

55. See above, p. 118. Jeffrey demonstrated his appreciation of Macaulay's outlook by offering him the editorship of the *Edinburgh Review* in 1829: [Margaret Macaulay], *Recollections by a Sister of T. B. Macaulay* (1834) (London: Privately printed, 1864), p. 56.

56. G. M. Young states that at Cambridge Macaulay was converted to the Whigs by Charles Austin and Lord Carnarvon: *Daylight and Champaign* (London: Cape, 1937), p. 17. "At Cambridge, however, his opinions changed. In the upshot after some hesitation he became what one may term a Whig, though that word does not convey very much": Mark A. Thomson, *Macaulay* (London: The Historical Association, 1959), p. 7. G. P. Gooch assumes he was a Whig when, in 1822, he wrote the "Essay on William III": *History and Historians in the Nineteenth Century* (London: Longmans, 1961), p. 282. Another example of the assumption that he became a Whig while still at Cambridge is the biography in the English Men of Letters series by J. Cotter Morison, *Macaulay* (London, 1889): At university "occurred his single change of opinions throughout life" (p. 10); "in the heyday of youth and spirits and talent, he took his side with the old and practical Whigs. . . . He was a Whig by necessity of nature, by calmness of passion, combined with superlative common sense" (p. 12). It would be helpful to know the identity of the newspaper whose offer of a job as political writer Macaulay turned down in 1822: TBM to his mother, 16 February 1822, Pinney, *Letters, 1,* 171.

57. For what it was worth, Jeffrey said of the *Edinburgh Review* that "though agreeing in the main with their [the old Constitutional Whigs'] tenets, we do not profess to acknowledge their authority, or to be guided in our opinions by any thing but our own imperfect lights": *Edin. Rev., 45* (December 1826), 32.

58. He accepted patronage from the Tory lord chancellor in January 1828, when appointed a commissioner of bankrupts. However, he heard of the appointment in January 1828, between ministries, and he welcomed this, since he thought "it implies no political obligations": Trevelyan, *Life, 1,* 129. However, in May 1827 he would have welcomed the appointment while Canning's ministry was still in office: Selina Macaulay's Journal, 7 May 1827, Huntington Library. Brougham asked the lord chancellor to appoint Macaulay "on account of the new Government we both support [i.e., Canning's]...; you do a lasting service to *our* Ministry. His father is an old friend of mine, but I should have written this letter if I never had seen him, on account of our common cause": Margaret Knutsford, *Life of Zachary Macaulay* (London, 1900), p. 442. Date not given, but reference to this letter was made in Selina's Journal, 1 May 1827.

59. Caroline Robbins, *The Eighteenth Century Commonwealthman,* pp. 7, 20, 320–21, 357; see also Foreword to paperback reprint (New York: Atheneum, 1968), p. ix.

60. "Hallam," *Edin. Rev., 42,* 99: "The cause for which Hampden bled on the field and Sidney on the scaffold is enthusiastically toasted by many an honest radical who would be puzzled to explain the difference between Ship-money and the Habeas Corpus act ...; as in religion, so in politics, few even of those who are enlightened enough to comprehend the meaning latent under the emblems of their faith can resist the contagion of the popular superstition." Another example, from a later period, is found in *History, 6,* 2734: "though an ardent, it was at the same time a corrupt and degenerate Whiggism...; [Spencer's] imagination had been fascinated by those swelling sentiments of liberty which abound in the Latin poets and orators; and he ... meant by liberty something very different from the only liberty which is of importance to the happiness of mankind. Like them, he could see no danger to liberty except from kings. A commonwealth, oppressed and pillaged by such men as Opimius and Verres, was free, because it had no king." See also *History, 6,* 2736, where John Trenchard is depreciated as spokesman for "malcontent Whigs" and is contrasted to Macaulay's hero, Somers. See also above, pp. 148–49. An exception appears in Macaulay's 1839 Edinburgh election speech, where it is the Whig party that "forced Charles the First to relinquish the ship-money ... destroyed the Star Chamber.... The good old cause, as Sidney called it on the scaffold, ... is still the good old cause with me": *Speeches,* 183–84. Far from endorsing the idea of a commonwealth in 1830, he thought that, apart from religious policy, the government of Charles I was not so bad. "In spite of the illegal proceedings of the Stuarts, the civil government had been in the main good. The ecclesiastical government had been intolerable": "The History of France, from the Restoration of the Bourbons to the Accession of Louis Philippe," p. 9, Longman Archives at University of Reading. I am grateful to Longman Group Ltd. for permission to quote from this. For conventional definitions of Whiggism that had historical importance but were clearly not relevant to nineteenth-century politics, see *History, 3,* 1284, 1323; "Mackintosh," *Edin. Rev., 61,* 319–20.

61. On Burke, see above, pp. 182-88. G. M. Trevelyan, *History of England* (London: Longmans, 1945), pp. 568-69. The connection with Holland House perhaps restrained Macaulay's judgments of Fox. There is a neat balance in his comparison of Fox's *History* with Mackintosh's; as a historian Mackintosh is better, but as an orator Fox excels: "Mackintosh," *Edin. Rev., 61,* 265-67. In the 1839 Edinburgh election speech he said, on the one hand, that he did not mean by a Whig "one who approves the whole conduct of any statesman, though that statesman may have been Fox"; on the other hand, he praised the Whig party for opposing the war against the French Republic: *Speeches,* p. 183. Macaulay was reluctant to write about Holland on the occasion of his death; Russell was not satisfied with Macaulay's estimate and published his own: TBM to Allen, 4 May 1841, Holland Papers, BM, Add. MSS 52193, unfol.; Lord John Russell, Preface, in *Memoirs, Journals, and Correspondence of Thomas Moore,* ed. Lord John Russell (London, 1854), *6,* xv-xvii. It is necessary to dispute Acton's statement that Macaulay was a Foxite Whig: Acton, *Essays on Church and State,* ed. D. Woodruff (London: Hollis & Carter, 1952), p. 434, also p. 433. It is only necessary to compare Macaulay's views on either Burke or Somers. On Somers, see *History, 6,* 2736-37, 2878. For a direct comparison of Fox and Burke, see "William Pitt," *Misc. Wr., 2,* 314.

62. Pitt was the man of liberal opinions who shifted positions because of changing circumstances. But he was unable to meet the highest test for a statesman: he did not manage a great crisis. With the rise of Jacobinism and the threat from France, he was not vigorous enough in prosecuting the war and was too vigorous in prosecuting radicalism at home. He had the misfortune to be a moderate statesman in immoderate times. He was "preeminently qualified, intellectually and morally, for the part of a parliamentary leader, and capable of administering with prudence and moderation the government of a prosperous and tranquil country, but unequal to surprising and terrible emergencies, and liable, in such emergencies, to err grievously, both on the side of weakness and on the side of violence": "William Pitt" (1859), *Misc. Wr., 2,* 346-47, 373. Already in 1832 Macaulay said of Pitt that, had he "lived in 1832, it is our firm belief that he would have been a decided reformer": "Mirabeau," *Edin. Rev., 55* (July 1832), 557. Pitt is held up as an example, and it is noted that Burke largely influenced him: *Hansard, 72,* 1183 (19 February 1844).

63. *Speeches,* p. 75 (16 December 1831). In another account, describing France but with categories based on British experience, he said, "fanatics of one kind might anticipate a golden age, in which men should live under the simple dominion of reason, in perfect equality and perfect amity, without property, or marriage, or king, or God. A fanatic of another kind might see nothing in the doctrines of the philosophers but anarchy and atheism, might cling more closely to every old abuse": "Walpole," *Edin. Rev., 58* (October 1833), 234.

64. [Margaret Macaulay], *Recollections by a Sister,* p. 96 (entry of 15 [March? 1832]). Compare above, p. 124.

65. It might be said in passing that it was one of Macaulay's most significant failures of political judgment that he did not discern the way

Peel's flexibility in tactics and conciliatory and reformist goals would be imposed on the Tory party. It was not evident in the way that Peel and Wellington yielded to the demand for Catholic Emancipation. In the end, Macaulay came to recognize Peel's qualities, but this came very slowly. Recent scholarship on Peel emphasizes the flexible, conciliatory character of his leadership; see Gash, *Reaction and Reconstruction,* pp. 45-47, 70, 83, 118-22, 130, 139-43, 149-54, 158, 166, 187. However, Macaulay was not altogether unrealistic, for the ultras were a problem for Peel; see *ibid.,* pp. 33-34, 46, 120, 143, 150-52. Macaulay in 1827 was not unaware of Peel's "propensity to innovation" and "tendencies to liberality": "Present Administration," *Edin. Rev., 46,* 260. On personal relations with Peel, see Trevelyan, *Life, 2,* 103, 212; they served together as trustees of the British Museum.

66. Gladstone, *Gleanings, 2,* 267-68; see also p. 270. Referring to the introduction of the Reform Bill in 1831, Macaulay called it "an epoch in my life as well as in that of the nation": Journal, vol. 8, fol. 16 (13 February 1854).

67. [James Grant], *Random Recollections of the House of Commons,* 3d ed. (London, 1836), pp. 170-72. He was compared to Burke: Trevelyan, *Life, 1,* 287. After the 1824 antislavery speech, Mr. Wilberforce compared him with Pitt and Fox: Alice C. C. Gaussen, ed., *A Later Pepys: The Correspondence of Sir William Weller Pepys* (London, 1904), *2,* 382. A friend who heard one of his Reform speeches recalled that "the House was entranced, almost breathless ... absorbed as the opera house is by a first-rate singer": J. L. Adolphus to Milman, 14 December 1861, Munby Collection, Trinity College Library. Edward Lytton Bulwer remembered one of his speeches at the Union as something that "still lingers in my recollection as the most heart-stirring effort of that true oratory which seizes hold of the passions, transports you from yourself, and identifies you with the very life of the orator": *Life of Edward Bulwer, First Lord Lytton* (London, 1913), *1,* 79. The eulogies seem endless, especially for his Reform Bill speeches; see *Three Early Nineteenth Century Diaries,* ed. A. Aspinall (London: Williams & Norgate, 1952), pp. 100, 130, 149-50, 169, 171, 255. However, occasionally there were dissenting views, including complaints about the quality of his voice. See n. 83, this chapter.

68. Broughton [John Cam Hobhouse], *Recollections of a Long Life,* ed. Lady Dorchester, 6 vols. (London, 1911), *4,* 156; *Hansard, 82* (9 July 1845); on another occasion Graham complained of "some spirit of word-catching" in Macaulay's "bitter party speech": *Hansard, 70,* 810-11 (7 July 1843). Gladstone said Macaulay "never had any idea of proportion, and often would absolutely despise an opponent who the world thought nearly his equal; and this was the case with Croker": Sir Algernon West, *Recollections 1832 to 1886* (New York, 1900), 280. His animosity for Croker preceded their political confrontation. As early as 1826 there is a clue as to its origin. "We have observed that," Macaulay wrote, "since Mr. Croker, in the last session of Parliament, declared himself ignorant of the site of Russell Square, the plan of forming an

University in so inelegant a neighborhood has excited much contempt amongst those estimable persons who think that the whole dignity of man consists in living within certain districts": "The London University," *Edin. Rev., 43* (February 1826), 319. In 1823, because of financial difficulties, the Macaulay family moved from Cadogan Place to 50 Great Ormond Street.

69. Reported by his sister Margaret in *Recollections by a Sister,* p. 59. One college friend, John Moultrie, said of him,

> Of intellectual matter . . .
> . . . [he] turn'd, with ready tact,
> Its huge artillery on whatever point
> It pleased him to assail, — and (sooth to say)
> He was not over-scrupulous; — to him
> There was no pain like silence — no constraint
> So dull as unanimity: — he breathed
> An atmosphere of argument, nor shrank
> From making, where he could not find, excuse
> For controversial fight.

(*The Dream of Life; Lays of the English Church; and Other Poems* [London, 1843], p. 89).

70. For example, Southey was "the lowest and worst of men, his friend and ally Croker excepted": Journals, vol. 3, fol. 134 (12 January [1851]). A colleague on the board of control was "a fat, ugly, spiteful, snarling, sneering, old rascal of a slave-driver"; and there was "that hairy, filthy, blackguard Sibthorpe": TBM to Hannah and Margaret Macaulay, 25 June and [9] August 1832, Pinney, *Letters, 2,* 139, 174.

71. "Francis Atterbury," *Misc. Wr.,* 2, 215–16. He later regretted some of his published observations; had he known his reviews would be remembered, he said, "I would have abstained from expressing myself in that acrimonious and scornful manner which has always been but too fashionable in critical journals. I daily regret the asperity with which I inconsiderately treated writers": TBM to George M. Gleig, 22 June 1851, National Library of Scotland.

72. Gash, *Reaction and Reconstruction,* pp. 128–29. "The rage of faction at the present moment [1831] exceeds any thing that has been known in our time. Indeed I doubt whether at the time of . . . the desperate struggle between the Whigs and Tories at the close of Anne's reign, the rage of party was so fearfully violent": TBM to Hannah Macaulay, 15 July 1831, Pinney, *Letters, 2,* 70. "Read the file of the Times during some months of 1834. . . . I was struck by the savage ferocity of much of the writing": Journals, vol. 5, fol. 36 (27 April [1852]). In 1849, on reading in the *Morning Chronicle* for 1811, he noted, "How scandalously the Whig Press treated the Duke of Wellington, till his merit became too great to be disputed! How extravagantly unjust party spirit makes men!": Trevelyan, *Life, 2,* 197.

73. TBM to Hannah Macaulay, 12 August, 13, 15 September 1831, Pinney, *Letters, 2,* 87–88, 99–101. He claimed to be the one who planned and organized the back-bench pressure on the Ministry that culminated

in Lord Ebrington's motion in October 1831: *ibid.*, p. 106. He said that if the Whig ministers resigned without passing the Reform Bill, he would take the Chiltern Hundreds, and, he added, "I never will consent to follow their lead more": [Margaret Macaulay], *Recollections by a Sister,* p. 96 (entry of 15 [March? 1832]).

74. Southgate, *Passing of the Whigs,* p. xv.

75. Selina Macaulay's Journal, entry of 19 January 1830, Huntington Library; until 1832 there were "about eighteen voters": A. E. W. Marsh, *A History of the Borough and Town of Calne* (Calne, 1904), p. 41. The population was 4,973 in 1831; 188 electors voted for Macaulay's successor in 1832, when again the election was uncontested: F. H. McCalmont, *The Parliamentary Poll Book,* 6th ed. (London, 1906), p. 40.

76. There were other reasons, to be sure, notably, his father's financial position and his concern for his younger and dependent sisters. His fear of being dependent on his pen for income must also have played a part; such "literary drudgery" would be incompatible with politics. In this connection his image of Grub Street is of interest. He referred to it with pity that turned to contempt: there were bookseller's hacks, starving pamphleteers and index-makers, famished scribblers, "the society of the lower and coarser class of literary men," the "mere adventurer [such as Addison], a man who when out of office, must live by his pen": TBM to Hannah Macaulay, 5 October 1833; to T. F. Ellis, 28 November 1833, Pinney, *Letters, 2,* 314, 345; "Samuel Johnson," *Misc. Wr., 2,* 273. "Walpole," *Edin. Rev., 58* (July 1833), 257. Macaulay's continuing deliberations as to whether he should pursue politics or literature were affected by these considerations. He was careful to define his own literary role in a way that sharply distinguished it from the Grub Street image. In a discussion of Dryden, Addison, Swift, Cowper, and Johnson he referred to "our caste," and he thought himself responsible for the "due mainte-nance of literary police": Trevelyan, *Life, 1,* 438; *Edin. Rev., 49* (June 1829), 274.

77. TBM to Hannah Macaulay, 22 July 1833, Pinney, *Letters, 2,* 275-76. This theme is also discussed in Clive, *Macaulay,* pp. 216-18.

78. Journals, vol. 11, fol. 416 (8 January [1859]). He had been reading the novel *Peer and Parvenus* by Mrs. [Catherine] Gore (London, 1846). In the novel he would have found the university described as a place where "the winter sky is illustrated by brilliant comets . . . and the seats of learning acquire sudden illustration from some Northern light or Macaulay of the minute," and "A member of the university having recently rendered his high college honours prefatory to unparalleled triumphs in the senate, had just then brought learning into vogue; and no distinction exceeded in influence the distinctions of talent" (vol. 1, p. 155). "He supplied an example rather rare of one who, not having been a Whig by birth, became one": Gladstone, *Gleanings, 2,* 288. It was said that "A Whig is like a poet, born not made. It is as difficult to become a Whig as to become a Jew": Sir F. Baring (*c.* 1840), in A. Beattie, ed., *English Party Politics, 1,* 97.

79. "Milton," *Edin. Rev., 42,* 318-19. "Hallam," *Edin. Rev., 48,* 99.

80. "A Speech delivered at Edinburgh on the 29th of May, 1839," in *Speeches,* pp. 182-84.

81. "Hallam," *Edin. Rev., 48,* 159.

82. Edward L. Pierce, *Memoir and Letters of Charles Sumner* (London, 1878), *1,* 364. One observer said that his speeches placed the subject "in an entirely new light. After he has spoken ... the debate usually takes a new turn. Members on both sides of the House, and of all ranks, are to be found shaping their remarks, either in confirmation or refutation of what Mr. Macaulay has said; so influential is his bold, uncompromising mode of handling a question": G. H. Francis, *Orators of the Age* (London, 1847), pp. 92-93.

83. *Three Early Nineteenth Century Diaries,* pp. 100, 346. Althorp thought that occasionally this quality was accompanied by the defect of insufficient detail and fact. Lansdowne to Brougham, 17 December [1833], University College, London, Brougham Papers, 38924. Bulwer-Lytton, who knew him from these years in the House of Commons, described the way Macaulay achieved intellectual leadership, although mainly with reference to his writings: "if he is not suggestive to men who wish to think for themselves, he is extremely convincing to men who dislike that trouble. He was really meant for an orator—an advocate": Bulwer-Lytton to Hayward, 26 November 1861: *A Selection from the Correspondence of Abraham Hayward,* ed. Henry E. Carlisle (London, 1886), *2,* 86. Sheil noted that Macaulay "has the power of coming forward on great occasions with a speech that commands the House" (*Three Early Nineteenth Century Diaries,* p. 169). Le Marchant thought the speech of 16 December 1831 "brilliant ... up to that time certainly his greatest, in which his noble vindication of the policy of the Whigs during their exclusion from office, and his crushing attack on Sir Robert Peel, were received with the most tremendous cheers": Denis Le Marchant, *Memoir of John Charles Viscount Althorp, Third Earl Spencer* (London, 1876), pp. 328, 382. To Mackintosh he was "the Orator of his Time": Mackintosh to Lady Holland, n.d. [1831], Holland Papers, BM, Add. MSS 51655, fol. 173b. Sydney Smith said that in 1839, after his return from India, Macaulay was "brought in for the express purpose of speechification": *The Letters of Sydney Smith,* ed. Nowell C. Smith (Oxford: Clarendon Press, 1953), *2,* 693. Macaulay's opponents also saw him cast in the role of leading spokesman for his party; see, e.g., Myron F. Brightfield, *John Wilson Croker* (Berkeley: University of California Press, 1940), p. 64; *The Critic in Parliament* (London, 1841), pp. 90-91.

84. *The Collected Works of Walter Bagehot,* ed. N. St. John-Stevas (Cambridge, Mass.: Harvard University Press, 1965), *1,* 400.

85. *History, 1,* 22. This view is the very opposite of William Madden's: "In his *History* ... Macaulay was seeking refuge in the past...; to have brought the history ... down to the real and threatening present, would have meant leaving that 'past and unreal' world in which ... his preconceptions were secure, his emotional life unthreatened, and his histrionic

temperament free to exercise itself without restraint. . . . Like Macaulay's Victorian reader, what we remember when we finish the book is the 'going back' . . . and the re-living of events the most memorable aspects of which have little to do with the history of England's material, moral, and intellectual progress": "Macaulay's Style," in George Levine and William Madden, eds., *The Art of Victorian Prose* (New York: Oxford, 1968), pp. 149-50.

86. Trevelyan, *Life, 1,* 408-9, 442-43; TBM to [Russell?], n.d. [*c.* January 1842], Russell Papers, PRO, 30/22/4B, fol. 258. One wonders whether Macaulay in 1838 feared that his characterization of Sir William Temple might apply to himself: "He was merely a man of lively parts and quick observation, a man of the world amongst men of letters, — a man of letters amongst men of the world. Mere scholars were dazzled by the Ambassador and Cabinet councillor; mere politicians by the Essayist and Historian": "Temple," *Edin. Rev., 68* (October 1838), 187.

87. Sydney Smith explained it differently: "Mcaulay [*sic*] had resolved to lead a Literary Life but cannot withstand the temptation—like Ladies who resolve upon celibacy if they have no offers" (1838): *Letters of Sydney Smith, 2,* 675.

88. Macaulay's sense of political responsibility was reflected in his harsh judgment of Sir William Temple for withdrawing from politics during the Exclusion crisis, when party spirit ran high and when, in view of the uncertainty of the outcome, it was dangerous to take sides. Temple explained his evasion: he would neither oppose the mighty nor try to stop the current of a river. This might be wise, Macaulay admitted, but added, "surely such wise and quiet men have no call to be members of Parliament in critical times": "Temple," *Edin. Rev., 68,* 76. Temple was "merely a neutral." Had he been a mediator, the judgment would have been favorable (pp. 176-77). In contrast, Robbins labels Temple a trimmer: *Eighteenth Century Commonwealthman,* p. 57. See also *History, 5,* 2316. Much later he claimed that had his penal code for India been adopted, he might have given more attention to legislation and less to literature; but in fact he had not neglected politics during much of the period before the penal code was adopted. See TBM to Hannah Macaulay, 4 October 1854, Trinity College Library.

89. Speech at Edinburgh, July 1847, Frederick Arnold, *Public Life of Lord Macaulay* (London, 1862), p. 310.

90. Trevelyan, *Life, 2,* 316; see also pp. 182-85, 212, 311-13, 335, 362. The People's Edition of the Essays had sold nearly three million copies by June 1867: *Lord Hanworth, Lord Chief Baron Pollock: A Memoir* (London, 1929), p. 201. *Extracts of the Journals and Correspondence of Miss Berry,* ed. Lady Theresa Lewis (London, 1865), *3,* 508; *The Croker Papers,* ed. Louis J. Jennings (London, 1884), *3,* 192. John Murray wrote to Croker in 1849, "I have not the least desire in any respect to see Mr. Macaulay spared—but the book is so clever, so entertaining, and has taken such a hold on the public mind and affections, that a critic that would begin by abusing M. or showing signs of irritation against him, would run little chance of *being read*": Brightfield, *Croker,* p. 373.

Henry Crabb Robinson's reaction is worth noting: "spent the greater part of the day reading Macaulay's eloquent Introduction [17 January 1849].... I remained reading Macaulay's third chapter with continued delight [21 January].... I could not resist the temptation to go on with it [22 January].... Though I had other things to do, yet I could not resist the temptation of reading the second volume [25 January]": *Henry Crabb Robinson on Books and Their Writers, 2,* 686-87.

91. *Gleanings, 2,* 315. He also was called "this great potentate in letters" and was said to be "at the head of our literature": [John Skelton], *Nugae Criticae* (Edinburgh, 1862), p. 437. Booksellers reported to the printer of the *Edinburgh Review* that the volume of sales depended on the presence of an article by Macaulay: TBM to Hannah Macaulay, 3 June 1833, Pinney, *Letters, 2,* 249. After reading the first two volumes of the *History,* Baroness Bunsen (née Waddington) felt "obligation to him for giving me *ten* reasons where I had *one* before, for holding opinions I have long held!": Augustus J. C. Hare, *The Life and Letters of Frances Baroness Bunsen* (New York, 1879), *2,* 126. It has been argued that "the influence which the writers of history thus exercise on public opinion is probably more immediate and extensive than that of the political theorists who launch new ideas. It seems as though even such new ideas reach wider circles usually not in their abstract form but as the interpretations of particular events.... There is perhaps no better illustration of the manner in which for more than a century the whole political ethos of a nation was shaped by the writings ... of men like Hallam and Macaulay, or Grote and Lord Acton": F. A. Hayek, *Studies in Philosophy, Politics and Economics* (London: Routledge, 1967), pp. 201-2. Olive Anderson has noted that the educated public's eagerness to draw lessons from the past was a "cultural fashion" of the time. She also describes Macaulay's specific influence on politicians' awareness of the reign of William III: "The Political Uses of History in Mid Nineteenth-Century England," *Past and Present,* no. 36 (April 1967), pp. 87-91, 95, 99.

92. Archibald Alison, *Some Account of My Life and Writings: An Autobiography,* ed. Lady Alison (Edinburgh, 1883), *2,* 331. Alison also described "the extraordinary *identity of thought* which prevailed in that celebrated party and the subjection in it of the many to the judgment and opinion of the few.... No such strange circumscribing of thought to their own circle was seen among the Tories" (pp. 331-32).

93. James Fitzjames Stephen, "Lord Macaulay," *The Saturday Review, 9* (7 January 1860), 9.

94. Henry Reeve, "Lord Macaulay," *Edin. Rev., 111* (January 1860), 273-76. Acton felt that as a young man he had been "primed to the brim with Whig politics," and he recalled that "it was not Whiggism only, but Macaulay in particular that I was so full of": quoted in Himmelfarb, *Lord Acton,* p. 25. Dicey said, "Macaulay Mill and Burke are I believe the three authors to whom as far as I can judge I owe more than to any other teachers I could mention": A. V. Dicey to Miss Wedgwood, 27 January 1893, Wedgwood Archives, University of Keele, 59/32729.

95. In mid-century, Bagehot "referred to the almost universal igno-rance which prevailed among the educated classes in England concerning the close of the seventeenth century. . . .   Macaulay has formed and instructed the national opinion of events from the death of Charles II to the Treaty of Ryswick": Herbert Paul, *Men and Letters* (London, 1901), p. 302. "I really do not think that there is in our literature so great a void as that which I am trying to supply. English history from 1688 to the French Revolution is, even to educated people, almost a *terra incognita*": TBM to Macvey Napier, 5 November 1841, *Selection from the Corre-spondence of the Late Macvey Napier,* ed. M. Napier (London, 1879), p. 367. One reader of Macaulay's essay on Mackintosh thought "the benefits derived from the Revolution of 1688 have never been so ably stated": Whishaw to Allen, 26 July [1835], Holland Papers, BM, Add. MSS 52179, unfol. On seventeenth-century historical memories, see Gash, *Reaction and Reconstruction,* p. 112, n. 3; "Nineteenth-Century Cromwell," *Past and Present,* no. 40 (July 1968). Vincent suggests that the "instilling of the traditional wisdom of Whiggery into the public mind was performed more by the Whig historians than by the Whig politicians": John Vincent, *The Formation of the Liberal Party, 1857-1868* (London: Constable, 1966), p. 22.

96. F. A. Hayek, *The Constitution of Liberty* (Chicago: University of Chicago Press, 1960), p. 469, n. 90.

97. Jeffrey to Empson, 20 March 1849: quoted in Henry Cockburn, *The Life of Lord Jeffrey* (Edinburgh, 1852), 2, 459.

Chapter 7. The Intellectual Context

1. "On the Royal Society of Literature," *Misc. Wr., 1,* 21. He added that "it is the great engine which moves the feelings of a people on the most momentous questions."

2. Gladstone, *Gleanings, 2,* 298; there was "an occasional tinge of at least literary vindictiveness" (p. 273).

3. H. R. Trevor-Roper, Introduction to Macaulay, *Critical and Histor-ical Essays* (London: Collins, 1965), pp. 16-17. There has been disagree-ment as to whether the essays are consistent with the *History.*

4. George Levine, *The Boundaries of Fiction: Carlyle, Macaulay, Newman* (Princeton: Princeton University Press, 1968), pp. 83-84, 159-60; Gladstone, *Gleanings, 2,* 311.

5. H. R. Trevor-Roper, Introduction to Macaulay, *History of England* (New York: Washington Square Press, 1968), pp. xxx-xli; J. H. Plumb, *Men and Places* (Penguin, 1966), pp. 287-88; John Paget, *The New "Examen"* (London: Haworth, 1934; 1st ed., 1861), passim; Sir Charles Firth, *A Commentary on Macaulay's "History of England"* (London: Cass, 1964), passim.

6. Eric Stokes, *The English Utilitarians and India* (Oxford: Clarendon Press, 1959), pp. 184-233; C. D. Dharker, *Lord Macaulay's Legislative Minutes* (London: Oxford, 1946), p. 132. Some have qualified the

conventional judgment of his political skill; see Plumb, *Men and Places*, p. 283; David Knowles, *Lord Macaulay, 1800-59* (Cambridge: At the University Press, 1960), p. 7.

7. Trevor-Roper, Introduction to *History*, p. xli.

8. *History*, *3*, 1204; Firth, *Commentary*, p. 138.

9. "Hallam," *Edin. Rev.*, *48* (September 1828), 99-100; *History*, *3*, 1277. See also *4*, 1978; "Lord Mahon's *War of the Succession in Spain*," *Edin. Rev.*, *56* (January 1833), 538: "speculation admits of no compromise."

10. *History*, *3*, 1386, 1388, 1390.

11. *Ibid.*, pp. 1389-90, 1392.

12. *Ibid.*, p. 1390. See also *Edin. Rev.*, *61*, 314.

13. *History*, *3*, 1389.

14. *Misc. Wr.*, *2*, 97-98.

15. *History*, *3*, 1204, 1304, 1306, 1310-12, 1339.

16. *Commentary*, pp. 138-39; Firth quoted Leslie Stephen. Macaulay implicitly rejected Locke in rejecting the contract theory: *Mirror of Parliament*, *10*, 554 (13 December 1830). See also above, p. 101.

17. "Machiavelli," *Edin. Rev.*, *45* (March 1827), 289, 291-92; "Utilitarian System of Philosophy," *Edin. Rev.*, *49* (June 1829), 295-97; Felix Raab, *The English Face of Machiavelli: A Changing Interpretation, 1500-1700* (London: Routledge, 1965), p. 249; however, for qualification, see pp. 250-51. An example of an extreme statement disparaging philosophy: "It is a mistake to imagine that subtle speculations, touching . . . the foundations of moral obligation, imply any high degree of intellectual culture. Such speculations, on the contrary, are in a peculiar manner the delight of intelligent children, and of half-civilized men": "Ranke," *Edin. Rev.*, *72* (October 1840), 229-30.

18. "Machiavelli," *Edin. Rev.*, *45*, 289; "Civil Disabilities of the Jews," *Edin. Rev.*, *52* (January 1831), 364-65.

19. "Mitford's History of Greece," *Misc. Wr.*, *1*, 158; "Mirabeau," *Edin. Rev.*, *55* (July, 1832), 573-74; "Croker's Boswell," *Edin. Rev.*, *54* (September 1831), 30. He was critical of J. S. Mill for thinking his era deficient in individuality. Macaulay thought there was a great display of genius, especially in science and technology, and a great deal of boldness and novelty, evident in such things as Comtism, St. Simonianism, Fourierism—which were "not indications of a servile respect for usage and authority." He did "not like to see a man of Mill's excellent abilities recommending eccentricity as a thing almost good in itself. . . . He is really crying 'Fire!' in Noah's flood": Trevelyan, *Life*, *2*, 379-80.

20. [Margaret Macaulay], *Recollections by a Sister of T. B. Macaulay* (1834) (London, 1864), p. 2.

21. TBM to Mrs. Sarah Austin, 27 February 1846, quoted in Janet Ross, *Three Generations of Englishwomen* (London, 1888), *1*, 203.

22. Journals, vol. 11, fols. 213-15 (13 November [1857]). There was "a most absurd article on Metaphysics in the new edition of the Encyclopaedia Britannica. . . . The author is named Mansell [*sic*]. He has now got into a controversy with as great a fool as himself on the highly interesting

and important question whether identity can properly be said to be a quality": TBM to Ellis, 22 July 1858, Trinity College Library.

23. "Bacon," *Edin. Rev., 65* (July 1837), 86.

24. *History, 1,* 110; *Speeches,* p. 281. Referring to the Jacobins: "It is absurd to say that any amount of public danger can justify a system like this, we do not say on Christian principles, we do not say on the principles of high morality, but even on principles of Machiavellian policy"; and the rule of Committee of Public Safety "was a tissue, not merely of crimes, but of blunders": "Barère," *Edin. Rev., 79* (April 1844), 311, 313. The Stamp Act was "unjust and impolitic, sterile of revenue and fertile of discontents": "Chatham," *Edin. Rev., 80* (October 1844), 574. "There was a fixed identity in the state—that public and private morals were the same—that honesty was the best policy . . . the state could not be guilty of a breach of faith . . . thus reducing itself to a situation at once disgraceful and perilous": *Hansard, 14,* 299 (12 July 1832).

25. Speech at General Meeting of Anti-Slavery Society, 15 May 1830, *Anti-Slavery Monthly Reporter, 3,* no. 61 (June 1830), 245-46. Macaulay was reproached by Rowland Hill for antinomianism: Diary of 7th earl of Carlisle, vol. 23, fol. 55 (12 March 1850).

26. John Morley, *On Compromise* (London, 1874), p. 18. Macaulay's unwillingness to act on moral principles without taking into account the immediate political consequences is even evident in his dealing with the slavery question: see *Hansard, 14,* 293 (12 July 1832); *77,* 1289, 1998-99, 1300-1302 (26 February 1845). His public position on slavery was partly a result of his wish to avoid displeasing his father; he was willing to resign his office on the question; however, he also wished to avoid causing difficulty to the ministry on an issue that he thought less significant than others it was dealing with: John Clive, *Macaulay: The Shaping of the Historian* (New York: Alfred A. Knopf, 1973), p. 235; Pinney, *Letters, 2,* 14, n. 5, 267, 274-75, 278. Far from feeling strongly about slavery, Macaulay applied his general suspicion of zeal to some of those who opposed slavery. "I hate slavery from the bottom of my soul," he wrote; "and yet I am made sick by the cant and the silly mock reasons of the Abolitionists": Journals, vol. 11, fol. 342 (8 July [1858]). One of his companions thought him "too favourable to the American Fugitive Slave Law, and too adverse to Sumner": Diary of the seventh earl of Carlisle, vol. 26, fol. 35 (27 May 1851).

27. "Essay on William III," p. 469; "Southey's *Colloquies,*" *Edin. Rev., 50* (January 1830), 552.

28. "Hallam," *Edin. Rev., 48,* 102. "The danger [from Puritans] was created solely by the cruelty [of the English Church]": *ibid.,* p. 104. *Hansard, 72,* 1183 (19 February 1844). However, Macaulay did not use Burke's moral argument; see *Tract on the Popery Laws* and *Letter to Sir Hercules Langrishe.* Civil disabilities "alienate from [the state] the hearts of the sufferers; they deprive it of a part of its effective strength in all contests with foreign nations": "Church and State," *Edin. Rev., 69* (April 1839), 276. "You make England but half a country to the Jews, and then you wonder that they have only half patriotism—you treat them as

foreigners, and then wonder that they have not all the feelings of natives": *Mirror of Parliament, 21,* 1274 (17 April 1833). Also see "Civil Disabilities of the Jews," *Edin. Rev., 52* (January 1831), 367-69; *Hansard, 23,* 1308-14 (5 April 1830).

29. "Warren Hastings," *Edin. Rev., 74* (October 1841), 225-26.

30. Matthew Arnold, "Joubert," *Essays in Criticism, First Series,* ed. T. M. Hoctor (Chicago: University of Chicago Press, 1968), p. 181. Carlyle thought Macaulay commonplace and limited: James Anthony Froude, *Thomas Carlyle: A History of His Life in London, 1834-1881* (New York, 1910), *1,* 369; *2,* 373.

31. Gladstone, *Gleanings, 2,* 272, 286, 295, 314.

32. John Morley, *Critical Miscellanies* (London, 1886), *1,* 267, 271-72. The complaint that Macaulay was not a genuine intellectual was often expressed, as with Morley, in the observation that he was middle class or that he was typical of his time and his class: see Gladstone, *Gleanings, 2,* 289; Walter Houghton, *The Victorian Frame of Mind, 1830-1870* (New Haven: Yale University Press, 1957), pp. 196-98; Knowles, *Macaulay,* p. 21. Also, he had "a great deal of talent, but no elevation of mind. There is not a novel or striking thought in the [*History*], not a new point of view from which to consider the events, and never one thrill or pulse of moral energy." "What a notable green-grocer was spoiled to make Macaulay!": *Journals of Ralph Waldo Emerson,* ed. E. W. Emerson and W. E. Forbes (London, 1913), *8,* 29, 462.

33. Mill, quoted in F. A. Hayek, *John Stuart Mill and Harriet Taylor* (London: Routledge, 1951), p. 223. Also: "It would certainly be unfair to measure the worth of any age by that of its popular objects of literary or artistic admiration. Otherwise one might say the present age will be known and estimated by posterity as the age which thought Macaulay a great writer": Mill's Diary, entry of 11 February 1854, in *The Letters of John Stuart Mill,* ed. H. S. R. Elliot (London, 1910), *2,* 370. Mill, favorable to codification, welcomed the Penal Code for India, but emphasized that it was not solely Macaulay's work and made mildly depreciative comments about Macaulay: "Penal Code for India," *London and Westminster Review, 29* (August 1838), 395, 403-4.

34. "Hallam," *Edin. Rev., 48,* 98. Macaulay noted that "Mandeville sets one thinking" and that "Rousseau is an object of unmixed aversion to me": marginal notes in vol. 2, pp. 441, 442, of William Field, *Memoirs of the Life, Writings, and Opinions of the Rev. Samuel Parr* (London, 1828); copy at Wallington.

35. Journals, vol. 11, fols. 369-70 (30 September [1858]). "I read Carlyle's Trash-Latterday something or other—beneath criticism.... Surely the world will not be duped for ever by such an empty headed bombastic dunce": Journals, vol. 2, fols. 279-80 (4 April [1850]).

36. Journals, vol. 8, fol. 143 (24 October [1854]); vol. 11, fols. 563-64 (17 September [1859]). On the other hand, when his feet are on the ground, he gains in Macaulay's esteem; "Now and then, when he writes like a man of the world, I read him with pleasure."

37. Journals, vol. 2, fols. 208-9 (18 January[1850]).

38. A. H. L. Munby, *Macaulay's Library*, Glasgow University Publications (Glasgow: Jackson, 1966), pp. 8, 10. "I have of late stolen a few minutes daily, while dressing and undressing, to make acquaintance with the theological writers of Germany. I admire their learning and ingenuity": TBM to Andrews Norton, 10 October 1840, Munby Collection, Trinity College Library. On the value of books: "as far back as I can remember, books have been to me dear friends; they have been my comfort in grief and my companions in solitude, — in poverty they have been to me more than sufficient riches, — in exile they have been my consolation for the want of my country, — and in the midst of vexations and distresses of political life . . . they have contributed to keep my mind serene and unclouded": *Report of a Public Entertainment held in the Waterloo Rooms . . . Sept. 2, by the Edinburgh Mechanics' Library; in which T. B. Macaulay, Esq., M.P. for the city . . . took part . . .* (Edinburgh, 1839), p. 9.

39. This explains Woodward's statement, "Few writers have had so great a fame and yet left so small a mark upon the development of English thought or upon the work of their intellectual equals": E. L. Woodward, *The Age of Reform, 1815-1870* (Oxford: Clarendon Press, 1949), p. 523.

40. For example, or at least sometimes, by Acton; see Gertrude Himmelfarb, *Lord Acton: A Study in Conscience and Politics* (London: Routledge, 1952), p. 73; and Stokes, *English Utilitarians and India,* pp. 191, 215. This outlook was reflected in Praed's observation, "I'm studying now, to please his taste, / MacCulloch, Bentham, Mill": in "The Young Whig," *The Political and Occasional Poems of Winthrop Mackworth Praed,* ed. Sir George Young (London, 1888), p. 169. However, some years later Macaulay told Whewell that Whewell's *Lectures* would not "terminate the state of suspense in which I have long been between the Utilitarian and Sentimental Systems": TBM to Whewell, 15 May 1846, Whewell Papers, Trinity College Library, Add. MS a.209[154]. He had been reading William Whewell, *Lectures on Systematic Morality, Delivered in Lent Term* (London, 1846).

41. Adam Ferguson, quoted in Duncan Forbes, "'Scientific' Whiggism: Adam Smith and John Millar," *Cambridge Journal,* 7 (August 1954), 654. Millar pointed out that significant features of the constitution, for example the separation of judicial and executive powers, were not introduced from any foresight of their beneficial consequences (p. 657).

42. *History,* 5, 2480, 2482. For other examples see *History,* 5, 2386; 6, 2698. For a statement of Macaulay's views as they reflect the teaching of the Scottish school, see "History,"*Edin. Rev., 47* (May 1828), 363.

43. Trevelyan, *Life, 2,* 74. For Jeffrey's exposure to Millar see Forbes, "'Scientific' Whiggism," pp. 663-64. On reading reprinted essays of Jeffrey's, Macaulay thought "the variety and versatility of Jeffrey's mind seems to me more extraordinary than ever. . . . When I compare him with Sydney [Smith] and myself, I feel, with humility perfectly sincere, that his range is immeasurably wider than ours . . . ; he is not only a

writer; he has been a great advocate, and he is a great judge. Take him all in all, I think him more nearly an universal genius than any man of our time": Trevelyan, *Life*, *2*, 95-96. Jeffrey reciprocated, and he demonstrated his sense of affinity with Macaulay in his approval of the articles on the Utilitarians and in his admiration of the *History*, which he also proofread: *Selection from the Correspondence of the Late Macvey Napier*, ed. M. Napier (London, 1879), p. 69; Henry Cockburn, *Life of Lord Jeffrey* (Edinburgh, 1852), *1*, 402; *2*, 458-59.

44. Forbes, " 'Scientific' Whiggism," p. 653.

45. Gladstone, *Gleanings*, *2*, 290.

46. "Machiavelli," *Edin Rev.*, *45*, 274-75, 289. The "peculiar immorality" of the *Prince* "belonged rather to the age than to the man" (pp. 288-89). See also *History*, *4*, 1949-50. Macaulay's early essay on Machiavelli did not reveal their affinities; it deals with Machiavelli's reputation, character, and career; his *Mandragola;* it compares him to Montesquieu (much to Machiavelli's advantage); it discusses Florentine history; and it comments on the character but very little on the political substance of Machiavelli's writings. According to Young, the essay was (in 1937) still reprinted in Italy as the best introduction to the study of Machiavelli: G. M. Young, *Daylight and Champaign* (London: Cape, 1937), p. 23. Macaulay acknowledged that "the[re] are 100 cas[es] wh justify falsehood one wh would even extenuate the gu[ilt] of assassina[tion]": marginal comment in vol. 1, p. 49, of Thomas M' Crie, *Life of John Knox* (Edinburgh, 1831); copy at Wallington.

47. Raab, *English Face of Machiavelli*, pp. 73-76, 239-54. Halifax's delight in Montaigne's writings (see n. 34 in chap. 4) is of course not inconsistent with his intellectual affinity with Machiavelli. According to Butterfield, Machiavelli "provides many formulas for what we have come to regard as the English mode of conducting politics; as when he says that political revolutions should be concealed by the retention of at least the forms of the ancient institutions.... Some of his maxims entered the English whig tradition—for instance his thesis that a constitution cannot be overturned unless the people themselves have become corrupt": *The Statecraft of Machiavelli* (New York: Collier, 1962), pp. 63-64.

48. *The Complete Works of Halifax*, ed. J. P. Kenyon (Penguin, 1969), pp. 209-10.

49. Kenyon places Halifax in the "tradition of British conservatism, or gradualism"; yet Foxcroft thought of him as a liberal. Macaulay (*History*, *1*, 234) recognized that Halifax was in temper a conservative, yet he clearly distinguished him from what he considered conservatism. Russell Kirk, labeling Macaulay a "liberal conservative," gives him a peripheral position in the history of conservatism; yet Macaulay has a prominent place in anthologies of liberalism, for example in Alan Bullock and M. Shock, eds., *The Liberal Tradition* (London: Black, 1956). Cf. Russell Kirk, *The Conservative Mind* (London: Faber & Faber, 1954), pp. 167-76; Kenyon, Introduction to Halifax, *Complete Works*, p. 32. Isaac Kramnick identifies the tradition of skepticism and gives Halifax and Burke important places in it, but makes no place for

Macaulay: "Skepticism in English Political Thought: From Temple to Burke," *Studies in Burke and His Time, 12* (Fall 1970), 1627-60.

50. "Essay on William III," p. 469 and n. 8; Journals, vol. 6, fol. 24 (22 January [1853]); Trevelyan, *Life, 2,* 97. There is a favorable allusion to Burke in a letter of 18 April 1818: Pinney, *Letters, 1,* 96. Macaulay spoke at the Union Society on 13 March 1822 in support of the proposal that Burke's political conduct deserved the approbation of posterity: *Laws and Transactions of the Union Society* (Cambridge, 1834), p. 21. Macaulay also considered writing on Burke in 1840 on the occasion of Croly's biography, but on reading it decided not to do it: TBM to Napier, 13 February and 18 April 1840, Napier Papers, BM, Add. MSS 34621, fols. 47, 102.

51. Benjamin Disraeli, *The Young Duke,* bk. V, chap. 6; also quoted in Trevelyan, *Life, 1,* 208, n. 1. The passage used by Disraeli is from Goldsmith's *Retaliation,* but he was most probably familiar with it from Boswell's *Johnson,* where it is quoted in a discussion of Burke; see *Boswell's Life of Johnson,* ed. George Birkbeck Hill and L. F. Powell (Oxford: Clarendon Press, 1934), *1,* 472, and n. 3.

52. "Hastings," *Edin. Rev., 74,* 229, 232; "Chatham," *Edin. Rev., 80,* 572-73; "Samuel Johnson," *Misc. Wr., 2,* 290; "William Pitt," *Misc. Wr., 2,* 314, 332.

53. "Hastings," *Edin. Rev., 74,* 232-34. Burke's passionate nature, he thought, was evident in his style, making it "ungracefully gorgeous": "Bacon," *Edin. Rev., 65,* 100.

54. "Southey's *Colloquies,*" *Edin. Rev., 50,* 528; Trevelyan, *Life, 1,* 236.

55. Peter Stanlis, *Edmund Burke and Natural Law* (Ann Arbor: University of Michigan Press, 1958), pp. 29-34.

56. Kenyon points to these continuities (and traces them to Pym as well): Introduction to Halifax, *Complete Works,* Penguin ed., pp. 24, 31-32, 34; he states that "it is in the highest degree unlikely that Halifax was directly influenced by Pym, or Burke by Halifax" (p. 32); see also n. 87. However, Burke does allude to Halifax in the very last sentence of the *Reflections;* see Harvey Mansfield, Jr., *Statesmanship and Party Government* (Chicago: University of Chicago Press, 1965), p. 241, where this passage is used to confirm the judgment that "Burke clearly is not just a party man." Macaulay's relation to Halifax was probably not a matter of direct influence, for Macaulay reversed an early, harsh judgment of Halifax only after he had fully developed his trimming outlook. See also chap. 4, n. 39. Compare Burke, *Reflections on the Revolution in France:* "As in most questions of state, there is a middle. There is something else than the mere alternative of absolute destruction or unreformed existence": in *The Works of the Right Honourable Edmund Burke* (London, 1887), *3,* 440.

57. "It is the part of wisdom to weigh, not indeed with minute accuracy, — for questions of civil prudence cannot be subjected to an arithmetical test, — but to weigh the advantages and disadvantages carefully, and then to strike the balances": *Speeches,* p. 172. "Let us look

at the question like legislators, and after fairly balancing conveniences and inconveniences, pronounce between the existing law ... and the law now proposed to us ... like most questions of civil prudence, [it] is neither black nor white, but grey": *ibid.*, p. 232. See above, p. 66. Compare Burke: "The rights of men in governments are their advantages; and these are often balances between differences of good, in compromises sometimes between good and evil, and sometimes between evil and evil": *Reflections on the Revolution in France*, in *Works* (London, 1887), *3*, 313; see also p. 457.

58. "Mirabeau," *Edin. Rev.*, *55*, 571–73. There are many other paraphrases of Burke in Macaulay's writings and speeches, often not accompanied by reference to Burke; see, e.g., *Hansard*, *48*, 467 (18 June 1839); *Speeches*, p. 324; Trevelyan, *Life*, *2*, 161 n.; *History*, 3, 1526. Macaulay modeled his 1833 speech on the East India Company Charter on Burke: Dharker, *Macaulay's Legislative Minutes*, p. 132.

59. "Mirabeau," *Edin. Rev.*, *55*, 573. Yet compare: "Revolution is, therefore, an evil; — an evil, indeed, which ought sometimes to be incurred for the purpose of averting or removing greater evils, but always an evil. The burden of proof lies heavy on those who oppose existing governments": "The History of France, from the Restoration of the Bourbons to the Accession of Louis Philippe," p. 48 (quoted above, p. 44); with Burke: "[with regard to] the case of a revolution in government, this, I think, may be safely affirmed, — that a sore and pressing evil is to be removed, and that a good, great in its amount and unequivocal in its nature, must be probable to certainty, before the inestimable price ... is paid for a revolution.... Every revolution contains in it something of evil": *Appeal from the New to the Old Whigs*, in *Works*, *4*, 81.

60. "Present Administration" (1827), *Edin. Rev.*, *46*, 260–65.

61. "Mirabeau," *Edin. Rev.*, *55*, 556–57. See also above, p. 45.

62. Quoted by Kenyon, Introduction to Halifax, *Works*, p. 32.

63. Quoted by Francis Canavan, "Burke as a Reformer," in *The Relevance of Edmund Burke*, ed. P. J. Stanlis (New York: P. J. Kenedy, 1964), p. 103.

64. *Hansard*, *72*, 1175–76 (19 February 1844); see also p. 1183. Woodward challenges Macaulay's analysis: *Age of Reform*, pp. 314–15.

65. "Hallam," *Edin. Rev.*, *48*, 164–67. In another example, Burke correctly assessed the consequences of the national debt where most of his contemporaries were wrong, including Hume and Adam Smith: *History*, *5*, 2284, 2286 n. 1. "Very slowly was the public brought to acknowledge ... that Burke was a great master of political science": *History*, *5*, 2408.

66. *Hansard*, *11*, 458 (19 March 1832). He also appeals to Burke's authority on 28 February 1832: *Speeches*, p. 90; see also p. 8. It will be recalled that he also said that Pitt, who had affinities with Burke, would have been "a decided reformer" in 1832: "Mirabeau," *Edin. Rev.*, *55* (July 1832), 557.

67. There are unusual references to capitalists in "Hallam," *Edin. Rev.*, *48*, 168, and in *Speeches*, p. 428. A comparison with J. S. Mill

shows how little Macaulay thought about economic questions. He was for free trade but criticized the Anti-Corn Law League for being doctrinaire on the issue. In 1846 he voted with the minority in supporting Fielden's Ten Hour Bill. More significant than his vote was the vigor of his argument "that where the health of the community is concerned, it may be the duty of the State to interfere with the contracts of individuals": *Speeches,* p. 440. Shaftesbury was particularly grateful for Macaulay's "true and noble speech"; see Edwin Hodder, *The Life and Work of the Seventh Earl of Shaftesbury* (London, 1886), *3,* 73; also *3,* 211.

68. For example, "Mr. Macauley [*sic*], A Legislator for the Hindoos," *Tait's Edinburgh Magazine, 4* (January 1834), 485-90 (probably by Roebuck); and *Blackwood's Edinburgh Magazine, 22* (October 1827), 403, 406.

69. *History, 2,* 886; *3,* 1339-40.

70. *History, 3,* 1340; see also "Hampden," *Edin. Rev., 54* (December 1831), 533.

71. "Essay on William III," p. 469. "No other society has yet succeeded in uniting revolution with prescription, progress with stability, the energy of youth with the majesty of immemorial antiquity": *History, 1,* 21.